Book   6

Book   5

Book   4

Book   3

Book   2

Book   1

Basic Skills in English

Book 6

Joy Littell, EDITORIAL DIRECTOR

McDougal, Littell & Company
Evanston, Illinois
Sacramento, California

AUTHORS

Joy Littell, Editorial Director, and
The Editorial Staff of McDougal, Littell & Company

Kraft and Kraft, Developers of Educational Materials

Marilyn M. Sherman, formerly, English teacher,
New Trier Township High School West, Northfield, Illinois

CONSULTANTS

Carolyn McConnell, formerly, English teacher, George C. Marshall High School,
Fairfax County, Virginia; and instructor, College of DuPage, Glen Ellyn, Illinois

Rebecca Williams, formerly, English instructor, Kennedy-King College, Chicago,
Illinois; and instructor of Special Programs, Indiana University

Editor-in-Chief: Joseph F. Littell
Managing Editor: Kathleen Laya
Senior Editor: Trisha Lorange Taylor
Director of Design: William A. Seabright
Design Associate: Lucy Lesiak
Associate Editor: Mary Schafer

Acknowledgments: See page 523.

ISBN: 0-88343-798-8

Composition

These eleven pages consist of additional writing assignments. There is an exercise for each Part. The exercises will give you extra practice in improving your writing skills.

Handbook

Developing an Effective Vocabulary

Close Encounters

Learning Word Meaning from Context

Here's the Idea Used by 400 million people all over the world, English is a continually changing language. In fact, English has a large, varied vocabulary that includes about 600,000 different words. In view of its flexibility and variety, English can be called a living and lively language.

The process of developing an effective vocabulary is lifelong. One important way in which you can build vocabulary is to examine words in context. Context means the words and sentences around a given word. There are several kinds of context clues that help you to figure out the meanings of unfamiliar words.

When a **definition** is given in context, the meaning of an unfamiliar word is stated directly. Look at this example.

> Many Americans are becoming interested in *ecology*. *Ecology* is the science that deals with the relations between living things and their environment.

When **restatement** is used, the meaning of a word is rephrased. Look for key words like *or, that is, which is,* or *in other words.*

> One review included many *caustic*, or sarcastic, comments expressing the critic's opinion of the new movie.

Sometimes you may be able to understand the meaning of a word through **examples** given. Look for key words like *especially, like, other, this, these, for example, for instance,* and *such as.*

> The punishments for murder, arson, and other *felonies* are more severe than those for minor crimes.

When **comparison** is used, a new word is compared with a similar word that is known to you. Look for the key words *as, like, in the same way,* and *similar to.*

> Korean *cuisine* is similar to the Chinese style of cooking.

When **contrast** is used, a word is compared with an opposite word that is known to you. Look for the key words *although, but, unlike, while, on the contrary,* and *on the other hand.*

Pamela Klein is *taciturn,* unlike her twin sister Paula, who is talkative.

If you make use of these context clues as you read, you will continually build your vocabulary.

Check It Out   Read the following sentences.

1. My ten-year-old brother enjoys *puns.* A pun is a humorous play on words that have the same sound but different meanings.

2. *Insomnia,* which is a difficulty in falling asleep, is a fairly common condition.

3. A *percussion instrument* such as a drum is as important to an orchestra as a string, brass, or woodwind instrument.

4. The *luge* is similar to a sled and it is raced in the winter Olympics.

- What is the meaning of each italicized word? What context clue is used in each sentence?

Try Your Skill   Choose four of these words: *drill, hammer, pliers, saw, screwdriver, wrench.* Write a sentence that explains each word. Use key words as context clues.

Keep This in Mind

- Develop your vocabulary by examining words in context. Useful context clues are definition, restatement, examples, comparison, and contrast.

Now Write   Choose four of the following words: *biography, drama, essay, novel, poem, short story.* Write a sentence for each, using a context clue to explain the word. Use key words to signal each context clue. Use a dictionary if necessary. Label your paper **Close Encounters**. Keep your paper in your folder.

A Hint of an Idea

Inferring Word Meaning from Context

Here's the Idea   You may not always be able to figure out the meaning of an unfamiliar word by relying on direct context clues. Sometimes you may have to examine the surrounding sentences, put clues together, and make a good guess at the meaning of the word. This process of reading between the lines in order to draw a conclusion about the meaning of a word is called **inference**.

The main idea of a short passage or of an entire paragraph may be related to the meaning of an unfamiliar word. In the following paragraph, for instance, try to infer the meaning of the word *lethargic*.

> I did not sleep well last night, and I awoke feeling drowsy. It seemed to take all of my energy just to get up and get dressed. I found myself dozing during the long bus ride to work. Even the thought of my first paycheck failed to excite me. I couldn't shake off my *lethargic* mood.

From this paragraph, you can infer that *lethargic* means "affected by a condition of abnormal drowsiness or inactivity."

Check It Out   Read the following paragraph.

> On Tuesday a *referendum* on the proposed school tax law will be held. Many residents have expressed strong feelings on this issue and are being urged to vote by local officials. This is an important civic event. Taxpayers have an opportunity to express their opinions in a way that can be effective.

> • What can you infer about the meaning of *referendum*?

Try Your Skill   As you read these passages, try to infer the meaning of the italicized words. Write definitions for them.

1. The reporter was struck by the *irony* of the news story. There had been a minor fire at the fire station. In fact, the fire had been caused by a firefighter who had been smoking in bed. Fortunately, the firefighter suffered no serious injury.

2. Mike is considering a career in *drafting*. He is a talented artist who has had a great deal of instruction in drawing. Moreover, he has always been interested in mechanical structures, especially in their design. The chance to combine his ability to draw and his interest in designing machinery appeals to him.

3. Rita's *credentials* for the job in the firm of architects were excellent. She had earned a degree from a leading university and a first-place award in a major national competition. In addition, she presented letters of recommendation from two well known and re-spected architects.

4. Unfortunately, there was a feeling of *apathy* about this year's class elections. There were no heated arguments about issues, little enthusiasm for any of the candidates, and no talk of victory parties. In fact, only a small number of students even bothered to vote.

Keep This in Mind

· Inference is the process of using clues to draw a conclusion. Inferences about unfamiliar words can be drawn from the main ideas of paragraphs.

Now Write   Suppose that you are telling a story about a *joyous* event. Write four or five sentences that suggest this quality without specifically defining it. Label your paper **A Hint of an Idea** and put it into your folder.

Up Front

Recognizing Prefixes

Here's the Idea Many English words are made up of parts that work together. If you can recognize some common word parts, you will be able to understand many unfamiliar words.

A **prefix** is a word part with its own meaning added at the beginning of a base word. The prefix *un-*, for example, means "not" or "opposite of." If you recognize this prefix and its meaning, you know that *unsteady* means "not firm or stable; changeable." You also know that *unpack* means "to open and remove the packed contents of." From these examples, you can see how the addition of prefixes affects the meanings of the base words *steady* and *pack*.

Study this list of common prefixes. Notice that some prefixes have more than one meaning.

Prefix	Meaning	Example
in- (also **il-**, **im-**, and **ir-**)	"not"	inactive, illogical, imbalance, irreligious
non-	"not"	nonfattening
pre-	"before"	prearrange
mis-	"wrong, bad"	mismanage
trans-	"across, through" or "changed"	transatlantic, transform
re-	"again" or "back"	reapply, replace
dis-	"opposite of" or "away"	disrespect, dislodge

Not all words contain prefixes, however. To determine whether or not a word contains a prefix you need to check the word and its history in a dictionary.

Check It Out Examine these words and their definitions.

> inapplicable — "not applicable; not suitable"
> illiterate — "not knowing how to read or write; uneducated"

immeasurable — "too large or too much to be measured; vast"
irrefutable — "that cannot be reputed or disproved"
nontoxic — "not poisonous"
prenuptial — "before a wedding"
miscalculate — "to determine or compute incorrectly"
transfix — "to pierce through, as with an arrow; to make unable to move, as if pierced through"
remodel — "to make over; rebuild"
retake — "to take again, to take back or recapture"
disavow — "to deny knowledge of, approval of, or responsibility for; repudiate"
discourage — "to cause to lose courage or confidence"

• What is the prefix in each? What is the base word?

Try Your Skill   Twelve of the following words have prefixes. For each word that has a prefix, write the prefix and its meaning, plus the base word. For example, for the word *incapable* you would write: in (not) + capable.

1. refurnish	6. restful	11. displace
2. nonresident	7. inadmissible	12. transact
3. disobey	8. immature	13. irreversible
4. mission	9. repay	14. misrepresent
5. illegal	10. predetermine	15. inning

Keep This in Mind

• A prefix is a word part with its own meaning added at the beginning of a base word. Learn to recognize common prefixes and their meanings.

Now Write   Using a dictionary, find seven unfamiliar words each of which contains a different one of the seven prefixes shown in this lesson. List the words, define them, and study them. Then write seven sentences, each using one of the new words you have learned. Label your paper **Up Front** and keep it in your folder.

Afterwards

Recognizing Suffixes

Here's the Idea   A **suffix** is a word part added at the end of a base word. A suffix is similar to a prefix in two respects. Like a prefix, a suffix has a meaning of its own that affects the meaning of the base word. Also like a prefix, a suffix may have more than one meaning or more than one form. For example, the suffix *-able* or *-ible* means "can be; having this quality." Thus, *manageable* means "that can be managed or controlled" and *reasonable* means "having the quality of reason or sense."

However, suffixes are unlike prefixes in one important respect. Sometimes the addition of a suffix changes the spelling of a base word. A final consonant may be doubled. For example, *run* becomes *runner*. The final letter may be dropped. For example, *sense* becomes *sensible*. The final letter of the base word may be changed. For example, *pity* becomes *pitiful*. Therefore, when you add a suffix to a word, check the spelling of the word in a dictionary.

Study this list of common suffixes.

Suffix	Meaning	Example
-ful	"full of, having"	shameful
-ous	"full of, having"	mysterious
-y	"tending to be, characterized by"	sleepy
-ness	"the state or quality of being"	weakness
-ion	"the act, result, or condition of"	celebration
-ment	"the act, result or state of"	movement
-less	"without"	weightless

Check It Out Examine these words and their definitions.

> soulful — "full of or showing deep feeling"
> malicious — "having malice, the desire to harm another"
> catty — "of or like a cat; mean; malicious"
> willingness — "the state of being ready to do gladly"
> rejection — "the act of refusing to take, use, or believe something"
> achievement — "the result of doing something successfully"
> tasteless — "without taste or flavor (as for something eaten); also, lacking the ability to judge what is beautiful and appropriate"

- What is the suffix in each? What is the base word?

Try Your Skill Find the suffix in each of the following words. Write the base word and the meaning of the suffix for each word. For example, for the word *translation* you would write: translate + the act of.

1. nervous	6. spiteful	11. funny
2. wavy	7. tenderness	12. gracious
3. friendless	8. development	13. reflection
4. improvement	9. misty	14. tactless
5. handful	10. correction	15. eagerness

Keep This in Mind

- A suffix is a word part added at the end of a base word. Each suffix has its own meaning. Check the spelling of a word when you add a suffix.

Now Write Using a dictionary, find seven unfamiliar words each of which contains a different one of the seven suffixes shown in this lesson. List the words, define them, and study them. Then write seven sentences, each using one of the new words you have learned. Label your paper **Afterwards** and keep it in your folder.

The Centerpiece

Using Roots from Latin

Here's the Idea As a means of developing an effective vocabulary, you have been studying word parts. You have learned that a prefix, such as *trans-*, can be added to a base word, such as *form*. The new word, *transform*, means "to change the form, appearance, or condition of." You have learned that a suffix, such as *-y*, meaning "tending to," can be added to a base word, such as *art*. The new word, *arty*, means "pretending or trying to be artistic." You have also learned that base words are separate words with their own meanings. What are the base words in *inconsiderate*, *heaviness*, and *misstatement*?

Some words are formed from a different kind of word part, called a **root**. A root has a particular meaning of its own. Usually, a root is not a word by itself. Instead, a root forms the main part of a word. Since half of the words in English come from Latin, the most common roots also come from Latin.

Study these four Latin roots.

Latin Root	Meaning	Example
flect, flex	"bend"	*flex*, meaning "to bend (an arm, leg)"
grat	"thank" or "favor"	*gratitude*, meaning "thankfulness"
gress, grad	"step" or "go"	*grade*, meaning "a step; stage; degree; rating"
rupt	"break"	*abrupt*, meaning "broken off; sudden"

Check It Out Examine these words and their definitions.

flexible — "able to be bent; adjustable"
deflect — "to bend or turn aside; swerve"

gratuity — "a gift of money for service; a tip"
ingratiate — "to work (oneself) into another's favor"
aggressive — "ready to start fights or engage in direct action"
transgress — "to overstep a limit; to break a law"
disrupt — "to break apart; to disturb the orderly course of"
erupt — "to burst forth, as from some restraint"

- Point out the Latin root in each example. How is the meaning of the root related to the meaning of the whole word?

Try Your Skill   Copy the following pairs of words and circle the Latin roots. Use the meanings of the roots to help you figure out the meanings of the words. Then check the history and the meaning of each word in a dictionary. Finally, use one word from each pair in a sentence of your own.

reflect	congratulate	graduate	interrupt
inflexible	ingrate	progress	rupture

Keep This in Mind

- A root is part of a word and has a meaning of its own. Learn to recognize the many common roots that come from Latin.

Now Write   Using a dictionary, find four new words containing each of the four Latin roots you have studied. List and define the new words. Then use each one in a sentence. Label your paper **The Centerpiece**. Keep your work in your folder.

On the Mark

Using Precise Words

Here's the Idea   Choosing the right word has two benefits. First, it makes your writing more precise. For example, did the dog *bark* or *snarl*? Was the chore *strenuous* or merely *time-consuming*? Choose a word that expresses the precise meaning you intend. Second, using the right word makes your writing more vivid. For example, avoid using a general word like *said*. Select a more specific word, like *whispered, bellowed, claimed*, or *questioned*.

To choose the right word, learn to choose among synonyms and antonyms. **Synonyms** are words with nearly the same meaning, like *strong, stout, sturdy, tough*, and *stalwart*. A *synonymy*, a list of synonyms and their shades of meaning, is given at the end of some entries in a dictionary. Synonyms are also given in a reference book called a *thesaurus*. **Antonyms** are words with opposite meanings, like *strong—weak, correct—wrong*, and *rare—common*. Antonyms are given in some dictionaries as well as in a thesaurus.

Check It Out   Examine these synonymies.

SYN.—**healthy** implies normal physical and mental strength and freedom from disease, weakness, disorder, etc.; **sound** suggests a condition of perfect health in which there is no sign of disease or weakness; **hale** is close to **sound** in meaning and is used esp. of elderly people who are lively and free from the weaknesses of old age; **robust** implies great bodily health and strength that can be seen in firm muscles, good color, large reserves of energy, etc.; **well** implies simply freedom from illness —*ANT.* **ill, diseased, infirm, frail**

SYN.—**sick** and **ill** both express the idea of being in bad health, having a disease, etc., but **sick** is more commonly used than **ill**, which is somewhat formal [he's a *sick* person; he is *sick*, or *ill*, with the flu]; **ailing** usually suggests poor health that lasts a long time or never improves [she has been *ailing* ever since her operation]; **indisposed** suggests a slight, brief illness or feeling of physical discomfort [*indisposed* with a headache] —*ANT.* **well, healthy**

- Which synonym for *healthy* is the right word to describe an elderly person who is in perfect health?
- Which antonym for *healthy* suggests poor health that lasts a long time?

Try Your Skill Choose the synonym that best fits the meaning of each sentence. Use a dictionary or thesaurus if necessary.

1. Although Beth (asked, begged, demanded, requested) angrily that her money be refunded, the clerk responded politely.
2. The jackhammers below (trembled, shook, disturbed, upset) the windows of the third-floor apartment.
3. Because I was not used to the standard transmission, the car (lurched, moved, jumped, advanced) forward when I shifted gears.
4. The racers' (silly, foolish, unwise, foolhardy) attempt to sail during the rainstorm ended when the boat capsized.

Keep This in Mind

- Choose precise words. Check their meanings in a dictionary or thesaurus.
- Synonyms are words with similar meanings. Antonyms are words with opposite meanings.

Now Write Using a dictionary or thesaurus, find four synonyms for one word. Write a separate sentence for each of the four words. Be sure that the sentences indicate the differences of meaning among the synonyms. Then write one sentence using an antonym of one of the words. Label your paper **On the Mark** and put it into your folder.

Extrasensory Description

Building a Vocabulary of the Senses

Here's the Idea   In order to present your experiences in the most vivid way, you need to sharpen two skills. First, you must develop an awareness of sensory details. That is, train yourself to be aware of the specific sights, sounds, textures, smells, and tastes around you. Second, you need to develop a vocabulary to describe sensory details. If something is pleasant to the taste, for example, is it *buttery*, *sweet*, or *spicy*? Become familiar with sensory words such as those listed on pages 16 and 17 at the end of this lesson. Select sensory words that describe an experience precisely.

Through the use of sensory details, you can write vividly about familiar experiences or extraordinary ones. For example, notice the use of sensory details in the following paragraphs.

> I had been wandering about the fairgrounds for hours, simply following wherever the most interesting sights and sounds had taken me. I drew in a deep breath and held it, savoring the smell of rich earth and sweet, damp hay. I found myself on the edge of a quiet crowd. I craned my neck and glimpsed a pair of horses. I was told that these work horses were preparing to move a two-ton weight.
>
> Suddenly, at a shrill "Haw!" from their trainer, the horses lunged forward. Straining into the creaking leather harness, they grunted and snorted. Their hooves thundered as the animals drove at the ground. Slowly the horses inched the ponderous weight forward. With a final effort, they dragged the weight across the finish line. I joined the crowd, roaring and clapping in approval.

Check It Out   Examine these examples of sensory words.

Sight:	crimson, tapered, mottled, robust
Hearing:	screech, bray, whir, guffaw
Touch:	tepid, waxy, leathery, gritty
Taste:	hearty, bland, tangy, medicinal
Smell:	aromatic, briny, acrid, dank

- Which of these sensory words are new to you? What do they mean? Think of something that might be described by each of these words.

Try Your Skill   Think of a particular place that fits one of these general categories. List as many sensory words as you can think of about the place. Be specific. Try to use all of your senses.

a hospital   a park
a shopping center   a bus terminal
a zoo   a busy intersection

Keep This in Mind

- When you write, use vivid sensory details that bring an experience to life. Build a vocabulary of the senses.

Now Write   Think of a place where you would like to be. List as many sensory details about the place as you can. Choose specific words that relate to all of your senses. You may want to refer to the sample lists on the following pages. Label your paper **Extrasensory Description** and put it into your folder.

A List of Sight Words

colorless	round	mottled	transparent
white	flat	freckled	sheer
ivory	curved	wrinkled	opaque
yellow	wavy	striped	tall
gold	ruffled	bright	lean
orange	oval	clear	muscular
green	angular	glossy	handsome
olive	triangular	shimmering	robust
turquoise	rectangular	jeweled	fragile
azure	square	fiery	pale
pink	hollow	muddy	small
crimson	wide	drab	tiny
maroon	long	dark	large
lavender	narrow	grimy	massive
purple	tapered	worn	immense
gray	crooked	messy	attractive
silver	wiry	cluttered	perky
beige	swollen	tidy	showy
brown	lopsided	fresh	lacy
black	shapeless	flowery	elegant

A List of Hearing Words

crash	squawk	crackle	chime
thud	whine	buzz	laugh
bump	bark	clink	gurgle
boom	bleat	hiss	giggle
thunder	bray	snort	guffaw
bang	blare	bellow	sing
roar	rumble	growl	hum
scream	grate	whimper	mutter
screech	slam	stammer	murmur
shout	clap	snap	whisper
yell	stomp	rustle	sigh
whistle	jangle	whir	hush

A List of Taste Words

oily	rich	bland	ripe
buttery	hearty	tasteless	medicinal
salty	mellow	sour	fishy
bitter	sugary	vinegary	spicy
bittersweet	crisp	fruity	hot
sweet	savory	tangy	burnt

A List of Smell Words

sweet	piney	acrid	sickly
scented	pungent	burnt	stagnant
fragrant	spicy	gaseous	musty
aromatic	gamy	putrid	moldy
perfumed	fishy	spoiled	dry
fresh	briny	sour	damp
earthy	sharp	rancid	dank

A List of Touch Words

cool	wet	silky	sandy
cold	slippery	velvety	gritty
icy	spongy	smooth	rough
lukewarm	mushy	soft	sharp
tepid	oily	wooly	thick
warm	waxy	furry	dry
hot	fleshy	feathery	dull
steamy	rubbery	fuzzy	thin
sticky	bumpy	hairy	fragile
damp	crisp	leathery	tender

Some Critical Points

Developing a Vocabulary of Criticism

Here's the Idea   *Criticism* is "the act of analyzing and of making judgments." You may not be aware of it, but you are being critical all the time. You are being critical when you choose a friend, a book, or a TV program. You are being critical when you shop for vegetables, apply for a job, or vote for a political candidate. In these and many other situations, you must be able to judge the good and the bad qualities of what is around you. Moreover, for each of your judgments, you need specific words that can help you to express your findings.

Developing a vocabulary of criticism does not mean merely learning to express an opinion. For example, you may describe a movie as "great." However, by doing so you are merely giving your *subjective*—or personal—opinion of it. That judgment is weak if you have said nothing about why the movie was "great." Such criticism supplies very little information.

The most informative and valuable criticism attempts to be *objective*—fair and impersonal. Objective criticism is concerned with explaining why an opinion is held. Its main purpose is to convey information. Therefore, it is based on words that convey information rather than opinion.

Your first step in developing a vocabulary of criticism must be to discard such empty words as *good, okay, great, terrible, terrific,* and *neat.* These are all vague words that tell a reader nothing about what you are evaluating except that you liked or disliked it. Instead, choose specific words that express the qualities of something in an informative way.

Check It Out   Compare the following criticisms.

1   "Presenting the Candidates" was a great TV show. Last night's program was well done. It was interesting and enjoyable. Most important, I learned a lot.

2   "Presenting the Candidates" was an informative and impartial review of the Democratic and Republican presidential candidates. In the first segment of the two-hour special, brief biographies outlined the background of each candidate. Their education and public service records were covered in detail. In the second segment, film clips revealed informal glimpses of the candidates relaxing with their families. In the final and most important segment, each member of the panel of candidates responded in turn to questions dealing with major national issues. This well organized factual presentation is the most comprehensive television program of its kind shown to date in this campaign.

 • Which criticism is subjective? Which is objective?

Try Your Skill   Rewrite the following sentences that contain empty subjective words. Write sentences that show objective judgments. Invent details if necessary.

1. The party was fun.
2. Mr. Jackson is a very nice neighbor.
3. The soccer game was interesting.
4. Juan is a good athlete.
5. The play we saw was wonderful.
6. That was the dumbest movie I have ever seen.
7. Sarah bought a fantastic bike.

Keep This in Mind

 • In making judgments, avoid empty, subjective criticism. Use specific words that convey information objectively.

Now Write   Write several sentences that reflect your objective judgment about something that actually exists. It can be a book, a movie, a TV program, a restaurant, a record, a band, a car or anything else you choose. Use precise, specific judgment words to describe the qualities of your subject. Label your paper **Some Critical Points**, and put the paper into your folder.

Writing Effective Sentences

Direct Action

Using Sentences

Here's the Idea Through your study of vocabulary, you have been learning to use words that are vivid and precise. In order to express an idea, you must learn to combine words effectively. Learn to write good sentences.

A **sentence** is a group of words that expresses a complete thought. A good sentence expresses a complete thought clearly and directly. It also makes a point in an interesting and imaginative way.

Read these examples of effective sentences.

The difficulty in life is the choice.—GEORGE MOORE

Love is love's reward.—JOHN DRYDEN

The dictionary is the only place where success comes before hard work.—ARTHUR BRISBANE

Things don't change, but by and by our wishes change.
—MARCEL PROUST

To be what we are, and to become what we are capable of becoming, is the only end of life.—ROBERT LOUIS STEVENSON

Notice that each of these sentences expresses an idea in a direct and original way. You can see that a single sentence can be powerful. Whenever you write a sentence, use your imagination to express an idea in an effective way.

Check It Out Read the following sentences.

1. General Kelly stretched his tired arms over the ledge and lowered the canvas supply bag to Corporal Fellows.
2. The sun dropped behind the hill, setting the clouds ablaze.

3. After you have put the car in gear, release the brake, and let out the clutch—slowly.

4. Art should reflect real life.

5. A feature of many American barns is the cupola, a small, domed structure on the roof.

· Does each sentence express a single, complete thought? Is each sentence clear and interesting?

Try Your Skill   Write one sentence in response to each of the following directions. Use real or imaginary details to make your sentences clear and effective.

1. Tell an event that happened in the news this week.
2. Describe a quiet place.
3. Explain how to be happy.
4. Explain why friends are valuable.
5. Explain what courage is.
6. Describe a person whom you respect.
7. Tell one event that you will always remember.
8. Explain what a good job is.

Keep This in Mind

· A sentence is a group of words that expresses a complete thought. A good sentence is clear and interesting.

Now Write   Write five original sentences. One should tell something that happened. One should describe something. One should explain one step of a process. One should explain an opinion. One should explain what something is.

Choose your words carefully. Be specific and direct. Label your paper **Direct Action** and put it into your folder.

Point-Blank

Keeping to the Point

Here's the Idea   An effective sentence expresses one idea clearly and directly. Consider these examples.

> I read an informative article about careers in electronics.

> The Sloans spent an enjoyable vacation in California.

Related details may be added to a sentence. Related details are those that support the main idea. By adding related details, you may add interest and meaning to a sentence. Look at these examples.

> I read an informative article about careers in electronics in the Sunday *Tribune*.

In this sentence the added detail is related to the article.

> The Sloans spent an enjoyable vacation at Big Sur in California.

Here, the added detail is related to the vacation.

When you include details in a sentence, be sure that they are related to the main idea. Unrelated details confuse the meaning of a sentence. Look at these examples.

> I read an informative article that was eight pages long about careers in electronics.

> The Sloans, who are our neighbors, spent an enjoyable vacation at Big Sur in California.

In the first example, notice that the added detail adds no real meaning to the main idea of the sentence. In the second example, notice that the added detail is related to the Sloans, but not to their vacation, which is the main idea.

Whenever you write sentences, keep to the point. Use only specific and meaningful details that are related to the main ideas.

Check It Out   Read these sentences.

1. My sister Ginny, who is nearly six feet tall, won three events in the track meet.

2. Taking a bus to Chicago, which is a five-hour trip, is less expensive than taking a plane.

3. Arnold Tyler, who was born in Oklahoma City thirty-eight years ago, announced that he had designed a plan for solving the energy problem.

4. We visited Salt Lake City, which is the largest city in Utah, and we like the city very much.

- In each sentence what unrelated detail should be omitted? What related details might you add?

Try Your Skill   Read the following sentences and decide which ones contain unrelated details. Rewrite those sentences, using related details.

1. The weather forecasters were concerned that the cold front would damage the orchards located near Jacksonville, where I was born.

2. Jill Roberts, president of the amateur sports club, told us about opportunities in athletics for young men and women.

3. The Voyager 1 spacecraft sent back to earth new and revealing pictures of Jupiter, the largest planet in the solar system, and its moons.

4. The members of the photography club, which meets every two weeks, will display their photographs in the auditorium.

Keep This in Mind

- Use related details that add interest and meaning to the main idea of a sentence. Keep to the point of the sentence.

Now Write   Write five effective sentences about subjects that interest you. Use related details that support the main idea of each sentence. Label your paper **Point-Blank** and put it into your folder.

No-Show

Avoiding Empty Sentences

Here's the Idea   Effective sentences express ideas clearly and completely. Some sentences, however, do not express ideas effectively. Some of these sentences are **empty sentences**.
One kind of empty sentence repeats an idea.

> My history teacher came to my assistance and helped me with my report.

To be assisted means to be helped. Therefore, the sentence unnecessarily states the same idea twice.
To improve this kind of empty sentence, you must eliminate the repetition. Sometimes you may choose to simplify the sentence. More often, you will want to add related information.

> My history teacher helped me with my report.
> My history teacher helped me with my report by showing me several informative magazine articles.

There is also another kind of empty sentence. This type of empty sentence states a strong, but unsupported, opinion. A strong statement is made, but no reasons or facts that explain it are presented. In this way, the sentence is incomplete and empty of meaning for a reader.

> Spring is a fascinating season.

To improve this kind of empty sentence, you must add supporting evidence that completes the idea. Supporting evidence may be given in the same sentence or in another sentence.

> Spring is a fascinating season because it is a time of continual awakening in nature.
> Spring is a fascinating season. It is a time of continual awakening in nature.

Check It Out   Read these empty sentences.

1. The book was dull because it seemed boring.
2. Craig's personality is pleasant and he is always nice.
3. Camping is the ideal hobby.
4. Susan is talented and can do many things.
5. Cities are dangerous.
6. Melinda's clothes are fashionable and she dresses stylishly.

• Which sentences repeat an idea? Which state an unsupported opinion? How would you improve each of these empty sentences?

Try Your Skill   Rewrite each of these empty sentences.

1. Margaret Mead wrote an autobiography of her life.
2. Biology is the most interesting science.
3. Individual sports are better than team sports.
4. You have been given the wrong information and you are misinformed.
5. Define each word and tell what it means.
6. The United States is a strong country.

Keep This in Mind

• Sentences that repeat ideas or state unsupported opinions are empty sentences. Improve a sentence that repeats an idea by simplifying it or by adding related information. Improve a sentence with an unsupported opinion by adding reasons or facts that support the opinion.

Now Write   Label your paper *Empty Sentences*. Write, or find, three examples of each kind of empty sentence. Improve the sentences by avoiding repetition or by including supporting evidence. Keep your work in your folder. Continue to check for empty sentences in your writing.

Battle of the Bulge

Avoiding Padded Sentences

Here's the Idea   An effective sentence contains no more words than are necessary. A **padded sentence** contains useless phrases that bury the main idea. The common phrases that signal padded sentences should be avoided. Look at these examples.

what I mean is	well, you see
what I'm saying is	you know
the reason that	in my opinion, I think
my feeling is that	because of the fact that
the point is	owing to the fact
the thing is	on account of the fact that

Usually you can improve a padded sentence simply by eliminating the unnecessary expressions. Sometimes, however, you will need to revise the sentence completely.

Padded   In my opinion I think that television programming should be improved.

Improved   Television programming should be improved.

Padded   Ann's help was valuable to the success of the program on account of the fact that she had experience as a fund raiser and she was willing to volunteer her time.

Improved   Ann's experience as a fund raiser and her willingness as a volunteer contributed a great deal to the success of the program.

Some groups of words using *who is, which is,* or *that is* may also be used unnecessarily in sentences. Use such expressions only when they add to the meaning of the sentence.

Padded   Carmen, who is my best friend, is moving to New York.
Improved   My best friend, Carmen, is moving to New York.

Padded   We attend a dance class that meets on Saturdays.
Improved   We attend a dance class on Saturdays.

Check It Out   Read these padded sentences.

1. Mom will be late for work due to the fact that she overslept.

2. Early covered wagons were called Conestoga wagons because of the fact they were first built at Conestoga, Pennsylvania.

3. What I wish is that I could go with you.

4. It seems to me that some people are always complaining about the weather although it is one of those things that they can't do anything about anyway.

• How would you improve each of these padded sentences?

Try Your Skill   Rewrite these padded sentences. Improve them by eliminating useless phrases or by revising the sentence completely.

1. For three years we lived in New Orleans, which is, as you know, in the state of Louisiana.

2. I think that Gwen should be elected because she is, in my opinion, the most qualified of the candidates running for treasurer.

3. Hal is a dependable employee owing to the fact that he is always at work on time.

4. What I mean is I like ice-skating on account of the fact that it makes me feel as if I'm flying.

Keep This in Mind

• Sentences that include unnecessary phrases are padded sentences. Improve a padded sentence by eliminating the useless expression or by revising the sentence totally.

Now Write   Label your paper *Padded Sentences*. Write, or find, five examples of padded sentences. Improve the sentences by deleting useless phrases or revising the sentences completely. Keep your paper in your folder. Check for padded sentences in your writing.

Think Small

Avoiding Overloaded Sentences

Here's the Idea   You need to limit the number of ideas you express in a single sentence. Sentences containing too many ideas are **overloaded sentences.**

Overloaded sentences usually contain several thoughts loosely joined by *and*. However, the word *and* is used incorrectly when it is used to connect ideas that are not related.

> Carrots are a practical vegetable to buy, and they are inexpensive and they are a good source of Vitamin C, and they can be eaten raw or cooked in a variety of ways, and there are many recipes for delicious carrot cakes.

From this example, you can see how confusing an overloaded sentence is. Too many ideas run together. Which is the main idea? It is difficult to tell. You should avoid such confusion. Separate an overloaded sentence into several shorter sentences.

> Carrots are a practical vegetable to buy. They are inexpensive and a good source of Vitamin C. In addition, they can be eaten raw or cooked in a variety of ways. There are even recipes for delicious carrot cakes.

There may be times when you need to express a complex idea in writing. However, be sure that a single sentence contains only one main idea or related ideas.

Check It Out   Read this overloaded sentence.

> Overloaded   On the first day of our trip, we crossed the Mississippi River into St. Louis, and just as we were about to stop for the night our car sputtered and stopped, and we located a mechanic, and he said that it would take two days to repair the engine, and we did some unexpected sightseeing in St. Louis.

Improved On the first day of our trip, we crossed the Mississippi River into St. Louis. As we were about to stop for the night, our car sputtered and stopped. We located a mechanic, who told us that it would take him two days to repair the engine. As a result, we did some unexpected sightseeing in St. Louis.

• How has this overloaded sentence been improved?

Try Your Skill   Improve the following overloaded sentences.

1. I searched everywhere for my missing wallet and I looked in the house, outside, and in the car and then I retraced my steps and finally found the missing wallet in a drawer of my desk at work.

2. The horseshoe crab is found on the eastern shores of the United States and it has a large, rounded body and a stiff, pointed tail, and it is also called "king crab."

3. The Cheshire cat is a fictional character, and it is always grinning, and it gradually disappears with only its grin remaining visible, and the cat is in the book *Alice's Adventures in Wonderland*, and it is written by Lewis Carroll.

4. Some people think that the federal government should deregulate oil prices and that would probably cause gas and oil prices to rise, but if gas and oil prices rose, then people would buy less, and the country would have to import less, and maybe that would help control inflation.

Keep This in Mind

• Sentences that contain too many ideas are overloaded sentences. Improve an overloaded sentence by separating it into shorter sentences.

Now Write   Label your paper *Overloaded Sentences*. Write four examples of overloaded sentences. Improve them by separating the main ideas into several shorter sentences. Keep your paper in your folder.

Balance of Power

Making Sentences Parallel

Here's the Idea   When you write a sentence, you must express a complete thought. You should also keep to a point, avoid repetition and unnecessary phrases, and limit the number of ideas in the sentence. In addition, you should join the parts of the sentence in a smooth and balanced way.

Usually, the word *and* is used to join similar sentence parts. These equal sentence parts should be in the same form. When they are, they are **parallel**. Sentences containing parts that are not parallel are faulty. These faulty sentences are awkward and confusing. Look at the following sentence.

> Maria is intelligent, ambitious, and likes to study.

You can see that the parts *intelligent, ambitious,* and *likes to study* serve the same function in the sentence. Therefore, these three parts should be in the same form. Notice the improvement in the sentence when the parts are parallel.

> Maria is intelligent, ambitious, and studious.

Many sentences with faulty parallelism can be corrected in more than one way. Any of the similar parts may be changed, although one change will probably sound most natural. Compare these examples.

> **Faulty**   Making the swim team requires skill, practice, and you have to want to.
>
> **Parallel**   Making the swim team requires you to be skillful, to practice, and to want to make it.
>
> **Parallel**   Making the swim team requires skill, practice, and desire.

Notice that both sentences with parallel structure are correct. However, the shorter parallel sentence sounds more natural. Thus, that sentence is more effective.

32

Check It Out   Compare the following pairs of sentences.

Faulty   This year we are going to take a vacation by bus, train, or fly.

Parallel   This year we are going to take a vacation by bus, train, or plane.

Faulty   The referee explained the rules that he would follow and that he would use certain signals.

Parallel   The referee explained the rules that he would follow and the signals that he would use.

· How has each faulty sentence been made parallel? Can any sentence be corrected in a different way?

Try Your Skill   Rewrite the following sentences, making the similar parts parallel.

1. The dogs in the show are judged on their appearance, their breeding, and how they behave.

2. The teacher explained the lesson and that the assignment was due in two days.

3. I like movies with suspense, dramatic music, and filled with colorful scenery.

4. For the part of the mother, we need a person with some acting experience and who has an alto voice.

Keep This in Mind

· Sentence parts serving the same function should be parallel. Many sentences with problems in parallel structure can be corrected in more than one way.

Now Write   Write, or find, four examples of sentences containing similar parts that are not parallel. Rewrite the sentences, making the parts parallel. Be sure that your revised sentences are clear and smooth. Label your paper **Balance of Power** and keep it in your folder.

Variations on a Theme

Varying Your Sentences

Here's the Idea Any sentence idea may be stated in a variety of ways. Each way may emphasize a different aspect of the idea. You must decide which way expresses most precisely a particular idea as you mean it.

In a series of sentences, variety becomes especially important. When you write a series of sentences that are too similar, your writing seems monotonous and ineffective. To strengthen your writing and make it lively, add variety. Vary the order in which you present ideas. Vary the ways in which you combine ideas. Vary the length of your sentences.

One way to vary sentences is to rearrange the word order. For example, use different beginnings. Look at the following sentences. The first sentence is written in the most common order. The other sentences express the same idea but with a variety of beginnings.

> Leo practiced the guitar faithfully for two hours each day.
> For two hours each day, Leo faithfully practiced the guitar.
> Faithfully, Leo practiced the guitar for two hours each day.
> Each day, Leo practiced the guitar faithfully for two hours.

Another way to strengthen your writing is to vary the structure of sentences. For example, the two ideas *Carla got up early* and *she wanted to be on time* can be combined into an effective sentence in a variety of ways.

> Carla wanted to be on time, so she got up early.
> Wanting to be on time, Carla got up early.
> Because she wanted to be on time, Carla got up early.
> Carla wanted to be on time; therefore, she got up early.

Finally, a series of sentences of the same approximate length can also be monotonous. Try to vary sentence length within a group of sentences.

Check It Out   Read the following paragraph.

When Linda bought her first car, she didn't realize the extent of her financial responsibility. She had thought only about keeping the gas tank filled and about enjoying the convenience. However, Linda soon learned otherwise. Filling the tank every week cost more than she had expected. Oil changes and tuneups added a great deal to the cost of maintaining the car. Since she was under twenty-five, her insurance bill was considerable. As soon as Linda had paid that bill in full, she received one for excise tax. After six months, Linda sold her car and began taking the bus.

• How have these sentences shown variety?

Try Your Skill   Rewrite each of the following sentences or pair of sentences. Use a variety of beginnings and structures to express these ideas. Invent necessary details.

1. We had dinner late. The traffic delayed us.
2. I was disappointed when I heard the bad news.
3. Mark worked hard at his first job. Mark was successful.
4. I stepped off the curb. I fell down.
5. The President repeatedly urged adoption of wage and price controls.
6. Many people today are finding jobs in the field of computer technology.
7. In 79 A.D. Mt. Vesuvius erupted, pouring molten lava down the mountainside. The lava destroyed the city of Pompeii.

Keep This in Mind

• A sentence idea can be expressed in more than one way. Sentences can be varied by using different beginnings, structures, and lengths.

Now Write   Write three original sentences. Rewrite each of your sentences in two different ways, striving for variety. Label your paper **Variations on a Theme**. Put it into your folder.

Analyzing
the Paragraph

Part 1 **Make a Stand**

Defining a Paragraph

Here's the Idea You have analyzed words and sentences. Now you are ready to analyze paragraphs. A **paragraph** is a group of sentences dealing with one main idea. For example, notice how the sentences in each of these groups work together.

1   Last Saturday I took my date to the new Takahashi Restaurant. It was my first Japanese meal. I ordered sukiyaki, and a young woman in a black and white kimono brought us a platter of thinly sliced meat, onions, and other vegetables. She quickly grilled these items at our table and filled our plates with the hot foods. Then she broke a raw egg into a bowl, handed it to me, and stepped back, waiting. I didn't know what to do. In desperation, I nodded in thanks and picked up a spoon to sip the egg. When my date giggled, I looked up. Then, the waitress explained to me how to dip the hot food into the egg. The meal was delicious, but I vowed to ask questions before I try another new dish.

2   The near-empty auditorium echoed. The only sounds were the whispers of the few campaign workers too exhausted to move. Crushed paper cups and shreds of paper streamers covered the floor. Scattered amid the debris were dozens of discarded campaign buttons. Suddenly, the door opened and the candidate herself entered the room. Her disappointed supporters clapped, but Ellen Collins looked truly defeated.

3   Taxes keep rising in our city, and taxpayers keep complaining. However, the higher taxes have bought us improved services. We are able to maintain our good schools, a well equipped fire department, and a municipal pool and public tennis courts. A great deal of money is needed continually. If residents want lower taxes, they will have to learn to do without many services. Taxpayers simply cannot demand something for nothing.

38

Check It Out Examine the three groups of sentences. The first group tells a story. The second group describes a scene. The third group explains an opinion.

• Are these groups of sentences paragraphs? Does each group of sentences deal with one idea?

Try Your Skill One of these groups is a paragraph. One is not. For the group that is a paragraph, write the main idea. For the group that is not, explain why.

1   During periods of warm weather, many people wish they owned a motorcycle. Of course, it is precisely at such times that most motorcycle owners do not want to sell. Therefore, it makes more sense to buy a motorcycle during the winter. The prices of used motorcycles are lower then, and there are more vehicles for sale. In addition, it is most sensible to shop by searching through the classified ads. Once I found a good used bicycle through the classified ads, and last winter I found a part-time job there, too.

2   The United States is a nation of watchers. Of the sixty million homes in the United States, ninety-five percent have television sets. One of every four homes has more than one set. The average television set is turned on five and three-quarters hours per day. An American child can expect to view enough television to total 3000 days, or nine years of his or her life. On a winter evening, half of all Americans are at home in front of their television sets. Television-watching seems to be a national addiction.

Keep This in Mind

• A paragraph is a group of sentences dealing with one main idea.

Now Write Analyze the group of sentences in **Try Your Skill** that is not a paragraph. Rewrite it so that it is. Label your paper **Make a Stand** and put it into your folder.

In Unison

Recognizing Unity in a Paragraph

Here's the Idea   A paragraph is an organized unit of sentences. When all of the sentences of a paragraph work together and relate to one main idea, a paragraph has **unity**.

Notice how these sentences relate to an unsettling experience.

> I had been nervous about entering my drawings in the Seattle spring art show. However, I was even more nervous when I walked into the lecture hall at the museum where the entries were being displayed. I started circling the hall slowly, pausing in front of each picture. I pretended to study them, but I was really only looking for my own work. I was too excited to concentrate anyway. By the time I had worked my way halfway around the room, I was truly upset. I could not find my drawings. Had someone lost them? I finished my search in despair. My work was definitely not there. Gathering my courage, I asked one of the judges whether all entries were displayed. She pointed across the hall to a door and told me that there were more in there. Then I saw the sign over the door. It read: Award-Winning Drawings.

Check It Out   Now read this paragraph.

> Thousands of years ago, sometime after the end of the Ice Age, tribes of people came to the New World from Asia. They traveled across the Bering Strait into Alaska and by the fifteenth century they had spread throughout all of North and South America. These people were hunters, fishers, and food-gatherers. They wandered around the land to find food, and they developed many cultures and many languages. By the time Christopher Columbus arrived in the New World there were over thirteen million Indians there. The approximately one million Indians of North America lived in seven major areas: the Eastern Woodlands, the Southeast, the Plains, California, the Southwest, the Northwest Coast, and Alaska.
> —ROSEBUD YELLOW ROBE

· Do all of the sentences relate to one main idea? Does the paragraph have unity?

Try Your Skill   Read the following paragraphs. Decide if each has unity. If a paragraph does not have unity, write the sentence or sentences that do not belong.

1   A recording artist does not always make a lot of money by making a record. When a record is purchased, only about ten percent of the price goes to the artist. The artist must split that money with managers, producers, arrangers, and any backup musicians. Barry Manilow was once a backup musician for Bette Midler. Nevertheless, because this is a period in history when an album can easily sell ten million copies, huge profits are possible.

2   There are many kinds of microphones used in radio broadcasting today. There are microphones that pick up all the sounds in an area, and others that absorb only the sound of the announcer's voice. There are also microphones for interviews, and remote microphones for news reports. Many people rely on the radio for daily news updates.

3   Mimes are trained in the art of portraying characters through movement. They use a combination of acting and dancing, but they never speak any lines. They work without props and in simple costumes. Mimes tell stories that can be understood by anyone from any country because these artists speak through body and facial expressions rather than words.

Keep This in Mind

· All of the sentences in a paragraph should relate to one main idea. Then a paragraph has unity.

Now Write   Name a public figure you respect. Write one sentence that sums up your thoughts about him or her. Below that sentence, list five more sentences related to the main idea. Label your paper **In Unison**. Keep your work in your folder.

What's the Point?

Using a Topic Sentence

Here's the Idea   The **topic sentence** of a paragraph states the main idea in a clear, direct, and interesting way. Because it tells what a paragraph is about, the topic sentence is often the first sentence in a paragraph. Placed in this position, it prepares a reader for what is to follow. However, the topic sentence may be placed anywhere in a paragraph where it expresses the main idea most effectively.

The topic sentence must state an idea that can be developed by the other sentences in the paragraph. For example, the sentence "Boston is the capital of Massachusetts" is too limited to be a good topic sentence. It makes a simple statement of fact that cannot be developed meaningfully. However, suppose you were writing a paragraph about Boston. A more effective topic sentence might be "Boston, Massachusetts, is known as the 'Cradle of Liberty.'" This topic sentence offers an idea that promises more. A sentence like this could be developed by other sentences in the paragraph.

Check It Out   Read the following paragraph.

Some animals are associated with a particular character trait. For example, a dolphin is associated with intelligence and a fox with slyness. An animal that has a reputation for fierceness is the mongoose. Mongoose is the name given to several related animals native to Africa and southern Asia. The common mongoose is only about sixteen inches long with a slender body and a long tail. This small, speedy animal is most noted for its ability to fight and kill poisonous snakes like the cobra. This ability makes the mongoose a fierce enemy.

• Which is the topic sentence? Is it too narrow? State the main idea of the paragraph.

Try Your Skill   Read each paragraph below. Write the topic sentence. If the topic sentence is too limited, label it *Narrow*. Then rewrite it so that it is a better topic sentence.

1   Charlie Chaplin is identified with a derby hat and a bamboo cane. One of the most famous stars in movie history, Chaplin was called "the funniest man in the world" during the era of silent comedies. The character he made famous was "the Tramp." He always wore a coat that was too small and baggy pants that were too large. The little Tramp was usually penniless, but he was always spirited and ready for mischief.

2   Many American portrait painters in the eighteenth century had a practical approach to painting. The artists traveled with canvases that were painted with bodies, but without heads. When customers wanted their portraits painted, they simply chose from the bodies available, and the painter would fill in the face while the customer waited. This unusual method offered convenience to the customer and increased sales to the painter.

3   Cloves were once thought to be a cure for headaches. These dried flower buds, used most often as spices, were also used as breath fresheners. Chinese messengers once had to place cloves in their mouths before speaking to their emperors. This nail-shaped spice has even been suggested as a cure for toothaches and for coughs.

Keep This in Mind

· A topic sentence states the main idea of a paragraph. The sentence should deal with an idea that can be developed in a meaningful way.

Now Write   Think of three topics that you might develop in paragraphs. For each one, write a topic sentence that states the main idea you have in mind. Label your paper **What's the Point?** Keep your work in your folder.

Multiple Choice

Ways of Developing a Paragraph

Here's the Idea Sentences that follow a topic sentence should develop the main idea of the paragraph. One of three basic ways of developing paragraphs will probably be best.

Use lively, specific **details** to make a subject come alive.

> The man came out of the house and stood quite still, listening. Behind him, the lights glowed in the cheerful room, the books were neat and orderly in their cases, the radio talked importantly to itself. In front of him, the bay stretched dark and silent, one of the countless lagoons that border the coast where Florida thrusts its green thumb deep into the tropics. It was late in September. The night was breathless; summer's dead hand still lay heavy on the land.—ARTHUR GORDON

Use one or more **examples** to develop a general statement.

> Most construction workers specialize in certain building materials. For example, carpenters use wood in constructing buildings and such building features as floors and frames. Metalworkers perform such jobs as pipe fitting and welding. They also install plumbing, heating, and air-conditioning systems. Masonry workers use bricks, cement, stones, and similar materials to build foundations, sidewalks, walls, and other structures. They also plaster surfaces and lay tiles. Electrical specialists install wiring and electrical fixtures. Finishing workers paint, wallpaper, landscape, install windows or floor coverings, and do other tasks to complete a building.—*The World Book Encyclopedia*

Use **facts and figures** to make an idea or opinion clear.

> Romanian Nadia Comaneci, the nineteen-year-old favorite of the 1976 summer Olympics in Montreal, astounded spectators and judges alike by performing seven perfect 10.0 routines. She performed four times on the uneven bars and three times on the beam. She is the first athlete in Olympic history ever to achieve a 10.0

score in any event. It had been considered unattainable, but not by Nadia. Indeed, she had achieved the 10.0 score sixteen times in the Olympic qualifying events alone.

—*The Women's Book of World Records and Achievements*

Check It Out   Read the following paragraph.

As Chris entered the forest he was surrounded by sound. A stream of water gurgled over the rocks. Branches of birch trees clacked together in the wind like gossiping neighbors. The older limbs of the stately evergreens creaked as they bent. Nearby, a woodpecker drilled a message into the bark of a tree. In the distance, an owl hooted a warning. The forest seemed a lively, noisy place.

• Is the paragraph developed by details, by one or more examples, or by facts and figures?

Try Your Skill   What is the main idea of this paragraph? Copy the topic sentence. Then write *Details*, *Examples*, or *Facts and Figures* to tell how the paragraph is developed.

Long before the metric system was developed in Europe, kings could set their own standards of measurement. For instance, one king's foot was used as a measure for length. One king's favorite cup was the standard measure for liquids in his country. In England, a yard was measured as the distance from the tip of King Edgar's nose along his outstretched arm to the tip of his middle finger.

Keep This in Mind

• The main idea of a paragraph may be developed by details, by examples, or by facts and figures.

Now Write   From your folder, take out the paper labeled **What's the Point?** Choose one of your three topic sentences. List three details, examples, or facts and figures to develop the main idea stated in the topic sentence. Label your paper **Multiple Choice** and put it into your folder.

The Name of the Game

Recognizing Three Kinds of Paragraphs

Here's the Idea   Every paragraph—whether it is about something real or something imaginary—fits into one of three basic categories. A paragraph might be a story, a description, or an explanation. Each kind of paragraph deals with an idea in a different way.

A **narrative** paragraph tells a story or relates a sequence of events. All events are usually told in the order in which they happened.

A **descriptive** paragraph is a word picture of an object, a scene, or a person. Its sensory details usually create a particular mood.

An **explanatory** paragraph explains something. It may explain a process, state an opinion, or state a definition. This kind of paragraph is also called an *expository* paragraph.

Check It Out   Read the following paragraphs.

1   Mr. Sherlock Holmes was leaning back in his chair, unfolding his morning paper in a leisurely fashion. Suddenly our attention was caught by a tremendous ring at the bell. This sound was followed immediately by a hollow drumming sound, as if someone were beating on the outer door with his or her fist. As it opened, there came a noisy rush into the hall. Rapid feet clattered up the stair, and an instant later a wild-eyed and frantic young man— pale, disheveled, and trembling—burst into the room.
—SIR ARTHUR CONAN DOYLE

2   One cloudy winter evening I sat in the corner of a second-class car of a Tokyo train and waited for the starting whistle. In the car there was no passenger but myself. On the platform, there was not a single person who had come to bid someone good-bye. The only sound was that of a puppy whining sadly from time to time. All of these things seemed wholly suited to my mood. Fatigue and boredom surrounded me with their dull and heavy shadows, like a

gray and shadowy sky. With both hands deep in my pockets, I
didn't even feel like taking the evening paper out of my pocket.
—RYUNOSUKE AKUTAGAWA

3   We put together a unique example of Americans. There were
Jews, Catholics, Protestants, agnostics, white men, black men. The
only thing we had in common was an Irish name—The Celtics.
We did the Irish name proud. Through it all we never had a
quarrel. We simply considered ourselves a proud group of men who
bore the distinction of being something no one else could be in
basketball—the champions of the world.—BILL RUSSELL

· Which paragraph is narrative? Which is descriptive?
Which is explanatory?

Try Your Skill   As you read these possible topic sentences,
decide what kind of paragraph they would most likely be part of.

1. Many adolescents develop poor eating habits.
2. My desk looks chaotic, but it is actually a masterpiece of
organization.
3. A hush fell over the crowd as the conductor mounted the
podium.
4. The first step in baking is to assemble all necessary ingredients.

Keep This in Mind

· A narrative paragraph tells a story or relates a sequence of events.

· A descriptive paragraph creates a word picture.

· An explanatory paragraph explains a process, states
an opinion, or states a definition.

Now Write   Review your work labeled **Multiple Choice**. Write
which of the three kinds of paragraphs you would use for this
topic. Explain why this choice seems best. Label your paper **The
Name of the Game**. Keep your work in your folder.

Writing a Paragraph

A Limited Edition

Narrowing a Topic

Here's the Idea To write an effective paragraph you must begin with a specific topic. A topic as general as "travel," for example, can only lead to a paragraph that is vague and dull.

> Traveling can be an educational experience. Going to a foreign country is certainly educational. Visiting an area with a different climate within your own country can be instructive, too. It is good to see how people work and live in other places.

However, if you narrow a topic, you can write a lively and informative paragraph. One simple way to narrow a general topic is to ask questions about it. Ask *who, what, when, where, why,* and *how* questions, and jot down details.

Who?	I
What?	learned about the southwestern U.S.
When?	one week last July—120°F.
Where?	Yuma, Arizona
Why?	family trip to visit cousins
How?	traveled through desert, across Colorado River

By narrowing the general topic "travel" to a specific experience, you can write a detailed, lively paragraph.

> My favorite geography lesson was a one-week family trip to Yuma, Arizona. Last July we traveled to visit cousins who live in that desert community. A native of Maine, I was fascinated by the southwestern United States. I saw desert areas surrounded by low, barren mountains. I saw lush green areas irrigated by the Colorado River and planted with vegetables, fruits, and cotton. I endured the region's intense summer heat, with highs between 108 and 120 degrees Fahrenheit. For the first time, I realized the powerful effect of geography on our daily lives.

You may not be able to answer all six questions every time you narrow a topic. However, if you try to answer as many questions as you can, you'll find your writing becoming more vivid and interesting.

Check It Out Notice how the topic "first aid" might be narrowed.

Who?	class of 20 adults
What?	learned CPR (Cardiopulmonary Resuscitation)
When?	last Saturday
Where?	Evanston Hospital
Why?	to save choking and heart attack victims
How?	by taking this 6-hour course
Specific topic:	CPR course offered recently by Evanston Hospital

• Could this topic lead to an informative paragraph?

Try Your Skill Choose two of these general topics. List *Who? What? When? Where? Why?* and *How?* Narrow each topic by answering these questions.

jobs   hobbies   families   friends   cities   mountains

Keep This in Mind

• Narrow a general topic by asking *who, what, when, where, why,* and *how* questions. Be sure that your specific topic will lead to a detailed paragraph.

Now Write In this section you will be writing a paragraph on your own. In each lesson you will be completing one step of the process. The first step is to choose a topic. Think of two general topics that interest you. Narrow both topics by answering *who, what, when, where, why,* and *how* questions. Write the specific topics. Label your paper **A Limited Edition**. Keep your work in your folder.

Set Your Sights

Writing a Topic Sentence

Here's the Idea You have learned that a topic sentence states the main idea of a paragraph. To be effective, a topic sentence must be direct and lively. Its directness helps both the writer and the reader to organize their thoughts. Its liveliness helps the writer to capture the reader's interest.

To make a topic sentence direct, get to the point quickly. Avoid using unnecessary words to introduce the subject or you, the writer. Such rambling or personal statements are not effective topic sentences.

> A cactus is the popular choice of many indoor gardeners who can choose from among some 2,000 species with various shapes, sizes, and colors.
> I'd like to write about cactuses, which grow so well in a sunny window in my apartment.

It is far more effective to write a direct topic sentence.

> Cactuses, with their striking shapes, are popular plants among indoor gardeners.
> An indoor gardener should consider the cactus—a plant often oddly shaped, but always easily cared for.

To make a topic sentence lively, find a striking or unusual way to express the main idea. There may even be ideas that you want to express in a humorous way.

> A cactus is a prickly, peculiar, living sculpture.
> A cactus thrives on what seems to be too much light and too little water.

As you have learned, there are many ways to express an idea in a sentence. When you write a topic sentence, try various ways to state the main idea. Make your topic sentence direct and lively.

Check It Out   Read the following topic sentences.

1. My first driving lesson was almost my last.
2. The first course, mud-colored soup, was the highlight of the meal.
3. You can save time and money by changing the oil in your car.
4. The potholes on Lake Street are a hazard to drivers and pedestrians.

- Which of these sentences are direct? Which sentences state the main idea in a lively way?

Try Your Skill   Rewrite these eight ineffective topic sentences. Use real or imaginary details. Make each one a direct and lively topic sentence.

1. I am going to tell you about the first meal I ever cooked.
2. This paragraph will tell you how to get a good job.
3. Molly, my sister who was thirteen in May, broke her arm.
4. I would now like to describe my invention.
5. The purpose of this report is to argue for a lower speed limit on superhighways.
6. Many people are interested in daredevil activities, and one such activity is parachuting.
7. I know what patriotism is.
8. There are many sports to play, but basketball is my favorite.

Keep This in Mind

- Write a topic sentence that states the main idea of a paragraph in a direct and lively way.

Now Write   You are ready for the next step in the writing of your own paragraph. From your folder, take out the topics you narrowed in the last lesson, **A Limited Edition.** Write a good topic sentence for each topic. Experiment by trying to express each idea in several different ways. Write your final topic sentences. Label your paper **Set Your Sights** and put it into your folder.

Selective Service

Developing a Paragraph

Here's the Idea   You know how to narrow a topic for a paragraph and how to write an effective topic sentence. How will you develop your main idea?

In **Multiple Choice** you learned to recognize three basic methods of paragraph development. In that lesson, you analyzed the use of details, examples, and facts and figures. You saw how the use of specific, sensory **details** creates a strong, vivid paragraph. You saw how the use of one or more **examples** illustrates a general statement. You also saw how the use of **facts and figures** helps to prove a point or to make an idea clear.

When you write a paragraph, you must decide how to develop the main idea. Select the method of paragraph development that seems best suited to each real or imaginary topic.

Check It Out   Read these paragraphs.

1   My fondest childhood memories are of my Saturday morning trips to Aunt Jean's house. First, we'd cook a special breakfast. We created rich banana milkshakes or animal-shaped pancakes topped with fresh strawberries. Then we'd be ready for adventure. We went to the planetarium, or to the park, for rollerskating, or to funny little antique shops where we searched for treasure. Wherever Aunt Jean's imagination led us, we usually found a little bit of magic and a great deal of laughter.

2   Some of the most popular and famous characters in literature have been animals. For example, there have been dogs, like Lassie, created by Eric Knight, and Old Yeller, created by Fred Gipson. There has been the horse Black Beauty in Anna Sewell's story, and the wolf White Fang, in Jack London's book. Perhaps the most unusual animal character has been Moby Dick, the great white whale in Herman Melville's famous novel.

3   Nearly one thousand different languages are spoken on the continent of Africa. Four of the most common are Arabic, Berber, Swahili, and Hausa. Swahili and Hausa, for example, account for more than 10,000,000 speakers each. Some African languages are used by as few as 2,000 people, although the average local language has about 200,000 speakers.

  · Which paragraph is developed by details? by example? by facts and figures? Do the choices fit the ideas? Why?

Try Your Skill   Here are five possible topic sentences. Decide how each idea might best be developed in a paragraph. Write *Details*, *Examples*, or *Facts and Figures*. Be prepared to explain your choices.

1. A baseball pitcher must master several types of pitches.
2. The woods were alive with the horde of hunters.
3. Astronauts are twentieth-century pioneers.
4. Americans eat too much.
5. In the depths of the coal mine, the world was dark and cold.

Keep This in Mind

  · You may develop a paragraph by using details, examples, or facts and figures. Select the method of paragraph development that best fits a particular idea.

Now Write   Review the topic sentences that you wrote in **Set Your Sights**, the last lesson. Select your best topic sentence and the most appropriate method of paragraph development. Write a paragraph that expresses your idea in a clear and interesting way. Label your paper **Selective Service**. Keep your work in your folder.

The Bottom Line

Writing a Good Ending

Here's the Idea An ending sentence is an important part of an effective paragraph. Its purpose is to sum up, or to tie together, the related ideas. In this way, an ending helps readers to understand the ideas presented.

A good ending makes a clear, final statement that works with the other sentences in the paragraph. A good ending should not introduce new information. In fact, often an ending may restate the idea of the topic sentence in a slightly different or more complex way.

A good ending should also be interesting. Sometimes it may be appropriate for an ending to be surprising or humorous. In every paragraph you write, try to express your idea in an ending sentence that is clear and effective.

Check It Out Read this paragraph.

> I left home this morning as usual, never suspecting anything was wrong. However, a group of schoolchildren who passed me on the sidewalk turned and ran. Then the clerk at the news stand stared at me, horror-stricken. Alarmed, I raced home, slammed the door, and dashed to the bedroom mirror. When I saw my face, I tried to scream. No sounds came out. Only the buzzing of my alarm clock rescued me from this nightmare.

> • Does the ending sentence tie together the ideas of the paragraph? Is the ending effective?

Try Your Skill Read these paragraphs with ineffective ending sentences. Rewrite or replace the endings. Make your endings clear and interesting.

1   It's hard to believe that the ostrich and the hummingbird belong to the same family. They are both birds, but they represent the extremes of the species. An ostrich can stand as tall as eight feet and can weigh as much as 300 pounds. Its clumsy size prevents it from flying. On the other hand, the hummingbird is the smallest of birds. This agile creature weighs less than a penny. *There are both tiny and huge members of the monkey family, too.*

2   When the branch of First Bank opened near our apartment building, the convenience of its location was overshadowed by inconvenience at first. At the main bank, I had been accustomed to instant recognition. At the branch, none of the tellers knew me. Every time I cashed a check, I had to show a pocketful of identification and account numbers. *The bank certainly has a strong security system.*

3   I hope to be the engineer who designs the perfect car. The body of my car would be completely rust-proof. The tires would never wear out, and they would be as safe on icy roads as on dry ones. The frame of the car could withstand a severe crash with only minor damage. Best of all, the car would run on a small electric battery that would require recharging only once a year. *Maybe the perfect car will be developed soon.*

Keep This in Mind

· A good ending sentence should tie together the related ideas of a paragraph. It should also be clear and interesting.

Now Write   It is your turn to write a strong ending to your own paragraph. Review what you have written. You will find it helpful to read your work aloud, at least to yourself. Then write an ending that sums up your idea in an interesting way. Write your paragraph in final form and proofread it. Label your paper **The Bottom Line**. Keep your work in your folder.

A Writer's Choices

Who's Watching?

Using Point of View

Here's the Idea As a writer, you control what a reader will know by your choice of a point of view. Point of view means the eyes and mind through which something is written.

One point of view you may choose is the **first-person point of view**. You use the pronoun *I* to represent the narrator. A reader will know only what the *I* character knows, but the reader will feel close to that character. Suppose you wrote about a race. Your story might say, "I can remember only pain and the arms of my family. I know that I crossed the finish line and collapsed."

Another point of view is the **third-person point of view** using the pronouns *he, she,* and *they*. Your story is told by an observer who sees and hears everything but who cannot know thoughts or feelings. Told from this point of view your story might say, "As Kate crossed the finish line, the crowd cheered. She threw her arms around her family and smiled weakly."

Another choice is the point of view called **omniscient**, meaning "all-knowing." The pronouns *he, she,* and *they* are used by a narrator who observes everything but who also knows what every character is thinking or feeling. Told from this point of view, your story might say, "As Kate crossed the finish line, she felt a throbbing pain. However, at that moment she was thinking only of her victory and of her family."

Check It Out Compare these paragraphs.

1   I have never forgotten the Christmas when I was four. One look at my parents' faces told me I was in trouble. Thinking that everyone was asleep, I had crept downstairs by myself. Unable to wait any longer, I had opened all of the packages under the tree. I was too young to read then, but I found my presents easily when everything had been unwrapped.

2   Anne Johnson was awakened by the sound of paper rattling. She grabbed her robe and headed downstairs. Her husband Phil followed her. They both stopped and stared when they saw the pile of torn wrapping paper. Opened packages were scattered all over the room, and four-year-old Michael sat in the middle of the mess.

3   A rattling noise had awakened Anne and Phil Johnson. Apprehensively, Anne decided to investigate. Phil felt too exhausted to move, but he thought he'd better follow Anne. Downstairs they were both shocked to discover the messy living room. Amidst the pile of opened presents sat their four-year-old son—who suddenly realized he was in trouble.

> • What is the point of view of each paragraph? What can you see and hear as you read each one?

Try Your Skill   Suppose that you were shopping in the supermarket. While you were deciding which soups to buy, a nearby shopper pulled out a can from the bottom, causing the entire display to crash noisily around you. First, write two sentences that relate these events from the first-person point of view. Next, relate these events from the third-person and omniscient point of view.

Keep This in Mind

- From the first-person point of view, what is written is seen through the eyes of the character *I*.
- From the third-person point of view, the narrator tells whatever can be seen and heard.
- From the omniscient point of view, the narrator tells everything—actions, thoughts, and feelings.

Now Write   Think of a situation in which you were involved with other people. Use two different points of view to write two short paragraphs about the situation. Label each. Then label your paper **Who's Watching?** Keep your work in your folder.

One or the Other

Expressing Real and Imaginary Ideas

Here's the Idea   There are two main types of writing, termed nonfiction and fiction. *Nonfiction* is based on real events. It is the type of writing that appears, for example, in news accounts, biographies, research reports, and encyclopedia articles. *Fiction* is based on imaginary events. It appears, for example, in novels, short stories, many movies, and most television programs.

Whenever you write, you must decide whether to write about a real subject—nonfiction—or about an imaginary one—fiction. You may choose to write narratives about real or imaginary events. You may write descriptions of real or imaginary people, places, or objects. You may write explanations of processes, opinions, or ideas that are either real or imaginary.

When you write nonfiction, you must be accurate. Use **facts** to present your real-life topic. You must be sure that all names, dates, and figures are correct. Use reliable sources to check information.

When you write fiction, you are free to invent a world of your own. You have the power to create people, places, and situations. Use meaningful specific **details** to make your creations believable and vivid.

Check It Out   Compare the following paragraphs.

1   In terms of human casualties, the Civil War cost more than any other American war. About one million men were killed or wounded. Deaths, including those from disease, totaled 529,332. By comparison, about 116,500 Americans died in World War I and 405,500 in World War II. The North lost 364,511 men; the South, 164,821. Disease killed more men than bullets did. About 140,000 Union men and 75,000 Confederates died in battle.
   —*The World Book Encyclopedia*

2   Suddenly, the guns on the slope roared out a message of warning. A spluttering sound of a new battle had begun in the woods. It swelled with amazing speed to a profound clamor that involved the earth in noises. The splitting crashes swept along the lines until an interminable roar was developed. To those in the midst of it, it became a din fitted to the universe. It was the whirring and thumping of gigantic machinery. The youth's ears were filled up. They were incapable of hearing more.
    —*The Red Badge of Courage*

- Which paragraph is based on factual statements? How can they be checked for accuracy?
- Which paragraph is based on imaginary details? Which details make the experience vivid?

Try Your Skill   First, choose a well known city and list five facts about the city. Check your facts in a reliable source. Then, create an imaginary city in your mind. List five specific and meaningful details that reveal the character of your city. Save your lists.

Keep This in Mind

- Use facts to write nonfictional narratives, descriptions, or explanations. Check all information, using reliable sources.
- Use details to write fictional narratives, descriptions, or explanations. Create meaningful specific details that will express an idea vividly.

Now Write   Compare the lists you wrote about real and imaginary cities in the **Try Your Skill** exercise. Use each list to write a short paragraph about each city. You may choose to write narrative, descriptive, or explanatory paragraphs. Make final copies of your paragraphs. Label your paper **One or the Other** and put it into your folder.

What's in a Word?

Creating a Mood

Here's the Idea   You know that there are many ways to
express an idea. By choosing specific words, you can express an
idea in a precise and vivid way. By choosing words carefully, you
can also convey a particular mood, or feeling.

First, you must choose specific verbs. A verb is a word that tells
what *happened* or what *is*. Use strong, specific verbs that express
an idea precisely. For example, compare these sentences.

> The children *were* happy as they *walked* on stage to claim their
> prizes.

> The children *beamed* as they *hurried* on stage to claim their
> prizes.

Notice how the use of strong verbs in the second sentence helps
to express the idea in a livelier way. Notice also how the use of
more specific verbs helps you to see the children more clearly.

In addition to specific verbs, you must also choose specific
adjectives. An adjective is a word that describes. A food, for
example, might be described as *sweet* or *sour*. A friend might be
described as *thoughtful* or *inconsiderate*. A decision might be *just*
or *harsh*. Notice the positive effect created by *sweet, thoughtful,*
and *just*. Notice the negative effect of *sour, inconsiderate,* and
harsh.

Take your time when you write. Consider words carefully.
Select strong, specific words to express an idea or to create a
mood. Select words that will show what you have in mind and
bring the idea to life.

Check It Out   Compare the following paragraphs.

1   Robin awoke feeling as if she were inside a blast furnace. The
blinding glare of the noonday sun forced her to close her eyes. The

intense rays were scorching her skin. Her throat was parched, and she was drenched with sweat. Robin watched the intense waves of heat flickering around her like a breath of an angry dragon. The gritty sand sizzled under her feet as she fled the beach.

2 Robin closed her eyes and snuggled under the warm blanket of sunlight. She stretched her arms and legs on the soft mattress of sandy beach. The sun seemed to be shining on her alone, and she wanted to soak up all of its warmth. Robin felt as cozy as a kitten stretching out for its nap, and as the gentle waves of heat relaxed her she fell asleep.

   · Which strong, specific words help to create the mood of each paragraph?

Try Your Skill   Suppose that you have recently eaten in two different restaurants. One experience was pleasant, and the other unpleasant. Write a brief paragraph about each experience. Choose strong, specific verbs and adjectives. Try to create different moods.

Keep This in Mind

· Select strong, specific verbs and adjectives that will help you to express an idea precisely or to create a particular mood.

Now Write   Write a paragraph dealing with a person or place about which you have strong feelings. Try to express your feelings by selecting strong, specific words. Keep revising your paragraph until you feel you have captured the most meaningful qualities of your subject. Label your paper **What's in a Word?** Keep your work in your folder.

Identity Crisis

Writing an Effective Title

Here's the Idea You have been learning about the choices you must make as a writer. Whenever you write, you must decide whether to write about a real subject or to create an imaginary one. You choose to write a narrative, a description, or an explanation. You choose a point of view from which to write. You select a method of paragraph development that fits a particular idea. You select strong, specific verbs and adjectives that will express your idea or create a particular mood. Making these decisions will be part of the process of writing each time you write.

For some forms of writing, you will also need to make other decisions. One decision you may be making fairly often is choosing a title. Short pieces of writing, like paragraphs, do not usually have titles. However, longer pieces of writing, like compositions and reports, do require titles.

A title should be informative and interesting. The best title may sometimes be a simple one that suggests the main idea. "The Lottery" by Shirley Jackson, for example, is such a title. Simple, straightforward titles are generally most appropriate for pieces of explanatory writing, especially those about real topics. Sometimes the best title may be a surprising or unusual one. "The Man Who Could Work Miracles" by H. G. Wells, for example, is this kind of title. Unusual titles are often appropriate for narratives or descriptions, especially those based on imaginary ideas.

Check It Out Read the following titles of stories you may have read.

"The Office" by Alice Munro
"The Lost Phoebe" by Theodore Dreiser
"The Jilting of Granny Weatherall" by Katherine Anne Porter

"The Summer of the Beautiful White Horse" by William Saroyan
"The Dill Pickle" by Katherine Mansfield
"The Mountain" by Martin Hamer
"The Lie" by Kurt Vonnegut, Jr.
"The Leader of the People" by John Steinbeck
"Neighbor Rosicky" by Willa Cather
"Total Stranger" by James Gould Cozzens

· Are these good titles? Why?

Try Your Skill Choose four of the following possible topics for longer pieces of writing. For each topic, write two titles that might work.

1. a narrative about working as a short-order cook
2. a description of a flooded town
3. an explanation of how to care for contact lenses
4. an explanation of why the U.S. needs the draft
5. an explanation of what black holes are
6. a report on careers in fashion designing
7. a story about a boating experience
8. a report on solar energy
9. a description of a mountain cabin
10. a report on the Olympic games

Keep This in Mind

· Use a title for longer pieces of writing. A good title is informative and interesting.

Now Write Review the five paragraphs you have written for **Now Write** assignments in this section. Suppose you were going to write compositions or reports on two of those topics. Write the two topics on your paper and write three possible titles for each. Be sure the titles are informative and interesting. Label your paper **Identity Crisis**. Keep your work in your folder.

The Process of Writing

The Process of Writing

From this point on, you will be learning, and practicing, the skills of writing. You will be able to write often about what is important to you. You will be able to practice different kinds of writing.

There will be lots of variety in your writing experiences. Whenever you write, however, there will be something that remains the same: **the process of writing.** There are three steps you will follow—**pre-writing, writing,** and **rewriting.** As you follow these steps, you will be learning to write.

On these four pages you can follow the process of writing from beginning to end. First, read about each step in the process. Then look at the example that shows how one person might have followed each step.

Pre-writing Sometimes you write in response to an assignment. Sometimes you choose to write in order to communicate something important to you. Whatever you write, and whenever you write, you will find the beginning steps, called pre-writing, very important.

Before you write, you need to focus on your subject. Take your time at this point in the process of writing. Narrow the topic so that you can handle it in a given length.

Think about your audience. Think about whether you want to use a personal point of view or an outsider's point of view. Use all of your senses to bring your subject clearly into focus.

Make a list of interesting details. Jot down any notes or ideas related to your topic. You don't have to use them all. If you need to learn more about your topic, do that, too.

topics

the hail storm — our cactus garden
my newest cousin — my hospital
the Olympics — experience

specifics

waking up, groggy — dry throat
sound of buzzer — no clock
weight on arm — nurse enters
cast, ice bag — Memorial Hospital
tube on arm — skating accident
bottle overhead — mild concussion

notes

kind of paragraph — descriptive
point of view — first-person
develop with details to show mood

You list possible topics.

You select a topic.

You list, in any order, details about your topic.

You plan what you want to write.

Writing   At this point in the process of writing, you are ready to write. Simply put your pencil to paper and write. Don't fuss with the writing. Don't worry about organizing ideas. Don't fret about spelling or punctuation. Just write.

You write a paragraph about your topic.

I woke up in a strange room. I heard a bell ringing and a strange voice. Feeling a weight on my arm, I forced my eyes open. My left arm lay straight beside me. It was wrapped in a cast. An ice bag was resting on the cast. My right arm had a tube taped to it, stretching from my wrist to a bottle. My throat was dry and my lip felt sore. I looked for a clock but couldn't find one. A door opened suddenly, and I tried to sit up. A nurse told me that I was at the hospital and that I would be all right. In a fall while skating, I had suffered a broken arm and a mild concussion.

Notice how this paragraph tells about the topic.

Rewriting Stop. At this stage of the process you will need to work more carefully. Read what you have written. Did you include everything you wanted to? Do you like what you've written? Is it interesting? Think about your topic.

It is possible that you may not like what you've written, and if so, you may want to begin again. It is likely, though, that you generally like your idea. Then you can rewrite whatever you need to change, or want to change.

Concentrate on every word. Is an idea clearly expressed? Did you *show* your reader what you want to say? Is your writing organized logically? Is there a beginning, a middle, and an end to the development of your idea? Is the writing lively and direct? Is each word the right word? Take time to read your writing and to select words thoughtfully.

<table>
<tr><td>

You rewrite. You express your idea in a different way.

</td><td>

I woke up~~, in a strange room~~. ^{feeling groggy} I heard a bell ringing and a ~~strange~~ voice~ ^{on a loudspeaker.} Feeling a ~~weight~~ ^{heaviness} on my arm, I forced my eyes open. ~^{I found myself in a strange room.} My left arm lay straight beside me /, ~~It was~~ wrapped in a~ ^{hard, white} cast. An ice bag was ~~resting~~ ^{perched} on the cast. My right arm had a tube taped to it, stretching from my wrist to a bottle~ ^{of clear liquid over my head.} My throat was ~dry ^{parched} and my lip felt~sore ^{split and}. I looked for a clock but~~, couldn't find one~~. ^{found none} I had lost all track of time.

A door opened suddenly, and I tried to sit up. A~nurse~ told me that I ^{starched-white, smiling gently,} was at~the hospital and that I would ^{Memorial H} be all right. In a fall while skating, I had suffered a broken arm and a mild concussion. I lowered myself carefully onto my pillow and ~ fell asleep.

</td><td>

Notice how this lively paragraph *shows* your idea clearly.

</td></tr>
</table>

Now, you need to look at how you have expressed your idea. It is important to make your writing correct as well as clear and lively. Check capitalization and punctuation. Use whatever references you have available to check your work.

Finally, when you are satisfied that your writing is clear and correct, write it out in its final form. Write carefully. Make your work as neat as possible.

When you have finished your final copy, proofread your work. Read your writing aloud, to yourself, one final time.

I woke up feeling groggy. I heard a bell ringing and a voice on a loud speaker. Feeling a heaviness on my arm, I forced my eyes open. I found myself in a strange room. My left arm lay straight beside me, wrapped in a hard, white cast. An ice bag was perched on the cast. My right arm had a tube taped to it, stretching from my wrist to a bottle of clear liquid hanging over my head. My throat was parched, and my lip felt split and sore. I looked for a clock, but found none. I had lost all track of time. A door opened suddenly, and I tried to sit up. A starched-white nurse, smiling gently, told me that I was at Memorial Hospital and that I would be all right. In a fall while skating, I had suffered a broken arm and a mild concussion. I lowered myself carefully onto my pillow and fell asleep.

You can learn to write only by writing. In each writing section you will be learning an idea about writing, checking your understanding of the idea, practicing your skill, and then writing on your own. Whenever you write, try to follow the steps in the process of writing. Each time you write you will be learning something about writing, and about yourself.

The Narrative Paragraph

In the Beginning

Using Chronological Order

Here's the Idea A narrative paragraph tells a story. The most logical way to tell a story is to present the events in the order in which they happened. This natural time sequence is called **chronological order**. Most narratives, either real or imaginary, are told in chronological order. Notice the order of events in the following true account.

> On a moonless night in August, 1961, my schooner lay moored to a rotting dock in an island harbor near the south coast of Newfoundland. About midnight I went on deck to smoke a pipe and enjoy the silence. The quiet was soon broken by what sounded like a gust of heavy breathing in the waters almost alongside. Startled, I grabbed a flashlight and played its beam over the dark waters. The calm surface was mysteriously stirred up in great, spreading rings. As I puzzled over the meaning of this phenomenon, there came another burst of heavy breathing. I swung the light to port and was in time to see one, three, then a dozen broad, black whales smoothly break the oily surface, blow, then skip away into the depths again.—FARLEY MOWAT

You tell a narrative so naturally that you may not need to begin with a topic sentence that states the main idea. Write a strong, interesting sentence that begins the sequence of events. Other events should follow logically.

To make the order clear, use transitions. **Transitions** are words and phrases that help you show how much time has passed between events. Here is a list of transitions useful for narratives.

first	now	when	at the same time
then	before	soon	by the time
next	earlier	suddenly	at the beginning
while	after	immediately	in the middle
last	later	finally	at the end

Sometimes you may need to use more specific transitions than these. For example, you may need to say *after two hours*, *at noon*, or *in 1982*. Use a variety of transitions in any narrative.

Check It Out   Now read this imaginary narrative.

Eric blew his whistle and waited by the side of the boat. Soon, in an explosion of warm ocean water, Lily appeared. Laughing, Eric dived into the water beside the trained dolphin. For a while, they swam and floated and practiced diving together. Now and then Lily would leap high above Eric into the air. Suddenly, Lily uttered a series of barks and clicks. Eric answered immediately with his whistle. He let Lily know that he had understood her warning about the shark. By the time Eric was safely back on board the boat, Lily was nowhere in sight.

- Are the events of this narrative in chronological order?
- Point out the transitions.

Try Your Skill   Suppose you decide to have a special birthday party for a member of your family next weekend. In chronological order, list the steps you will take between now and then. Add transitions that show the passing of time between events. Use the list to write a clear, interesting paragraph.

Keep This in Mind

- Organize the events of a narrative paragraph in chronological order.
- In a narrative, use transitions that show chronological order.

Now Write   Write a narrative paragraph based on either real or imaginary events. Follow all the steps in the process of writing. Plan your idea carefully. List events in chronological order, using clear transitions. Write your narrative. Rewrite. Make a final copy. Label your paper **In the Beginning**. Keep it in your folder.

Part 2 **In Any Event**

Developing a Narrative Paragraph

Here's the Idea   You know that an effective narrative paragraph presents a well organized sequence of events. A good narrative is also interesting. What makes a narrative interesting is the use of vivid **details**. When you write a true account, you will recall details from your memory. When you write an imaginary narrative, you will invent details by using your imagination.

One direct way to develop a detailed narrative is to ask yourself the questions that a reader might ask. Ask *who, what, when, where, why,* and *how* questions. Then answer each question with a specific detail.

It is likely that you will not find all of these questions appropriate for every topic. However, it will always be helpful for you to answer as many as you can. It is also likely that you may not want to use every detail in the final version of a narrative. However, it will always be easier for you to write a paragraph if you begin by jotting down all the details that you can think of. Later, in the process of writing and rewriting a narrative, you can select the most suitable and significant details.

Check It Out   Look at this list of details.

Who? I
What? lost my money—$48.00
When? last June
Where? on a bus into Hartford
Why? lost track of my coin purse
How? when the bus started unexpectedly

Now read the paragraph about the mishap.

Alicia and I started to get onto the bus. When she stumbled ahead of me, I bumped into her, and we both laughed. We were on our way into Hartford to shop for graduation dresses, and we were excited. Still laughing, I looked for my coin purse to get the exact change for the bus fare. Suddenly the bus lurched forward as it swung into traffic, and half the contents of my handbag went spilling down the aisle. I screamed and snatched up my heart-shaped purse. That purse had forty-eight dollars crammed in it, savings plus birthday money. I jammed the purse into my coat pocket, and Alicia helped me pick up the lipstick, change, pencils, and keys that had clattered to the floor. Then we took our seats and talked all the way to Constitution Plaza. As the bus pulled away from our stop, I reached in my pocket for my purse. It was gone! I checked both coat pockets and my handbag. My eyes filled with tears as I realized I had lost my dress money somewhere on that moving bus.

- Is this narrative developed by details?
- Does it show *who, what, when, where, why,* and *how?*

Try Your Skill   Think of a situation in which you lost something important to you. On your paper, list *Who? What? When? Where? Why?* and *How?* Recall and list details about the situation. Then use the details to write a narrative paragraph.

Keep This in Mind

- Develop a narrative by using vivid details from your memory or your imagination.
- To develop details, answer *who, what, when, where, why,* and *how* questions about your topic.

Now Write   Write a lively narrative paragraph. Follow all the steps in the process of writing. Choose either a real or imaginary topic. Organize the events in chronological order, using clear transitions. Develop vivid details by answering *who, what, when, where, why,* and *how* questions. Use your pre-writing notes to write your paragraph. Rewrite. Make a final copy of the paragraph and proofread it carefully. Label your narrative **In Any Event** and put it into your folder.

The Descriptive Paragraph

Part 1 **Impressions**
Using Your Senses in Description

Part 2 **Direction Finders**
Using Spatial Order in Description

Impressions

Using Your Senses in Description

Here's the Idea   A descriptive paragraph is a word picture. Through description you are able to reveal a person, a scene, or an object—either real or imaginary. Through a well written description you will be able to share a vivid experience.

In order to write an effective description, you need to explore both the details and the feelings related to your experience. Begin by selecting details that appeal to all the senses—sight, hearing, touch, taste, and smell. Because your senses are what tell you about your surroundings, use them to provide the vivid details of a description. Select specific sensory words that will bring an experience to life. Work from the vocabulary of the senses that you have been building.

Notice the sensory details in this description.

> In my Wisconsin, the leaves change before the snows come. In the air there is the smell of wild rice and venison cooking. When the winds come whispering through the forests, they carry the smell of the leaves. In the evenings, the loon calls, lonely. Birds sing their last songs before leaving. Bears dig roots and eat late fall berries, fattening for their long winter sleep. Later, when the first snows fall, one awakens in the morning to find the world white and beautiful and clean.—THOMAS S. WHITECLOUD

By using specific details, you will also be able to create a mood, or special feeling. For example, you may want your readers to feel peaceful, sad, happy, or frightened. Select sensory words and descriptive words carefully to create the mood or effect you want.

Check It Out   Read the following description.

The high gray-flannel fog of winter closed California's Salinas Valley from the sky and from all the rest of the world. On every side it sat like a lid on the mountains and made of the great valley a closed pot. On the broad, level land floor the plows bit deep and left the black earth shining like a metal where they had cut. On the foothill ranches across the Salinas River, the yellow stubble fields seemed to be bathed in pale, cold sunshine; but‚there was no sunshine in the valley now in December. The thick willow scrub along the river flamed with sharp and positive yellow leaves. It was a time of quiet and of waiting.—JOHN STEINBECK

· What sensory details does this description use?
· What mood does the paragraph create?

Try Your Skill   Think of particular persons, scenes, or objects that fit two of the following general topics. Consider your feelings for each topic you choose. Then list sensory details related to each.

| a friend | a celebration | a hospital |
| an employer | an accident | a theater |

Keep This in Mind

· Use sensory details to create a vivid description.
· Choose specific sensory words to create the particular mood you want.

Now Write   Write a descriptive paragraph. Choose a person, an object, or a scene that you have strong feelings about. List as many sensory details about your subject as you can. Then select the details that will help you to create a particular mood. Organize the details in a natural order. Write the paragraph. Rewrite. Make a final copy. Label your description **Impressions**. Keep it in your folder.

Direction Finders

Using Spatial Order in Description

Here's the Idea An effective description creates a vivid impression through the use of sensory details. An effective description is also well organized.

One clear way to organize a descriptive paragraph is to use **spatial order**. In other words, show how the various parts of a subject are related to each other in space. Start from one significant part and describe everything else in relation to it. Choose any logical pattern. For example, you may describe a subject from top to bottom, from side to side or in a circle. Choose a pattern suitable for a particular subject.

Notice the use of spatial order in this description.

> Roger, exhausted but pleased, inspected the results of his Saturday afternoon labor. The chrome parts of the grille and headlights were brightly polished. The yellow hood reflected his image clearly. The whitewall tires were snow white, for a change. The windows sparkled. The trunk and the rear bumper gleamed mirror-clean. Even the back license plate shone like new.

There are **transitions** that will help you to make the spatial order clear. Here is a list of transitions often used in description.

above	beside	in the center	over
across	between	near	side by side
against	by	next to	south
ahead of	down	north	throughout
at the end of	east	on	to the left
at the top	facing	on the bottom	to the right
around	in	on the corner	under
behind	in back of	on the edge	up
beneath	in front of	outside	west

Check It Out   Read this description.

> Lined up across the stage stood the ten finalists. Smiling nervously, they were avoiding looking at the front row of seats where the group of judges sat huddled. Instead, those dancers who had survived the final audition stared straight ahead. They watched the orchestra directly in front of them filling the tense moments with soft music. Sometimes, their eyes wandered over the heads of the musicians to the sea of faces filling the hall. There they hoped to spot the warm, encouraging smile of a mother or cousin or friend.

• How does this description use spatial order?
• Point out the transitions.

Try Your Skill   Examine the photograph at the very beginning of this book. Study the relationship of people and objects and decide on a logical spatial order that fits the picture. Then write a descriptive paragraph based on the picture. Use clear transitions.

Keep This in Mind

• Use spatial order to organize a description. Focus on something and describe everything else in relation to it.
• In a description, use transitions that show spatial order.

Now Write   Write a descriptive paragraph. Follow all steps in the process of writing. Choose either a real or imaginary subject, and list sensory details related to it. Organize the details in an appropriate spatial order. Write your description. Rewrite. Make a final copy of the paragraph. Label your paper **Direction Finders** and put it into your folder.

The Explanatory Paragraph

How About That?

Writing a Paragraph That Explains a Process

Here's the Idea   Besides narrative and descriptive paragraphs, there are explanatory paragraphs. Explanatory paragraphs explain a process, state an opinion, or state a definition. Most explanatory paragraphs are factual, based on real subjects.

A paragraph that explains a process must be detailed and accurate. The explanation may tell how to do something or how to make something. Choose a simple process, such as a household task or a sports activity, that you know well. For example, you may want to explain how to make candy, plant a flower garden, frame a picture, or repair rust damage to a car.

You need to explain the entire process **step-by-step**. Write each step as a single, specific direction. Organize the steps in the natural time order of the process. Be sure to note any steps that depend on one another.

> Hot, buttered corn on the cob fresh from a charcoal grill can be the highlight of a summer meal. To make corn that is neither tough, soggy, nor charred, try the following steps. First, peel back the outer layers of husk and remove the corn silk. Next, replace the husks and soak the corn in water for one hour. Finally, remove the corn from the water, shake it, and put it on a hot grill. Let the ears roast for about thirty minutes, turning them two or three times. Then enjoy this delicious treat.

Use **transitions** that will help you show step-by-step order. These include such words as *first, second, next, until,* and *finally.* These also include such phrases as *at first, after that, at the same time,* and *the last step.* Whenever necessary, use transitions that show a specific time sequence.

Check It Out   Read the following paragraph.

You can create personalized and artistic gifts by learning the art of decoupage. Decoupage, a French word meaning "a cutting up," is the art of decorating with paper cutouts. Decoupage consists of five steps. First, cut out the designs or pictures to be used. Lovely and suitable selections can come from magazines, old greeting cards, photographs, or even wrapping paper. Second, sand the outside of the object to be decorated. Then coat the cutout with a sealer and glue it to the object. Next, apply many coats of varnish to the decorated surface. Finally, wax and polish the last coat of varnish. You can turn lamps, small boxes and trays, and furniture into works of art through decoupage.

• Does this paragraph explain a process in a detailed way? Which transitions show step-by-step order?

Try Your Skill   Write the steps of these jumbled instructions for washing windows in the correct order. Add clear transitions.

1. Remove water with horizontal wipes of the squeegee.
2. Using a sponge, wash windows with the vinegar-water mix.
3. Polish corners and stray streaks on the windows with a dry rag.
4. Collect clean smooth rags, a sponge, a rubber squeegee, a pail of water, a measuring cup, and a bottle of vinegar.
5. Stir two cups of vinegar into a pail of water.

Keep This in Mind

• An explanatory paragraph may explain the process of doing or making something. Be sure the steps in the process are detailed and accurate. Use transitions that show step-by-step order.

Now Write   Write an explanatory paragraph that explains a process. Choose an activity and list the steps in the process. Include transitions that show step-by-step order. Label your final copy **How About That?** Put it into your folder.

I Believe

Writing a Paragraph That States an Opinion

Here's the Idea   You have strong feelings about many subjects that affect your life. You may want to write an explanatory paragraph that states a certain opinion. Begin an explanatory paragraph by stating your opinion in a direct and specific topic sentence. Then present convincing reasons or facts to support your opinion. Organize supporting evidence **in order of importance,** from the least important point to the most important.

Use two kinds of **transitions** to help you develop an opinion. One group of transitions helps you to state reasons or facts. This group includes *because, so, since, if, therefore,* and *as a result.* The other group helps you put the reasons or other facts in order of importance. This group includes *the first reason, second, most important,* and *finally.*

The concluding sentence of the explanatory paragraph should sum up your argument strongly and clearly.

Check It Out   Examine these notes.

Opinion: Everyone should become more involved in recycling.

Reasons: to reduce litter, to save money, to extend the earth's resources

In a second pre-writing step, the reasons can be written with appropriate transitions and arranged in order of importance.

everyone should recycle	*since* litter is becoming unmanageable	= *first of all*
will save money	*if* materials can be used again	= *more important*
will save natural resources	*as a result* of not having constantly to produce new materials	= *most important*

Now read the completed paragraph.

Every responsible citizen should become more involved in recycling. Let us all save newspapers, aluminum cans, and glass bottles. First of all, every city is becoming choked with litter. Recycling would greatly reduce the amount of trash and clutter now needing disposal. More important, by reusing materials, corporations can save money on production costs, and can pass this savings on to the consumer. Most important, as a result of widespread recycling, the nation will slow its consumption of natural resources. For example, we will save huge numbers of trees and barrels of oil now needed to make paper and aluminum. Recycling can help guarantee a more abundant future for everyone.

• Does the topic sentence state an opinion directly? Is the supporting evidence organized in order of importance? Which transitions are used? Does the concluding sentence sum up the argument?

Try Your Skill Think about one of the general topics below. Write a good topic sentence that expresses your opinion. List, in order of importance, three reasons or facts to support your opinion. Write a sentence to sum up your opinion.

driving   exercising   marrying   working   voting

Keep This in Mind

• An explanatory paragraph may state an opinion. State the opinion in a topic sentence. Support the opinion with reasons or facts. Use transitions that show their order of importance. Sum up your argument in the concluding sentence.

Now Write Write an explanatory paragraph that states an opinion important to you. Follow the steps in the process of writing. Make a final copy. Label your opinion **I Believe** and put it into your folder.

A Definite Answer

Writing a Paragraph that States a Definition

Here's the Idea   An explanatory paragraph may also state a definition. What is defined may be an object or something that really exists, such as *grits, a stockbroker,* or *pesticides*. What is defined might also be a term or idea, such as *rock-and-roll, recession,* or *patriotism*.

A good definition does three things. First, it gives the word to be defined. Next, it puts a subject in the general class to which it belongs. Then, by giving specific characteristics, it shows how the subject is different from all other members of its class.

Suppose you want to define a lemon. What is a lemon? First, you would state that a lemon is a fruit. That puts it in its general class. But how is a lemon different from other fruits? A lemon is a citrus fruit. That shows how a lemon is different from apples, berries, or bananas. Because there are several other citrus fruits, such as oranges and grapefruit, you might add that a lemon is small and tart in flavor. Because the lime is also a small, tart citrus fruit, you need to state that the lemon is yellow. Now you have a complete definition. You might state your complete definition as follows: A lemon is a small citrus fruit with a yellow rind and a tart flavor.

State a clear, specific definition in the topic sentence of an explanatory paragraph. Develop that definition as completely as possible in the rest of the paragraph. Use either facts and figures or details.

For example, if you define *pesticides*, you will probably develop the explanation with facts and figures. Check your information in a reliable reference. However, if you define an idea like *patriotism* you will probably use specific details based on personal experience to develop your definition. Be sure all definitions are clear and complete.

Check It Out Read the following paragraph.

An ambulance is a motorized vehicle used for transporting the sick or injured. Modern ambulances are equipped with cots designed to prevent jarring. They also contain medical supplies and equipment, such as oxygen, blood-transfusion equipment, and heart-monitoring equipment. Ambulances are used mainly to take patients to a treatment center or hospital, but they can also be used to move a patient back home or to another health care facility. There are both civilian and military ambulances. Civilian ambulances are constructed to be fast and comfortable. They usually hold one or two patients. Military ambulances, sometimes used on rough terrain, must be sturdy rather than speedy. These larger ambulances can hold four to six patients and more equipment for immediate emergency treatment.

· Is the topic sentence a definition? Is the paragraph developed with facts and figures or with personal details?

Try Your Skill Choose three of the following objects, terms, or ideas. For each one, write a good definition.

a wrench	a bog	a la carte	a novel
a barge	cold war	family	success

Keep This in Mind

· An explanatory paragraph may state a definition. The topic sentence should be a definition. A definition puts a subject in its general class and gives its specific characteristics. Develop the definition by using facts and figures or details.

Now Write Write an explanatory paragraph that states a definition of an object, term, or idea important to you. Write a good definition as the topic sentence. Develop the definition with facts and figures or with personal details. Label your paper **A Definite Answer**. Keep your work in your folder.

Analyzing the Composition

Group Dynamics

Defining A Composition

Here's the Idea   A **composition** is a group of paragraphs dealing with one main idea. In some ways, a composition is similar to a paragraph. Both deal with only one main idea that may be real or imaginary. Both have a logical beginning, middle, and end and are organized by the used of transitions. Although a topic for a composition is one that is too broad for a single paragraph, it must also be limited to the scope of one main idea.

Check It Out   Read the following composition.

A Driving Ambition

Getting my driver's license was a much more complicated process than I had expected. First came months of waiting impatiently for my sixteenth birthday. The hardest part of the waiting was watching my older friends. Some already had their licenses when I still had months to wait. At last summer came, and then my birthday. As a gift, my parents offered to pay for an inexpensive summer course in driver education offered by the local high school.

Instead of taking the easy, automatic, way out, I decided to learn how to drive a car with manual transmission. That is, I had to learn to shift gears. For my first lesson, my instructor, Marion McKenna, began with a lecture on the simple use of the three basic pedals—the gas, the clutch, and the brake.

However, three pedals proved to be one too many for me. For the first several lessons I wasn't sure whether I was learning to drive a car or ride a horse. I jolted the car so often that I felt bruised. It was the clutch that did me in. I couldn't seem to balance the tension between the clutch and the gas pedal.

Near the end of the course, my instructor commented quietly that some people are better at one thing, some at another. She remarked that I was probably expert at painting or tennis, or stamp-collecting. I decided that I needed a few more lessons.

Several hours of lessons later, I had gained skill and confidence enough to apply for my license. Marion drove me to the state license bureau. I passed my written exam, and faced the final hurdle—the road test. Suddenly, I realized that I would be using a different car, not the usual training car with its two sets of brakes, but I felt confident and ready to go.

Marion gave me a final smile of encouragement, and the driving examiner slid onto the seat beside me. I sat waiting, anxious to start the engine. Instead, I was told to turn on the windshield wipers. For the first time I noticed the dashboard. Four silver unmarked knobs faced me. I reached out and pushed one. Nothing happened. I tried pulling instead, and the wipers actually started waving. The examiner smiled and told me to start the car.

During the next twenty minutes, I followed all of the examiner's commands without difficulty. Finally, when I stopped the car in the parking lot of the license bureau, the examiner told me that I had passed the test. I sighed, realizing that I had traveled a long road to earn my driver's license.

· What is the main idea of this composition?

Try Your Skill Copy the following list of topics. Write *P* if the topic could be covered in a paragraph. Write *C* if the topic requires a composition.

1. how to insulate a house
2. the story of making a new friend
3. a description of Williamsburg, Virginia
4. how to park a car
5. why gerbils are good pets

Keep This in Mind

· A composition is a group of paragraphs dealing with one main idea.

Now Write List six possible topics for compositions. Label your paper **Group Dynamics**. Keep your list in your folder.

A Threesome

The Parts of a Composition

Here's the Idea   When you write a paragraph, you develop it in a logical order. Each sentence has a purpose. A composition also develops a topic in a logical order. Within the three main parts of a composition, each paragraph has a purpose.

The first paragraph is the **introduction**. In it, state your topic clearly and prepare your readers for what is to follow.

The middle paragraphs are the **body** of a composition. In a narrative composition, the body contains the events of a real or imaginary story. In a descriptive composition, it contains the sensory details of a word picture. In an explanatory composition, the body contains directions that explain a process, reasons that support an opinion, or details that develop a definition.

The final paragraph of a composition is the **conclusion**. Here you summarize your main idea. You may want to add a title.

Check It Out   Read the following composition.

An Uncommon Friend

Best friends can be childhood playmates, school friends, or fellow employees. I met my best friend a few years ago when I began jogging in the park. She sat on a bench while I ran past her day after day. After a few weeks of smiling and nodding, we started talking—and we haven't stopped since.

People often form friendships by having common interests or by sharing similar experiences. However, my best friend and I have almost nothing in common. I'm not yet old enough to vote and she remembers voting for the first time in 1932 for Franklin D. Roosevelt. My best friend is seventy years old, and her name is Millie. Millie is just five feet tall, but her careful, erect posture makes her seem taller. She has short, silver gray hair, naturally curly. Wire-rimmed glasses frame her twinkling blue eyes, for Millie always manages to find something to be cheerful about.

Millie, a widow, fills her life with others. She lives with her dog, her cat, two gerbils, four goldfish, and a steady stream of boarders. Her eldest son left the dog with her when he took a job in South America. The cat just wandered in one day and has never left. The gerbils were a gift from the boy next door, who learned that he was allergic to them, and the goldfish were a prize won at a carnival. The boarders are harder to account for. When I first met Millie, she had taken in Mrs. Parsons, a sickly woman in her eighties who was alone. From time to time, there are also foster children, teen-agers usually, whom Millie especially enjoys caring for.

Because she was studying painting when we met, Millie asked if she could sketch me as I jogged. That painting is now one of my favorite possessions. Today Millie and I are students together. Millie was studying Spanish, and she talked me into taking a course with her. She is learning more quickly, though, since she became friendly with a Spanish family who moved into her block.

No one listens to me the way Millie does. What I wish, what I fear, what I hope to be—she hears it all, and she always seems to understand. Maybe that's why Millie has become my best friend.

· Identify the introduction, the body, and the conclusion.

Try Your Skill Think of a special friend about whom you might write a composition. List at least fifteen details that reveal the character of your friend. Then write one sentence that expresses your main idea.

Keep This in Mind

· A composition has three main parts: an introduction, a body, and conclusion.

Now Write Review the composition topics you wrote for the last lesson. Choose one topic, and list three headings: *Introduction*, *Body*, and *Conclusion*. Then, for each of these parts write a few sentences explaining what you would include in a composition. Label your paper **A Threesome**. Keep it in your folder.

For Every Purpose

Recognizing Three Kinds of Compositions

Here's the Idea A composition may tell a story, describe something, or explain something. The form and content of any composition work together to do one of these things.

A **narrative** composition tells a story. The events of the story may be either real or imaginary. The important feature of a narrative is what happened. For this reason, the events are usually presented in the order in which they occurred.

A **descriptive** composition is based on sensory details. The details develop a word picture of an object, a place, or a person. The use of vivid, lively details brings a subject to life.

An **explanatory** composition explains something. It may explain how something is done, why something should be so, or what something is. Steps in a process, reasons, or facts are used to develop the explanatory composition. This kind of composition may also be called an *expository* composition.

Check It Out Read this composition.

Feet First

Two of the problems most talked about today are the rising costs of energy and the rising costs of health care. Thus, people are being urged to conserve energy and to keep healthy. However, a vital and simple form of exercise is being ignored—walking. Walking, both as a form of exercise and as a source of energy, should be revived.

First of all, walking is an activity available to more people than any other form of exercise. Walking does not require an expensive piece of equipment or a special outfit. Walking costs nothing! Also, it requires no track, rink, or other particular location. The busiest streets or the quietest woods are suitable arenas for walking.

Second, in most sports beginners are urged to make sure they are fit enough to take up an activity. Medical checkups are suggested and caution is advised. Walking, however, is safe for the young, the not-so-young, the strong, and the not-so-strong. Also, beginners need no expensive series of lessons. In other words, almost anyone, anywhere, at any time can enjoy walking.

Most important, walking strengthens the muscles, exercises the heart, expands the lungs, and burns up calories. However, in addition to these physical benefits, walking can do more. A half-hour daily walk can give people the chance to collect their thoughts, to reflect, to relax. A walk with a friend, parent, or child can offer valuable time for conversation and sharing. Also, taking a stroll in their neighborhoods provides people a chance to see familiar sights at a pleasant pace.

Finally, once people begin to enjoy the benefits of walking, they can use their new-found energy to save even more energy. Routine drives to the store around the corner, for example, can become walks. Many drivers could substitute some portion of their driving with walking. Such a saving of energy should indeed put this country back on its feet.

· What kind of composition is this? How do you know?

Try Your Skill Examine the compositions shown in this section in **Group Dynamics** and **A Threesome**. Write what kinds of compositions they are and explain your answers.

Keep This in Mind

· A narrative composition tells a story. A descriptive composition creates a word picture. An explanatory composition explains a process, states an opinion, or develops a definition.

Now Write Take out the topics you listed for **Group Dynamics**. Choose one topic for each kind of composition. Write your three topics under the headings *Narrative, Descriptive* and *Explanatory*. Jot down the events, sensory details, directions, reasons, or facts you would include in each composition. Label your plans **For Every Purpose** and put the paper into your folder.

The Narrative Composition

In the Event of

Planning a Narrative Composition

Here's the Idea   Before you write a narrative, spend some time thinking about events that interest you. A narrative that relates events that really happened is a **true account**. A narrative based on imaginary events that are invented is a **story**. Whenever you write a narrative composition, you must decide whether to write a true account or a story.

After you have chosen a topic—real or imaginary—you need to make your pre-writing notes. Plan the three parts of your composition. In the introduction, plan to introduce the most important element of your narrative in an interesting way. In the body of the composition, plan to tell a sequence of events in chronological order. In the conclusion, plan to resolve the main problems in the narrative and tie up any loose ends.

When you jot down notes for a true account, include details about the people, places, and events that you remember. When you jot down notes for a story, include details that you invent. Invent details about whoever is involved in the story, called the *characters*; about places, called the *setting*; and about events, called the *plot*.

Check It Out   Examine these notes for a narrative.

Topic	handling many responsibilities
Introduction	Carolyn is star of basketball team
	she hopes to get scholarship
	dreams of being a coach
Body	she has to get job to help family
	Carolyn goes to see her coach
	she says she is quitting team
	Coach tells her to think
	Carolyn talks to advisor
	she drops course and gets morning job

Conclusion	Carolyn works hard for semester
	her father gets his job back
	Carolyn gets scholarship
	chance to play on college team

- Does this seem to be a true account or a story?
- What is included in the introduction? the body? the conclusion? Are there notes about people, places, and events?

Try Your Skill   Here are several general topics suitable for a narrative composition. Choose one and narrow it to a specific situation, either real or imaginary. Make a set of detailed pre-writing notes.

an adventure	making a decision
a disaster	handling a disappointment
a victory	trying something new

Keep This in Mind

- You may choose to write a narrative composition that is a true account or one that is an imaginary story.
- Make a set of pre-writing notes. Plan the introduction, body, and conclusion of a narrative. For a true account, list details about people, places, and events. For an imaginary story, list details about characters, setting, and plot.

Now Write   Think of a topic suitable for a narrative composition. Choose a situation in which an interesting problem or decision is resolved. The situation may be either a real or imaginary one. Plan your narrative by making a set of detailed notes. Label your notes **In the Event of** and put your paper into your folder. You will need it for all of the following lessons in this section.

Be a Troubleshooter

Developing a Narrative Composition

Here's the Idea Before you begin a narrative, select a **point of view**. If you select the first-person point of view, the narrative will be told by the character you identify as *I*. From the third-person point of view, it will be told by a character who only observes the action. From the omniscient point of view, the narrative will be told by a character who knows everything.

Once you have selected the most suitable point of view, you are ready to write the **introduction**. In this first paragraph, present the most important element of the narrative. Introduce the person, place, or event that is to be the main focus.

In the **body** of the narrative, relate what happened. In a true account, develop the sequence of actual events by using accurate details. In a story, develop the imaginary plot by using details that present the conflict. It is the conflict—the major problem affecting the characters—that controls any story. Conflict may arise from a force in nature or from tensions between characters. Sometimes conflict arises within one character who must make a difficult choice.

As you develop the body of a narrative, be sure to include transitions that make the sequence of events clear.

Check It Out Read the beginning of this narrative.

Carolyn was on top of the world. She had just scored twenty-six points, leading her basketball team to another victory. The Weston Warriors remained undefeated and still in first place in the City League. However, Carolyn was especially excited tonight because there had been scouts from two local colleges at the game. If Carolyn could only gain an athletic scholarship, she would be able to pursue her dream of becoming a coach.

Full of these high hopes, Carolyn rushed home and into the kitchen. She stopped suddenly when she noticed the pained expressions on her parents' faces. Carolyn sat down at the table with them, but she wasn't prepared for the bad news they had to share. Her father was being laid off from work for several months. Her parents were hoping that Carolyn would be able to find a job in the afternoons and evenings after classes. In fact, Carolyn's mother had already looked into an opening at the dress shop where she worked.

Carolyn's hopes crashed. Of course she wouldn't mind working. However, working would mean that she would have to give up practice time and maybe even quit the team altogether. How could she manage to get a job, go to classes, and stay on the team?

- From what point of view is the narrative told?
- What important elements of the narrative are introduced?
- What conflict is established in the body?
- What transitions make the order clear?

Try Your Skill   Invent a situation in which a character must choose between two major courses of action that will affect his or her future career. Create specific and original details. Choose a point of view and write an introduction. Then write one paragraph of the body that presents the conflict.

Keep This in Mind

- Select a suitable point of view for a narrative.
- In the introduction, present an important element that draws readers into the narrative.
- In the body, develop the action with details.
- Include transitions that make the order clear.

Now Write   Review the set of notes labeled **In the Event of**. Select a point of view that fits the narrative and write an introduction. Write the body of the composition, developing the conflict. Include transitions that make the order clear. Label your paper **Be a Troubleshooter** and put it into your folder.

So to Speak

Using Dialogue

Here's the Idea   In order to develop a more realistic narrative, you may sometimes want to use dialogue. A dialogue is a conversation between people or characters. Using dialogue is an effective way to bring characters to life.

Try to make dialogue as realistic as possible. Keep in mind the way people actually talk. Also, keep in mind the personalities of your characters. Whenever you write dialogue, follow these rules.

1. Use quotation marks to show that you are using the exact words of a speaker. This is called a *direct quotation*.

2. Only a speaker's exact words are placed inside the quotation marks. Explaining words, like *Joy said*, are placed outside.

3. Separate a direct quotation from the explaining words by using a comma or other appropriate punctuation.

4. A direct quotation may be placed at the beginning of a sentence or at the end. It may also be divided into two parts.

5. Use explaining words for each line of dialogue. Try to vary the explaining words you use. They can help reveal character.

6. Begin a new paragraph every time a different person speaks.

7. If you do not use the exact words of a speaker, do not use quotation marks. This is called an *indirect quotation*.

Check It Out   Read the following dialogue about Carolyn.

Early the next morning, Carolyn walked into her coach's office.
"I might have to quit the team," she said quietly.
Mrs. Benson looked startled. "What on earth is the problem?"
Carolyn explained her parents' predicament.
"I certainly understand your parents' needs," Coach Benson sympathized. "It's too bad this happened now because I talked to the head coach from City College last night. He is definitely interested in seeing you play some more, and City offers just the

program you're looking for in coaching. In addition, they have some money available for athletic scholarships."

"It's too late," sighed Carolyn.

"Haven't I taught you any better than that?" the coach said rather sternly. "When you find one play blocked, what do you do? Give up? No, you regroup, rethink a new game plan. Now, before you take any drastic action, you spend the next few hours thinking."

That afternoon an energetic Carolyn returned.

"You were right, Coach," Carolyn exclaimed. "I did find a way. My advisor said there is an opening for a typist in the mornings in the placement office, and I am applying for the job. This way I can still play, and if I do get a shot at City College, I'll have the courses I need to get in."

"Well, don't just stand there," laughed Mrs. Benson. "Get out on that court and start shooting."

· What does the dialogue reveal about these people? Point out examples of rules for punctuating quotations.

Try Your Skill   Write the following dialogue correctly.

I can't get this machine to work complained Joe. That's ridiculous. Anybody can use an electric can opener answered his younger brother Bob. I've tried three times, Joe replied, but nothing happens. Why don't you try it. Bob looked at the can opener, smiled, and said It helps if you plug it in first, of course.

Keep This in Mind

· Use dialogue to reveal the thoughts of the characters in a narrative. Punctuate correctly.

Now Write   Review what you have written thus far for your own narrative composition. Find a place where the use of dialogue would make the characters and the conflict seem more realistic. Write the dialogue, following the rules for punctuating quotations. Label your paper **So to Speak**. Keep it in your folder.

A Final Offer

Completing a Narrative Composition

Here's the Idea The final paragraph of a narrative composition is the **conclusion**. There you must provide a clear ending to the complex sequence of events you have presented. Resolve any conflict that the characters have been facing and tie up all loose ends.

It is important that your conclusion be consistent with all of the events it follows. Relate how the characters in the narrative solved the problem, overcame the hardship, or made their important decision. If the characters were not successful in dealing with a situation, explain why not. In this resolution, however, the characters should not suddenly develop new habits—unless a character change is part of a surprise ending. Be sure that all elements of the conclusion are consistent with early development of the narrative.

Try to make your conclusion interesting. Sometimes you may want to use humor or surprise to add interest to your conclusion. At other times, you may simply want to sum up a character's reactions. Try to leave a final impression that is memorable.

After you have written a conclusion, review your composition. Write a title that suits the events and the mood of the narrative. Try to write a lively, interesting title.

Check It Out Read the following conclusion and title for the narrative about Carolyn.

Second semester was a blur for Carolyn. Between working, studying, practicing, and playing, she didn't have a minute to spare. However, it was worth every hectic day and every sore muscle. By the end of the term, Carolyn's father had gone back to work, and Carolyn had been offered a tuition scholarship to City College. She would have a chance to play on the basketball team there. When Carolyn shared the good news with Coach Benson, she congratulated Carolyn on her superb game plan.

Title: Shooting for a Goal

- Does the conclusion resolve the conflict presented in the narrative? Is the conclusion interesting?
- Is the title a good one for this story? Why?

Try Your Skill   Write the name of an exciting movie or television show you have seen or a story you have read recently. Write a summary of the ending. Then write a new and different ending. Try to make the conclusion sum up the events of the narrative in an interesting way. Finally, write a new title that reflects the new ending.

Keep This in Mind

- Write a conclusion that resolves the conflict. Tie all the elements of the composition together in a clear, lively ending.
- Write an interesting title that fits the narrative.

Now Write   Take your narrative composition from your folder. Write a conclusion that resolves the conflict. Tie up all loose ends of the story.

Read over the complete narrative. Is the composition well organized? Is the writing detailed and vivid? Is a conflict clearly presented and logically resolved? Make any revisions necessary to strengthen the story.

Write a title that is appropriate for the composition.

Make a final copy of the narrative. Label your paper **A Final Offer**. Keep your paper in your folder.

The Descriptive Composition

Behind the Scenes

Planning a Descriptive Composition

Here's the Idea   A descriptive composition creates a picture with words. However, a vivid description appeals not only to the sense of sight but also to the senses of hearing, touch, taste, and smell. For this reason, your first step in planning a description is to choose a suitable topic. An unusual person, object, or scene that appeals strongly to the senses or arouses strong feelings makes a good choice.

The next pre-writing step is to jot down your notes. Use your senses to discover how your subject looks, sounds, smells, tastes, or feels. List the lively and important sensory details. Then, organize them using spatial order. Show how the various features of your subject appear in space. You may want to include such transitions as *under, behind, to the right, in front of,* or *inside.*

The last of your pre-writing steps will be to arrange your notes in three parts. First, in the introduction, plan to present the subject of your composition. Second, in the body, plan to develop your picture of the subject by using selected sensory details. Third, in the conclusion, plan to summarize your ideas and feelings about the subject.

Check It Out   Examine these pre-writing notes.

Topic	Sal's Diner
Introduction	busy city block at morning rush hour
	Central Street, Somerville
	new, commercial area
	towering new businesses
	with one exception—Sal's
Body	diner is old-fashioned
	wooden, rectangular
	shabby, peeling paint
	squeaky old door
	window boxes full of geraniums

breakfast
    noisy, friendly
    heaping plates of homecooked specialties
neighborhood gathers
    buzz of conversations
    flow of customers
Conclusion   Sal's offers more than its appearance shows
    old-fashioned hospitality
    good food, conversation
    heart of the neighborhood

- What will be the main idea of this description?
- What details will describe the diner? Are the three parts of the composition clearly organized?

Try Your Skill   Choose one of the general topics below as the subject for a descriptive composition. Narrow the topic to a specific, vivid subject. Make a set of pre-writing notes, listing main ideas and sensory details. Arrange the notes into an introduction, a body, and a conclusion.

an animal shelter	a special collection	a storm
a supermarket	a waterfront scene	a special person

Keep This in Mind

- For a descriptive composition, choose and narrow a topic that appeals to the senses.
- List the main ideas and sensory details that you will use to describe your subject. Organize the notes into an introduction, a body, and a conclusion.

Now Write   Choose and narrow a topic for a descriptive composition. You may want to describe a vivid object, scene, or person. Make a set of pre-writing notes. List main ideas and sensory details. Organize the notes into three parts. Label your paper **Behind the Scenes** and put it into your folder.

Using Sensory Details

Here's the Idea   Once you have completed your pre-writing planning, you are ready to write. Begin by writing the **introduction**. Describe the surroundings of your real or imaginary subject. Set the scene and the mood. Try to stir the interest and imagination of your readers. As you describe a scene, be sure to state the specific subject of your description. This sentence in the introduction serves as a topic sentence for the entire composition.

Develop a complete description of your subject in the **body** of the composition. Use meaningful sensory details that will create a vivid word picture. Use language that is as detailed and as accurate as possible. For example, you might describe a certain object as being *wonderful* or *special*. Such general words only vaguely describe an object. However, more specific descriptions, such as *handcarved* or *gold-filled*, show an object more clearly. Always use your senses to help you describe a subject vividly.

Check It Out   Read this introduction and body.

Every morning I get off the Number Twelve bus on the same busy city block. Every morning Central Street bustles with activity. Commuters pass each other in a parade. They hurry, whether on foot or in dusty buses or in whizzing cars. Shops and offices open, welcoming the throng. As Somerville has grown, this block has changed from a quiet old neighborhood to a busy commercial area. Modern buildings reach up towards the sunlight, shiny and sleek —with one exception. Sal's Diner was here long before any of these new structures and still remains the heart of the neighborhood.

Sal's Diner is a tiny, rectangular wooden structure that looks like a railroad car. It is nestled between the twenty-five-story Commercial Bank building and the new Civic Building. Compared with them, the diner is shabby. The yellow paint is peeling. The roof is missing a few shingles. At the right side of the diner, two worn stone steps lead to a glass door, which squeaks and sags on its hinges. To the left of the door are three small windows. Under each window is a flower box overflowing with cheerful red geraniums.

Whenever I open the door and step inside, a tinkling bell sounds. Sal glances out from the grill window, smiling broadly to welcome me, as she does to each of her customers. Then she quickly turns her attention to the waiting breakfast orders. Silverware rattles and dishes clatter. Waitresses place heaping plates on the counter and empty ones into the tub of dirty dishes underneath. Bacon and eggs sizzle on the grill, giving off their tempting aroma.

Every morning I see the same people sitting in the red vinyl booths and at the counter. Voices blend together in a pleasant buzz. Customers come and go, often leaving behind creased sections of the morning paper. On their way out, they wave at Sal. Then they rejoin the working world outside the sagging diner door.

- Does the introduction show the location of the subject?
- Point out sensory details. What senses are included?

Try Your Skill   Choose three of the following objects and think of a particular example of each. List at least six sensory details that describe each object as specifically as you can.

a shaggy dog	a picture	a dandelion	a chair
a butterfly	a sweater	a pineapple	a campfire

Keep This in Mind

- In the introduction of a descriptive composition, describe the location of your subject.
- To develop the body of the description, use vivid and specific sensory details.

Now Write   Review your notes labeled **Behind the Scenes**. List sensory details that will make your description more accurate. Write the introduction. Then write the body of the composition. Label your paper **Full of Life** and put it into your folder.

In the Shape of

Organizing a Description

Here's the Idea A description must be organized in a clear, logical order. You may want to organize some descriptive compositions using **spatial order**. Follow any of the basic spatial patterns. For example, you may describe a subject from side to side or from top to bottom. There may be a subject you will want to describe using a circular pattern.

To make any pattern clear, use transitions. Using transitional words and phrases will help you to organize the details within each paragraph. Using transitions between paragraphs will also help you to show how the parts of your description are related.

To complete your word picture, write a **conclusion**. Consider the main ideas and details you have presented. How can you summarize your feelings about a certain subject? What impression do you want to leave with readers? Write a clear, strong conclusion that ties together your ideas and feelings.

As a final step, you may want to write an interesting and suitable title for your descriptive composition.

Check It Out Review the descriptive composition about Sal's diner that is shown in the last lesson. Notice how the description is organized. Then read the following conclusion and title.

> Sal's Diner looks out of place among its towering new neighbors. It doesn't seem to belong, it's true. Despite its old-fashioned appearance, however, Sal's continues to offer a pleasant haven. Whenever I walk by, I can't seem to resist stopping in for a cup of coffee and a bit of cheerful conversation. Most of the neighborhood shares my feelings and my routine. Sal's is the busiest spot on this busy block, and will probably remain so for quite some time.

Title: A Taste of Home

- In what order is the description organized? Point out the transitions used.
- Does the conclusion summarize the main idea?
- Is the title interesting?

Try Your Skill   Think about the objects listed below. Each one is a possible topic for a descriptive composition. Decide what is the most logical spatial pattern to use to describe each object. Write and explain the pattern you would use.

a gymnasium   a roller coaster   a church
a city block   a forest   a band

Keep This in Mind

- Use a clear, logical order to organize a descriptive composition. You may want to use transitions that show spatial order.
- In the conclusion, summarize your main ideas and feelings about your subject.
- Write a suitable title.

Now Write   Review the composition you have been writing in this section. Is your description organized in a logical order? Have you used clear transitions? Do any necessary rewriting.

Write a strong conclusion for your description. Summarize your main ideas and your feelings. Also, write a title.

Make a final copy of your composition. Label it **In the Shape of**. Keep your description in your folder.

The Explanatory Composition
Explaining a Process

Part 1 # How So?

Planning an Explanation

Here's the Idea   There are many everyday situations in which you may have given directions to someone. You may have given directions explaining how to make something, such as a patchwork quilt or a wood carving. You may have given directions explaining how to do something, such as tune up a car or use a potter's wheel.

To write an explanatory composition that explains a process, rely on the same skills you have used in everyday situations. Explain the steps in the process briefly and clearly. Start with the first step and proceed through all the steps in the order in which they must be completed. It is essential that the steps be presented in the correct sequence and that they be accurate and complete.

Before you write, choose and narrow a topic. The best ideas will reflect your own interests and special skills. Plan your idea in a set of pre-writing notes. List the major steps in the process. Be sure to include any tools, materials, or ingredients required.

An additional pre-writing step for this explanatory composition is to write a title. Write a title that indicates the process to be explained. For example, you may want to use the words *How To* as part of a title.

Check It Out   Read these pre-writing notes.

How To Trace Your Family Tree

1. Collect facts from those living
     write down what you know
     interview parents
     interview grandparents, relatives

2. Sort notes
     begin a file for each person
     compare information gathered thus far
     try to clear up confusion

3. Search family records
     photograph albums
     legal documents
     personal documents
     personal documents of other relatives

4. Check public records
     organizations
     library records
     town records
     newspapers

  · What process do these steps explain?
  · Do the notes clearly list the steps in the process and the materials needed?
  · Is the title appropriate?

Try Your Skill   Suppose you were writing an explanatory composition to explain one of the following processes. Make a set of pre-writing notes, listing the steps you would include for that process.

     cooking homemade soup   cleaning a house   washing a car

Keep This in Mind

  · Choose a special skill as a topic for an explanatory composition that explains a process.

  · In your notes, list the steps in the process and any equipment or materials needed.

  · Write a title that states the process clearly.

Now Write   Think of five processes you might explain in a composition. You may explain a process related to a hobby, a work activity, a sport, or an area of study that interests you. Write the topics, and a title for each. Label your paper **How So?** Put it into your folder.

Part 2

One, Two, Three

Using Step-by-Step Order

Here's the Idea   An effective way to organize an explanatory composition that explains a process is to follow this plan: introduction, steps in the process, conclusion.

In the first paragraph, introduce your topic. One sentence of the **introduction** should be the topic sentence for the composition.

In the paragraphs of the **body**, give a step-by-step explanation. Discuss each step in a paragraph, developing each one with details from your notes. Be specific and complete.

Develop the concluding paragraph from the final step. In your **conclusion**, include any additional advice or encouragement.

Check It Out   Read the body of the explanatory composition about the process of tracing a family tree.

To begin your search, you need only a notebook and a pencil. Like any good detective, start with the obvious clues at the scene—your own home. First, jot down everything you already know about yourself. Include where and when you were born, your parents' names, your mother's maiden name, and the schools you have attended. After that, interview each older member of your family. Find out where and when they were born, where they went to school or church, where they worked, and when they were married. Ask any questions that might lead you to others. Move back in time from your parents to your grandparents. Interview them if possible, or gather information from their closest living relatives.

The next step is to sort your notes and file them properly. You may wish to make separate files of notes for each person. For example, you may make a pile labeled *Mother* and another labeled *Mother's Mother*, and so on. Check to see if information from one source, such as a parent, agrees with information from another source, such as an aunt. Try to clear up any confusion.

124

After you have interviewed all living relatives, turn your search to silent witnesses. That is, search for family records stored in drawers, attics, or garages. Such records could include snapshots, diaries, newspaper clippings, diplomas, and birth and marriage certificates. Other records might be birth or death announcements, wills, deeds, contracts, citizenship papers, military records, passports, or a family Bible. Ask relatives in other cities to check their written records and family mementos as well.

Once you have exhausted your family's personal records, you can move on to public records. You may find information and clues from membership lists of public organizations, library records, newspaper stories about public events, and church and town records. Such a search may take some time.

- What steps are explained in the body of this explanatory composition?

Try Your Skill   Read these jumbled and incomplete notes for the body of a composition on baking a cake. Write them in the correct order.

Cream butter and sugar.	Put batter into hot oven.
Frost cooled cake.	Add dry ingredients and liquid last.
Assemble ingredients.	Cool the baked cake.
Add eggs to butter and sugar.	Beat batter for two minutes.
Spoon batter into pan.	Preheat oven.

Keep This in Mind

- Present your topic in the introduction.
- In the body, give a step-by-step explanation.
- Develop the conclusion from the final step.

Now Write   Review the processes you listed in **How So?** Choose one process and list the steps involved. Using step-by-step order, write the body of a composition that explains the process. Label your paper **One, Two, Three** and keep it in your folder.

In Connection with

Using Transitions

Here's the Idea   In an explanatory composition that explains a process, your directions should lead a reader through the process. By using transitions, you will be able to lead your reader more easily step-by-step. The most helpful transitions are similar to those used for narrative compositions because they indicate the natural time order of the process. For instance, you may want to use transitions like *the first step, the next step, while, when,* and *finally*. At times, you may need a more specific transition like *after twenty minutes*. Generally, it is best to make transitions as precise as possible.

Transitions will make the order clear within each paragraph, especially in the body of the composition as you explain the steps of a process. Transitions will also help to link ideas in all three parts of the explanatory composition.

Check It Out   Here are the introduction and the conclusion of the explanatory composition on tracing your ancestry. Before reading them, review the body of the explanation in the last lesson. Point out the transitions used to link the three paragraphs.

Introduction

From ancient times to the present day, people have asked themselves "Who am I?" One step in answering that question is to learn about where you came from and who your ancestors were. Ever since Alex Haley shared his search for his past with the American public in his book and in the television series "Roots," many more people have become interested in tracing the history of their own families. The study of ancestry, or the family tree, is called the science of genealogy. With only a few tools and some organization, you, too, can have the pleasure of exploring your own past.

Conclusion

Finally, you should be able to use the information from your notes to write about your family tree. Begin with yourself and go backwards to your parents, two sets of grandparents, four sets of great grandparents, and so on, until you reach the limits of your search. This fascinating tracing of your family tree will reward you by giving you a better sense of who you are.

- What transitions are used within the introduction and within the conclusion? What transitions link the introduction or the conclusion to the body of the composition?

Try Your Skill   Below, in proper order, is a list of directions for conducting a meeting. Rewrite the list in paragraph form, adding transitional words and phrases to make the order clear.

Call the meeting to order.
Ask that the minutes of the last meeting be read.
Ask for reports of the officers.
Call for reports of special committees.
Review unfinished business.
Call for new business.
Adjourn the meeting.

Keep This in Mind

- In an explanatory composition that explains a process, use time transitions to make clear the order of the steps in each paragraph. Also, use transitions to link paragraphs in all three parts of the composition.

Now Write   Review the body of the composition you wrote for **One, Two, Three**. Add any transitions necessary to make the order of the steps clear. Write an introduction and a conclusion for your explanation. Use transitions to link the paragraphs in all three parts of the composition. Make a final copy of the composition. Label your paper **In Connection with**. Keep your work in your folder.

The Explanatory Composition
Stating an Opinion

Look at It This Way

Stating an Opinion

Here's the Idea An explanatory composition may express an opinion and explain why others should accept that opinion. For example, you may explain why wildlife conservation is an issue that concerns everyone. You may argue that the United States needs to change its system of electing a President. Your opinion may be shared by many other people or only by those in a certain group. Your opinion may be a controversial idea. Whatever opinions you believe in strongly are likely to be suitable topics for your compositions.

To select a topic, think about your life. Think about your neighborhood, city, state, or country. What events and ideas concern you? What practices should be changed? Consider the issues that affect you most strongly.

After you have chosen a topic, make your pre-writing notes. Sort out your ideas and feelings. Plan to state your opinion clearly in the introduction. Plan to support your opinion with reasons or facts in the body of the composition. Plan to summarize your argument in the conclusion.

Check It Out Examine these notes for an explanatory composition stating an opinion on a community issue.

Topic   Foster School should become a community center

Introduction   Rutland forced to close Foster Elementary School
    like other towns
    to balance budget, for decreasing enrollments
    an unwise decision

Body   good reasons for community center
    1. offices would be waste of space
      school board doesn't need rooms
      gym, auditorium, and playground would
      not be used

2. senior citizens need facilities
    large number in that neighborhood
    active senior citizen group
    cafeteria could be used for meals for
        elderly
3. center could serve entire neighborhood
    park district could run center
    daytime and nighttime programs
    public gym
    rooms for adult education classes

Conclusion   community center is practical solution
    facilities would be used
    meeting place for everyone
    safer, more pleasant neighborhood

- Is the topic suitable for an explanatory composition that states an opinion? Is an opinion clearly expressed?
- Will these notes lead to a strong, lively composition?

Try Your Skill   Read local newspapers for one week. Identify two major current issues, which may be controversial. State your opinion on each issue in a strong, direct statement. Be prepared to support your opinion with reasons or facts.

Keep This in Mind

- Choose a personal belief as the topic for an explanatory composition that states an opinion.
- In your notes, jot down your opinion and supporting reasons or facts. Organize your notes into the introduction, the body, and the conclusion.

Now Write   Write several opinions that you hold. Choose one to be developed in an explanatory composition. List the reasons or facts that support your opinion. Organize your notes into the introduction, the body, and the conclusion. Label your paper **Look at It This Way** and put it into your folder.

And Here's Why

Developing an Opinion

Here's the Idea   If you intend to convince others that an opinion is based on sound judgment, you need to present sound evidence. In an explanatory composition, you need to present strong, specific reasons or facts. For example, you may want to use reasons to support the opinion that wildlife conservation should be everyone's concern. You may want to use facts to support the opinion that the United States should revise its system of electing a President.

The most effective way to present supporting evidence is to state the weakest reason or fact first, and the strongest reason or fact last. In other words, build your argument by organizing supporting evidence **in order of importance.**

Because the supporting evidence is so important, it must be presented in complete detail in the **body** of your composition. Develop each important reason or fact in a separate paragraph of the body.

Check It Out   Read the body of the composition about using Foster Elementary School as a community center.

First of all, the current school board plan calls for moving administrative offices into the vacant school. This plan will give a few extra feet of desk space to some individuals. However, it will largely be a waste of a facility that includes a fine auditorium, a gymnasium, and a playground. Administrators admit that they are not overcrowded in their present location, and the current budget calls for reducing their ranks in the future.

More important, Foster School was closed because of the dwindling number of children in this neighborhood, where a large number of senior citizens are living. The school would therefore be a perfect location for the park district's active senior citizens' organization. The building could be used both day and night for senior citizen programs. In addition, the cafeteria could also accommodate the hot lunch program for these citizens. The current program is severely limited by lack of space.

Most important, the school could serve the entire neighborhood in other ways. Afternoon and evening park district programs could offer a needed source of recreation for both elementary students and teen-agers. Foster School offers the only public gymnasium in the neighborhood, and it has always been the center of much sports activity. Adult evening classes could also be held at Foster.

- Is an opinion supported by specific reasons or facts? Is the evidence given in order of importance, from the least important to the most important?

Try Your Skill   Choose one of these opinions to support. List at least three specific supporting reasons or facts.

1. Community colleges are vital and valuable institutions.
2. There should be more public facilities for the handicapped.
3. Gasoline should be rationed.
4. Parents should supervise the televison viewing of children.

Keep This in Mind

- In the body of an explanatory composition that states an opinion, present specific supporting reasons or facts. Organize supporting evidence in order of importance, from the least important to the most important.

Now Write   From your folder, take out your composition notes labeled **Look at It This Way**. Examine the reasons or facts you have listed to support your opinion and arrange them in order of importance. Then, using your notes, write the body of your explanatory composition. Label your paper **And Here's Why** and put it into your folder.

A Sure Thing

Using Transitions

Here's the Idea When you write an explanatory composition stating an opinion, you may rely on a variety of helpful transitions. Using one group of transitions will help you to present supporting reasons or facts in their order of importance. These transitional words and phrases include *the first reason, second, most important,* and *finally.* You will want to use such transitions in the body of a composition.

Using a different group of transitions will help you to state reasons or facts. These transitions include *because, since, if, therefore,* and *as a result.* You will want to use these transitions in an introduction and in a conclusion.

In your **introduction**, express your opinion as directly as possible. Include a sentence that serves as the topic sentence for the entire composition. In the **conclusion**, summarize your argument as forcefully as you can. Finally, write a title that presents your topic in an interesting way.

Check It Out Read the introduction, conclusion, and title for the composition about the community center.

Introduction

Rutland is not alone in having been forced to close schools. Like other communities, it has had to balance the budget in response to shrinking enrollments. However, the recent decision of the school board to close Foster Elementary School was especially unwise. The young children in that district will now have to travel greater distances to any recreational facility as well as to school. One way to offset this danger is to turn the vacant school building over to the park district so that the school can become a neighborhood community center.

Conclusion

Therefore, it is much more practical that Foster School become a community center rather than an office building. The present facilities, including cafeteria, auditorium, gym, and playground, would be put to better use. As a community center, Foster School would become a focal point for the neighborhood—a place for young and old to meet and to get to know each other. Foster School is the key to a safer and more pleasant neighborhood.

Title: Classrooms for the Community

- Does the introduction state an opinion clearly?
- Does the conclusion summarize the argument?
- Which transitions help to state the reasons or facts?

Try Your Skill   Rewrite the following paragraph, adding appropriate transitions. You may also want to add details.

I believe everyone should learn to cook. One member of any household should not have the sole responsibility for preparing meals. Cooking is a creative skill, and it can be relaxing, challenging, and fun. Every individual should learn to be self-sufficient. To be self-sufficient requires knowing how to prepare nutritious meals. Cooking should be part of everyone's education.

Keep This in Mind

- In the introduction, state your opinion clearly.
- In the conclusion, summarize your argument.
- Use transitions to help state the reasons or facts and present evidence in order of its importance.

Now Write   Review the explanatory composition that you have been writing. Write an introduction that presents your opinion and a conclusion that summarizes your argument. Include clear transitions. Add a title. Make a final copy. Label your paper **A Sure Thing** and put it into your folder.

The Explanatory Composition

Stating a Definition

What in the World?

Planning a Definition

Here's the Idea You have learned that an explanatory composition may explain a process or state an opinion. An explanatory composition may also state a definition. For example, you may wonder what a *census* is, what *style* is, what a *lobbyist* does, or what the term *OPEC* means. Any of these subjects could be defined in an explanatory composition. In fact, any interesting object, idea, or special term may be a suitable subject to define.

You will discover many possible topics suitable for an explanatory composition. In school situations, for instance, you may be asked to define an *essay*, a *coalition*, or *sociology*. In other everyday situations you might have to explain a *soldering iron*, *microwaves*, or *arbitration*. There might also be situations in which you would need to explain something related to a job, a hobby, a household task, or a sport. For your definition, choose a topic that interests you and that you can develop in detail.

Plan an explanatory composition that states a definition by making pre-writing notes. In the introduction, plan to state a specific definition of your topic. In the body, plan to develop the main ideas of your definition with details or with facts and figures. In the conclusion, plan to summarize your definition.

Check It Out Read these pre-writing notes.

Topic	the draft
Introduction	defense is basic human need
	protection for all means service by all
	draft necessary to provide ample military force
Body	types of draft
	war time only
	war and peace time
	men only, men and women

history of draft in Europe
    ancient Greece and Rome
    Middle Ages
    modern draft from French Revolution

history of draft in U.S.
    used in American Revolution, Civil War,
       World War I, World War II, Korean War,
       Vietnam War
    Selective Service System
    return to volunteer army

Conclusion   each age, each country has different military needs
          draft has been one answer to need

- Do these notes include details or facts and figures that will define the subject clearly?

Try Your Skill   Suppose that you want to define something you use in everyday living. For example, you may want to define a car, a television, a bank, or a library. Make a detailed set of notes for an explanatory composition.

Keep This in Mind

- Choose an object, term, or idea as the topic for an explanatory composition that states a definition. In your notes, list details or facts and figures that will define your subject clearly.

Now Write   Choose a topic of interest to you for an explanatory composition that states a definition. You may want to define something related to a hobby or a job, for example. Make a detailed set of pre-writing notes. Plan the introduction, the body, and the conclusion of the composition. Label your paper **What in the World?** Keep it in your folder.

Class Consciousness

Stating a Definition

Here's the Idea   To write a good definition, you must do three things. First, name the word to be defined. Second, name the general class to which the subject belongs. Third, name the particular characteristics of the subject. By defining a subject you will be able to present a complete and informative picture of it.

Suppose you want to define a whale. You could begin by saying that a whale is an animal. You have named the word and its general class. However, an animal could be a mouse, a dog, a fish, a bird—even a human. You might add that a whale is a mammal. That distinguishes it from reptiles, insects, amphibians, and fish. However, there are many types of mammals including humans, horses, apes, bats, and squirrels. You might add that a whale is a marine mammal with a fishlike form and flippers. However, porpoises and dolphins are also marine mammals with the same general shape. Therefore, you need to add that the whale is the largest species of marine mammal. By using all this specific information you can now write a good definition like this one: A whale is the largest marine mammal, having a fishlike form, front flippers, and a flat, horizontal tail.

You should include a good definition as part of the **introduction** of an explanatory composition. Your definition serves as the topic sentence for the composition. Be sure that your definition is precise.

Check It Out   Read the introduction to the explanatory composition that defines the draft.

For as long as human beings have banded together in communities, there has been the need to defend these communities. The idea that all members of a group are responsible for its safety gave rise in earlier ages to the practice of conscription, or the draft. The military draft is the system of requiring people to serve in a country's military force for a certain length of time. The draft has been used whenever a government has needed a larger military force than it could assemble from volunteers.

- Does this introduction include a good definition? Is the definition a topic sentence that presents a suitable subject for an interesting composition?

Try Your Skill   Define three of the following objects. Name the word, its general class, and its particular characteristics. Check a reference book such as a dictionary or encyclopedia for more facts, if necessary.

a rose	a taxicab	a lime
a rifle	a quilt	a palm tree
a banjo	a shawl	a wok

Keep This in Mind

- To state a definition, name a word, its general class, and its specific characteristics. Include the definition in the introduction as the topic sentence for a composition.

Now Write   Review the pre-writing notes you labeled **What in the World?** Write a good definition for your chosen subject. Be sure you have named your subject, its general class, and its particular characteristics. Then write the introduction for your explanatory composition. Label your paper **Class Consciousness** and put it into your folder.

On the Whole

Developing a Definition

Here's the Idea   You define a subject in the introduction of an explanatory composition. You need to develop that definition as completely as possible in the **body**. The most informative way to develop a definition is with details or with facts and figures.

There are certain subjects that can be defined best in a factual way. Suppose you were defining a *primary election* or *nuclear radiation*. To define subjects like these you would want to use facts and figures. Use reference books for information.

There are other subjects that can be defined best in a personal way. Suppose you were defining *talent* or *equal opportunity employer*. To define ideas or terms like these you would want to use details related to your personal experiences.

Write a **conclusion** that sums up the main idea of your definition. Also, add a title that suggests your main idea.

Check It Out   Read this body, conclusion, and title.

Many countries use a draft only during a war. Some countries also draft people in peace time in order to maintain a standing army. People can be drafted for both military and civilian service. Some nations draft both men and women for national service; some draft only men. Other countries have never had a draft.

In ancient Greece and Rome, additional men were drafted in emergencies, but these societies relied mainly on professional armies. In Europe in the Middle Ages, armies were small. Warfare was considered the duty of the nobility who could afford the costly, scarce weapons. The modern idea of the draft stems from the French Revolution in the late eighteenth century. Then, the theory of equality for all led to the notion of universal service.

In the United States, the draft began with Colonial times. The American Revolution was fought by both drafted militia troops and volunteers. In the Civil War, both the North and the South drafted troops to swell the ranks of volunteers. The United

States drafted about two and one-half million men during World War I, ten million in World War II, two million in the Korean War, and more than one and a half million in the Vietnam War.

The Selective Service System was organized in America in 1940 to administer the draft. Men were classified as available for duty, deferred (postponed) by reason of studies or an essential job, or physically or mentally unfit. After public opposition to the draft increased during the Vietnam War, the United States stopped the draft in 1973 and began an all-volunteer army.

In each period of history a country must reexamine its military and civilian needs and determine how best to meet those needs. One method of providing military protection throughout history has been some form of required military service—the draft.

Title: The Need To Serve

- Is this definition developed in a factual or in a personal way? What facts and figures or personal details are used?
- Do the conclusion and title point out the main idea?

Try Your Skill Write definitions for two of these terms or ideas. Then list at least three facts and figures or personal details that you could use to develop your definition.

boycott	patriotism	work	superstar
opinion poll	home	hope	talent

Keep This in Mind

- Develop the body of a definition by using facts and figures or personal details.
- Summarize the main idea of your definition in the conclusion and in the title.

Now Write Review the notes and the introduction you have written. Write the body, using either facts and figures or personal details. Write a conclusion and a title. Make a final copy. Label your paper **On the Whole**. Keep your work in your folder.

Letters, Applications, and Résumés

Dear Friend

Writing Personal Letters

Here's the Idea A **personal letter**, which is any letter not written to a business, is informal and friendly. It is usually handwritten. Writing a personal letter allows you to stay close to an absent friend or to express your feelings in a certain social situation. Personal letters contain five parts.

The **heading** consists of three lines: one line for your street address; one for the city, state, and ZIP code; and one for the date. Do not abbreviate any of this information. Place the heading at the top right corner of your letter.

The **salutation** is your greeting, which you generally begin with *Dear*. Write the salutation on the next line below the heading. Start at the left margin and place a comma after the greeting.

The **body** of the letter is the main part. Write what you want to say in a detailed and conversational way. Begin on the line following the salutation. Indent each paragraph of the body.

The **closing** is your "goodbye." You may write *Love*, or *Your friend*, for example. Write the closing on the line below the last line of the body, placing a comma after it. Align the first word of the closing with the first words of the heading.

Your **signature** is the last part of the letter. Skip a line after the closing, and sign your name in line with the first word of the closing. Usually, you need only sign your first name.

Some forms of personal letters are written only for special occasions. These social notes include invitations and thank-you notes. These notes also have five main parts, although the heading may be shortened to the date only.

If you send an **invitation**, include specific information about the event. If you receive an invitation, reply immediately.

You may also send **thank-you** notes. Write a thank-you note after you receive a gift. Also write a thank-you note, called a **bread-and-butter** note, to thank someone for his or her hospitality if you stayed overnight as a guest. Be sure to write any thank-you note promptly and to express your appreciation graciously.

Check It Out   Read this personal letter.

- Identify the five parts of this personal letter.
- Is this a well written letter? Why or why not?

1012 Ocean Way
San Francisco, California 94109
March 15, 1981

Dear Rudy,

Today at a basketball game I saw your cousin Paul, who told me that your Grandfather Lane had died last week. I am writing to tell you how sorry I am. I know what a great friend he was to you. I remember the time when you both lived here that Mr. Lane took us camping and canoeing. Do you remember how he talked your mother into letting us go hiking? I will never forget that he said I could borrow him as my grandfather if I needed one.

Maybe, if you can visit again this summer, we can go fishing together at the pond where he used to take us. Since I can't be with you now, please know I'm thinking about you. Try to think about how lucky you have been to have had such a fine man for a grandfather.

Sincerely,
Joe

Try Your Skill Arrange the following information in the correct form for a personal letter. Add the information and details necessary to make it a good letter. Use capital letters and punctuation correctly.

106 willow st., flatbush kans. 67052, september 16, 1981, dear aunt lois and uncle vic, thank you for inviting me to your farm this summer. I had a wonderful time. I thought the country fair was especially exciting. I'd love to come back again soon. love, julia

Keep This in Mind

- Write personal letters that are conversational, detailed, and neat. Be sure that the heading, salutation, body, closing, and signature follow the correct form.

- Social notes are short forms of personal letters. Write invitations that are specific and thank-you notes that express your appreciation.

Now Write Write a personal letter. Use your own address and today's date in the heading. The body of the letter may be based on either real or imaginary events. Be sure all parts of your letter are in the correct form. Label your paper **Dear Friend**, and put it into your folder. Make a copy of your letter that you could send and save that also.

First Class

Preparing Letters for the Mail

Here's the Idea After you have written a letter, prepare it correctly for mailing. Begin by folding the letter neatly and selecting an envelope that matches the width of the stationery. Insert the folded letter and seal the envelope.

To make sure that your letter reaches its destination without delay, prepare the envelope accurately and neatly. First, address the envelope. Be sure to include your ZIP code. (You may review the correct use of ZIP codes and state abbreviations by turning to page 151.) Next, double-check all numbers to make sure they are correct. Then, put a stamp on the envelope. Be sure you have used enough postage for the letter or package. Finally, check every envelope or package for accuracy. If you need any more information, call your local post office.

Check It Out Examine the envelope below.

```
Bill Garber
3128 Eagle Boulevard
Denver, CO 80201


                    Ms. Sylvia Rosso
                    1915 Maple Avenue #111
                    New Orleans, LA 70140
```

- Who wrote the letter? Who will receive it? What state abbreviations are used? How could you check all of the information?

Try Your Skill Rewrite each of these jumbled addresses as it should appear on an envelope. Also write a return address. You may need to refer to the list of correct state abbreviations on page 151.

1. Henry Wright, 27 Rose Circle, Tucson, Arizona 95703
2. 5138 Enfield Avenue, Lincoln, Nebraska 68501, Nina Trovato
3. Miami, Florida 33116, 2241 M Street, Albert Vega
4. 9942 Long Road, St. Louis, Missouri 63114, Jan Weissburg
5. Isabel Saez, P.O. Box 2216, Vieques, Puerto Rico 00765
6. Dr. J. C. Chua, 14943 18th Street, N.W., Washington, D.C. 20036
7. Betty Casali, 645 Crain Street, Portsmouth, New Hampshire 03801
8. San Diego, California 92109, Dennis Boyd, 22 Parkway Drive
9. 1417 Greenwood Avenue, Michigan City, Indiana 46360, Leona Corby
10. Linda Rooney, Clarkston, Georgia 30021, 243 Elm Road

Keep This in Mind

· Prepare letters for the mail carefully. Check all information for accuracy.

Now Write Take out your personal letter labeled **Dear Friend**. On the other side of that paper, write the title of this lesson, **First Class**. Draw a rectangle to represent an envelope. Address it as if you were going to mail it to your friend or relative. Put this paper into your folder.

Copy your work onto a real envelope. Fold the copy of the letter that you can send and put it into the envelope. Add a stamp and mail your letter.

ZIP Codes and State Abbreviations

In order to make sure that your letter reaches its destination, check the address, including the ZIP code. The ZIP code is very important today. It enables the postal department to sort your letter for delivery as rapidly as possible. If you don't know a ZIP code, call your post office. Someone will give you the correct ZIP for any address in the United States and the territories.

The United States Postal Service has created a list of approved state abbreviations to be used on all envelopes and packages. You must use the ZIP code with these abbreviations.

Abbreviations of State Names

Alabama	AL	Montana	MT
Alaska	AK	Nebraska	NE
Arizona	AZ	Nevada	NV
Arkansas	AR	New Hampshire	NH
American Samoa	AS	New Jersey	NJ
California	CA	New Mexico	NM
Canal Zone	CZ	New York	NY
Colorado	CO	North Carolina	NC
Connecticut	CT	North Dakota	ND
Delaware	DE	Ohio	OH
District of Columbia	DC	Oklahoma	OK
Florida	FL	Oregon	OR
Georgia	GA	Pennsylvania	PA
Guam	GU	Puerto Rico	PR
Hawaii	HI	Rhode Island	RI
Idaho	ID	South Carolina	SC
Illinois	IL	South Dakota	SD
Indiana	IN	Tennessee	TN
Iowa	IA	Trust Territories	TT
Kansas	KS	Texas	TX
Kentucky	KY	Utah	UT
Louisiana	LA	Vermont	VT
Maine	ME	Virginia	VA
Maryland	MD	Virgin Islands	VI
Massachusetts	MA	Washington	WA
Michigan	MI	West Virginia	WV
Minnesota	MN	Wisconsin	WI
Mississippi	MS	Wyoming	WY
Missouri	MO		

Office Hours

Writing Business Letters

Here's the Idea   In many situations, you will need to write **business letters**. You may want to write to a school or college. You may need to write a letter seeking employment. You may need to write to an organization requesting information. You may have to write to a company to order a product or to complain about one. You may wish to write to the editor of a newspaper or to an elected official about major issues that affect your life. In all of these situations, you will be most effective if you follow the correct form for business letters.

In order to make the best impression, your business letters must be neat. Use plain white paper 8 1/2 x 11. Type your letters, if possible. Although it is not required that you type a business letter, it creates a better impression if you do so.

You may write any business letter following one of two standard forms. One form is the **block** form, which should be used only if you type a letter. Using the block form, begin every part of a letter at the left margin. Leave two lines of space between paragraphs and do not indent them. A second form, the **modified block**, may be used either for handwritten or typewritten letters. In this form, place the heading, closing, and signature at the right side of the page, as you do in personal letters. Indent the paragraphs and do not leave extra space between them.

Every business letter has six parts—the five parts of a personal letter, plus an **inside address**. The inside address is the name and address of the company to which you are writing. Whenever possible, include the name of a particular employee or department within the company. Place the inside address at the left margin, below the heading and above the salutation.

The language of business letters is more formal than that of personal letters. For the salutation, use Dear *Mr.*, *Mrs.*, *Miss*, or *Ms.* with the name of a particular employee. Otherwise, use a general greeting like *Dear Sir or Madam*. Place the salutation two lines below the inside address and use a colon (:) after it.

For the more formal closing, write *Sincerely, Yours truly*, or *Very truly yours*, followed by a comma. If you type a letter, leave four lines of space between the closing and your typed signature. Then, write your signature in the space.

Be sure a business letter is always polite, specific, and neat. Keep a copy of each business letter you write.

Check It Out Read this business letter.

```
          64 Vernon Street
          St. Paul, Minnesota  55107
          February 2, 1981


          The St. Paul Repertory Theater
          178 Summit Avenue
          St. Paul, Minnesota  55101


          Dear Sir or Madam:


          My neighborhood drama group is interested in
          attending your production of Dracula next month.
          There will be about fifteen of us.  Could you
          please send me information on ticket prices for
          this show and a schedule of performance dates.
          If you have group rates, please let me know.


          Sincerely yours,

          Lois Gordon


          Lois Gordon
```

- What is the purpose of this business letter?
- In what form is this letter?

Try Your Skill   Write a letter from Herbert Stann to Sheila Troy, Sales Manager of Soundwave Records, Incorporated. Have Herbert ask why his order for the "Golden Hits of the 70's" album has not yet been filled after eight weeks. Invent other necessary details. For the purpose of this exercise, use the block form, even though your letter will be handwritten.

Keep This in Mind

- You may write a business letter to apply to a school, to seek employment, to request information, or to ask about a product. Whether you write or type a business letter, be polite, specific, and neat. Keep a copy of every business letter.

- Use either the *block* or *modified block* form for a business letter. Either form has six parts, including an inside address.

Now Write   Write or type a business letter to a real organization regarding a particular product or requesting certain information. Also, draw an envelope and address it. Label your paper **Office Hours**. Keep it in your folder.

Schoolwork

Writing Letters to Colleges and Other Schools

Here's the Idea You may want to go to a vocational school or college. You can learn about some schools through a library, where you will find catalogs and scholarship information. You will also find valuable information about our nation's schools, including listings of their addresses, in references like *Lovejoy's Career and Vocational School Guide* and *Barron's Profiles of American Colleges*.

However, the best way to get specific information about a particular school that interests you is to write directly to the school. A letter to a school or college is a business letter. Address it to the Admissions Office of the school and follow either of the standard forms for business letters. As in any business letter, you must be specific and to the point. Briefly give the school the information it needs in order to provide you with the information you need.

The school that you may attend will want to know about you. In your letter, include information about the school you are attending, or any you have attended, and the date of your graduation. Include information about your general area of interest.

In addition, you want to know as much as possible about a school. Therefore, in your letter also include a request for information about entrance requirements, special programs offered, the size and location of the school, tuition costs, and scholarships. Include a request for a catalog. If there is any charge for a catalog, the school will notify you.

As you may know, the cost of education can be high. Therefore, you may also be interested in information about student loans and scholarships. If so, write also to the Office of Financial Aid. Ask about financial assistance available for the time you plan to enter. The school will send you information about its programs and any forms that must be completed.

Making a decision about continuing your education is an important one. You need to compare several schools carefully in order to make the best choice for you. Writing letters to schools is an effective way to learn all you can.

Check It Out   Read the letter on page 157.

· What specific information does this business letter include? What specific information does it request?

Try Your Skill   Choose one of the following situations and write a letter to the Admissions Office requesting the information mentioned. Add other necessary details. Use correct business letter form.

1. You are a high school graduate interested in becoming a computer technician. You want to find out if the Piedmont Regional Vocational School at 44 Marlboro Street, Peterson, New Hampshire 03233, offers courses suitable for you, and how much they cost.

2. You are a high school graduate interested in music. Write to State College, Western Avenue, Plattsville, West Virginia 25426, inquiring about whether it offers a major in music and what the course requirements are. Ask about entrance requirements, student housing costs, and scholarship availability. Request a copy of the catalog.

Keep This in Mind

· When you write to vocational schools and colleges, use the correct business letter form. Include specific information about yourself and request specific information from the school.

Now Write   Write a letter to a vocational school or college that interests you. Ask about the program in the field of your choice and request a catalog. Use either correct form for this business letter. Label your letter **Schoolwork** and put it into your folder. You may want to make a copy of your letter and mail it.

122 Broadway
Kenvil, New Jersey 07847
March 3, 1981

Admissions Office
Paxton School of Design
Amsterdam, New York 12010

Dear Sir or Madam:

I am a senior and will graduate from Westport
Technical School this coming June. I intend to
pursue a career in fashion designing, and I am
most interested in your program. Can I still
apply at this time for the fall of 1981, or will
I have a better chance by applying for 1982?

I need to know your entrance requirements to make
certain that I have taken the proper courses. I
can plan to attend summer school if necessary.
Also, I have worked part time for one year for a
local dress designing company. I would like to
know if such experience is either required or
helpful for applicants.

Please send me a copy of your catalog so that I
may study the tuition and fees and may investigate
your financial aid programs. Also, I would like
descriptions of specific courses offered in dress
designing.

Sincerely,

Brenda Rowlands

Brenda Rowlands

Working Papers

Writing a Letter Seeking Employment

Here's the Idea   The most important point to remember in writing a letter seeking employment is to present yourself in the best possible way. Be direct about stating what you can bring to a job. Your strengths may include valuable previous experience, reliable work habits, or an enthusiastic desire to learn. Be sure your letter presents your strengths clearly.

A letter seeking employment generally includes certain basic information related to the job. For instance, be sure to include the title of the job you are seeking. Be specific about the kind of position you want. Indicate whether you are looking for full-time, part-time, or temporary employment. If applicable, mention particular days or hours that you are willing to work. It is a good idea to include a starting date that you will be available. Finally, request an interview if the job is in your area.

In addition, a letter seeking employment usually includes information about yourself. You may want to make a brief statement about your education or your current situation. Briefly summarize your qualifications. Be sure to mention any related work experience or courses taken in school.

If you are sending your letter to a large company, write to the personnel department. If you are writing to a small company, write to the owner or manager. If you answer a newspaper advertisement, follow the instructions on how to reply. Many ads will ask you to reply to a box number in care of the newspaper. Others may contain the address of the company.

Be sure that a letter seeking employment follows the correct form for business letters. It should be informative, neat, and polite. The letter may be the first contact you have with an employer. You want to create a good impression. Also, be sure to proofread your letter carefully. Your attention to detail may lead to a job offer.

Check It Out   Read this letter.

2941 Grove Street
Lansing, Michigan   48927
April 14, 1981

Personnel Department
Valley Hospital
1600 Sherman Avenue
Lansing, Michigan   48927

Dear Sir or Madam:

I am interested in applying for a full-time
summer job as a clerk-typist in the business
office. I will be a 1981 graduate of Valley
High School. I have had courses in typing,
shorthand, and business machines. Last summer
I worked full time as a typist at the Municipal
License Bureau. I am currently working part
time in the school office.

For the past four years I have been a volunteer
Candy Striper at Valley Hospital and am very
familiar with the institution. I am considering
entering nursing school after graduation.

I will be available to work full time from June
15 until Labor Day. I can work any combination
of hours, including nights and weekends.

I plan to apply in person next week. I will be
available for an interview at your convenience.

Yours truly,

Ruth Myers

Ruth Myers

• Does this letter include all the necessary information? Is it courteous and neat?

Try Your Skill   Write a letter answering one of the following want ads in the newspaper. For the purpose of this exercise, invent information.

1. Wanted: Cafeteria help, 4:30-8:30 P.M. No experience necessary. Write C. R. Industries, P.O. Box 414, Duluth, Minnesota 55806.

2. Wanted: Part-Time Teller. Join organization that promotes from within. Will train. Must type and speak English well. Write to Glenbrook Savings and Loan, 5162 Howard Street, Topsfield, Massachusetts 01983.

3. Deliver suburban newspapers. Early morning hours. Must have valid driver's license. Write *Village News*, 158 Ogden Avenue, Hinsdale, Illinois 60521.

Keep This in Mind

• Write a letter that will create a good impression when you are seeking employment. The letter should be informative, polite, and neat. Include specific information about yourself and the job you want.

Now Write   Write a letter seeking employment at a restaurant, store, or business in your town. Ask to be considered for a particular position. Be sure to include all necessary information. Proofread your letter carefully. Label it **Working Papers** and put it into your folder. You may want to copy your letter and mail it.

The Subject Is You

Writing a Résumé

Here's the Idea When you apply for a job, you usually send a letter and a résumé (rez′ • σσ • mā′) to an employer. A **résumé** is a list summarizing information about you, your education, work experiences, and special skills. In seeking employment, you may want to prepare a résumé, make several copies, and send one to each employer.

Many employers and schools will request that you submit a résumé, often before you will be given an interview. Using résumés is one way in which they can narrow a large number of applicants. Thus, you must prepare a résumé that shows who you are in a clear, easy-to-read form.

No two résumés are exactly alike, but most are one page long and typewritten. All contain short phrases that summarize information. The order in which you choose to present the information, however, may vary as your skills and work experiences vary.

All résumés should begin by identifying you. At the top, state your name, address, and telephone number, including the area code. Below that, you will generally want to state your job objective. Identify the kind of position or general area of work that you are seeking.

Next, summarize your education. List your high school, its address, your date of graduation, and any courses related to a job. If you have attended more than one school, always list the most recent first. For example, if you have attended or are attending a college or vocational school, you would list that first.

Summarize your work experience next. State the dates of your employment, the name and address of your employer, the position you held, and your duties. Again, list your most recent jobs first. Also, list any related volunteer experience here.

Then, list significant personal achievements. Mention special skills, such as computer language, office skills, or community work. Also mention awards, societies or clubs, offices held, hobbies, or related special interests.

Finally, mention references. You may name two or three people who can give you good character or employment references. It is also standard practice to state simply that you will name references upon request. In either case, be sure you have asked people for permission to name them as references.

As your life and work change, so should your résumé. Revise your résumé so that it is accurate and up-to-date.

Check It Out   Examine the résumé on page 163.

- Is this résumé well organized and easy-to-read? Does it include all the necessary information?

Try Your Skill   Revise the résumé on page 163, adding the following information. On your paper, rewrite the appropriate sections.

1. Volunteered as camp counselor in Headstart day camp, Lansing, Michigan 48927. Summer, 1978.

2. Student Council member, 1978-1979.

3. Courses in business English and accounting.

Keep This in Mind

- A résumé summarizes basic information about your life in relation to work. Make sure your résumé is clear, well organized, and up-to-date. Include all information necessary to present you and your skills.

Now Write   Now you are prepared to write your own résumé. As a first step, jot down notes and organize them in a way that shows your talents best. Print or type a neat final copy. Label it **The Subject Is You**. Keep it in your folder.

Ruth Marie Myers

2941 Grove Street
Lansing, Michigan   48927
(317) 555-2549

OBJECTIVE   A summer job as a clerk-typist at
                 Valley Hospital.

EDUCATION   Valley High School
                 Lansing, Michigan
                 Member of senior class graduating
                 June 10, 1981, with courses in
                 typing, business machines,
                 shorthand, and office skills.

WORK EXPERIENCE Clerk
        Present Valley High School
                 Lansing, Michigan
                 after school hours.

Summer, 1980   Typist
                 Municipal License Bureau
                 Lansing, Michigan
                 Full time.

       Skills   Have experience typing, using
                 calculator, dictaphone, and adding
                 machine, and answering telephones.

PERSONAL   Volunteer Candy Striper, Valley
                 Hospital, 1977-1981. Won first place
                 Typing Award, 1981. Member of Valley
                 High Business Club.

REFERENCES   Will be provided upon request.

In Good Form

Completing a Job Application

Here's the Idea   Generally, whenever you apply for a job, you will be asked to complete a job application. The form of the application will vary, of course, from business to business. However, you will find many similarities in the information required and in the process you must follow.

You should always be prepared to answer several standard questions. For example, you will be asked to state your address, telephone number, date of birth, social security number, and your citizenship. You will be asked about your education, work experiences, and special skills. You will usually be asked to name references. Choose people best able to evaluate your strengths and abilities. For example, you may name former teachers or former employers who have given you permission to name them as references.

In answering these questions, it is important to be neat. Your application reflects your ability to follow directions and to work neatly. Print your answers carefully, using a good pen with blue or black ink. Because there is not much space to print information requested, plan your answers. Read all instructions thoroughly, especially those in fine print. If you do make an error, erase it carefully.

In completing an application, it is also important to fill in every item. There may be questions that do not apply to you. If an item is not applicable to you, write N.A. to show that it is not.

Finally, you must be honest in completing an application. You will be asked to sign your name to a statement that all information is accurate.

Check It Out   Examine the completed job application on page 165.

Valley Hospital

APPLICATION FOR EMPLOYMENT

Date _April 22, 1981_

Name _Myers,_ _Ruth_ _Marie_   Tel. No. _555-2549_
        Last   First   Middle

Present Address _2941 Grove Street, Lansing, Michigan   48927_
              Street   City   State   Zip

Do you rent? ☐   Own your home? ☐   Live with parents? ☒

Previous Address _N.A._
              Street   City   State   Zip

Soc. Sec. No. _689-31-2182_ Date of Birth _8-29-63_   Are you a citizen? Yes ☒ No ☐

Person to be notified in case of accident or emergency _Anita Myers, (mother)_

Address _Same as above_   Phone _same_

Position applied for _clerk-typist_   Date available for work? _June 15, 1981_

RECORD OF EDUCATION

School	Name and Address of School	Years Attended	Circle last year completed
Elementary	Wayne Elementary School Lansing, Michigan	1969-1977	5 6 7 ⑧
High	Valley High School Lansing, Michigan	1977-Present	1 2 ③ 4
College			1 2 3 4

Did you serve in the military? Yes ☐   No ☒   Which branch? _N.A._

Rank _N.A._   Date of discharge _N.A._

RECORD OF EMPLOYMENT   (List your last two employers, starting with the more recent one)

Dates	Name and Address of Employer	Salary	Position	Reason for Leaving
1980-81	Valley High School Lansing, Michigan	$4.00 hour	Clerk	Will graduate
June-August 1980	Municipal License Bureau Lansing, Michigan	$3.50 hour	Typist	to return to school

Check the following office operations with which you have had experience

☒ Adding Machine   ☐ Switchboard   ☐ Shorthand   ☒ Addressograph   Other_____
☐ Proof Machine (IBM)   ☒ Dictaphone   ☒ Typewriter   ☒ Bookkeeping Machine   _____

PERSONAL REFERENCES   (Not former employers or relatives)

Name and Occupation	Address	Phone No.
Ms. Martha Scott, Teacher, Valley High School, Lansing, MI 48927		555-7522
Ms. Jane Hamilton, volunteer Coordinator, Valley Hospital, Lansing, MI 48926		555-1313
James Milbank, M.D., 14 Hill Street, Lansing, MI 48927		555-4135

I hereby affirm that my answers to the foregoing questions are true and correct and that I have not knowingly withheld any information which would, if disclosed, be considered sufficient cause for dismissal.

In the event of my employment, I promise to comply faithfully with all the rules and regulations presently in effect, or which may hereafter become effective, relating to the conduct and performance of the employees of Valley Hospital.

Applicant's Signature _Ruth Marie Myers_

- Have all items on the form been completed? How might an employer check that the information is correct?
- Has the application been filled in neatly? Have all instructions been followed carefully?

Try Your Skill Suppose that you were applying to Valley Hospital for a summer job in the business office. You wanted to work full time and you were willing to work weekends. Refer to the application for employment on page 165. On a separate sheet of paper, list the correct information as you would write it on the application. Your teacher may give you a copy of this application to complete.

Keep This in Mind

- Answer all items on an application form honestly, correctly, and completely.
- Complete the application by printing neatly, using ink. Work carefully. Read all instructions.

Now Write Complete an actual employment application. Use a form given to you by your teacher or one from a business in your community. Complete the form, following the guidelines you have learned. Label the form **In Good Form**. Keep it in your folder.

Take the Credit

Completing a Credit Application

Here's the Idea   At some point in your life, you may want to apply for credit. *Credit* means "trust in a person's integrity in money matters and his or her ability to meet payments when due." There are several kinds of situations in which you may want to apply for credit. You may want to borrow money from a bank for a large purchase, such as a car or house, or for school or college tuition. You may want a credit card to use in a certain department store or one to cover expenses in an emergency. You may want check cashing privileges at a local supermarket. In these situations, you will need to complete a credit application.

There are two major parts of a credit application, one in which the business gives information, and one in which you give information. Perhaps the company's part of an application is the more important part; it states the terms of your agreement. In this section of any credit application, for example, you will find information about billing policies, including minimum monthly charges, finance charges, and penalties for defaulting on payments. If you are applying for a credit card, you will find a statement of your responsibility if the card is lost or stolen. Specific policies that vary from business to business will also be included here. This section of the application is often difficult to read. It may be complicated, or written in small print. However, your signature, a requirement on any application, indicates that you have not only read this information, but that you agree to these policies. Read this section carefully before you sign an application, and keep this information for your records.

On the form, you will be asked to give personal information, including your age, social security number, and length of residence at your present address. You will be asked to give employment information, including your salary and length of employment. You will be asked to give credit information, including the status of any monthly payments, loans, or other charge accounts. Finally, you will be asked to sign your name. Your signature indicates that the information you have given is true, that you authorize the company to investigate your credit, and that you agree to all policies stated in the agreement.

Once you submit a credit application, a business or store will investigate you and your credit history. The business will make a judgment about whether you will be given credit. If you are considered a good credit risk, you will be allowed a certain amount of credit based on a company's individual policies.

Check It Out Examine the portion of a credit application shown on page 169.

- What information has the applicant stated? What store policies are stated?

Try Your Skill Refer to the credit application on page 169 and answer the following questions.

1. If Rafael Ortega had had no previous employer, what would he enter in that blank?

2. Suppose Rafael had no present loan but had just finished paying off a $1500 loan. Would this information be relevant? Why or why not?

3. What does Rafael indicate when he puts his signature on the application form?

Keep This in Mind

- On a credit application, you state information about yourself, your employment and income, and your financial obligations. Also on a credit application, a business states information about its policies. By signing an application, you agree to all terms stated.

Now Write Complete an actual credit application. Use a form given to you by your teacher or one from a business or store in your town. Read the application thoroughly and then complete the form. Label it **Take the Credit**. Put it into your folder.

APPLICATION FOR CREDIT

J. B. Weber's
708 Fifth Street
Spokane, Washington

PERSONAL DATA

☐ MRS. ☐ MISS ☐ MS. ☒ MR.
Designation of title is optional

FIRST NAME
Rafael

INITIAL
J.

LAST NAME
Ortega

STREET ADDRESS
1526 Crawford

CITY
Chicago,

STATE
Illinois

ZIP CODE
60607

HOW LONG
12 yrs.

☐ RENT ☐ BOARD
☐ OWN ☒ WITH PARENTS

HOME PHONE
555-9634

AGE
20

SOC. SEC. NO.
698-51-7242

NEAREST RELATIVE, NOT LIVING WITH YOU
Juan Ortega

RELATIONSHIP
Brother

ADDRESS
914 East Watson

CITY
Chicago, Illinois

STATE/ZIP
60680

EMPLOYMENT AND INCOME

PRESENT EMPLOYER Lincoln Federal Bank

PHONE
555-1600

ADDRESS
212 Market Square

CITY
Chicago,

STATE
Illinois 60607

POSITION Teller

SALARY
$800/month

HOW LONG
1 year

PREVIOUS EMPLOYER
Ferman Drug Store

POSITION
Cashier (part-time)

ADDRESS
1223 Mason Street

CITY
Chicago, Illinois

STATE
Illinois 60607

CREDIT REFERENCES

LANDLORD OR
MORTGAGE HOLDER Mr. Juan Ortega

MONTHLY
PAYMENT $ 200.00

ADDRESS 1526 Crawford, Chicago

PHONE
555-9634

BANK Lincoln Federal Bank

CITY

☒ CHECKING
☒ SAVINGS

LOANS OWED TO
1. City National Bank

BALANCE
$1400.

MONTHLY PAYMENTS
$85.00 (car payment)

2.

MONTHLY CHARGE ACCOUNTS
1. Sherman's Dept. Store

ACCT. NO.
555-613-0987

BALANCE
$23.45

2.

The above information is for the purpose of obtaining credit and is warranted to be true. False or misleading information will cause revocation of any extension of credit.

I hereby authorize J. B. Weber's or any credit bureau employed by them to investigate the references herein listed pertaining to my credit responsibility and to report to proper persons and bureaus my performance of this agreement.

I agree to pay all charges made by any authorized person within fifteen days of statement closing date. This is a 30 day charge account to be paid in full upon receipt of statement, if the account becomes delinquent (60 days overdue), I agree to pay a finance charge of 1½% per month, which is an annual percentage rate of 18% applied to the past due balance after deducting payments or credits.

Credit cards, when issued, are the property of J. B. Weber's and are returnable on request.

The Federal Credit Opportunity Act prohibits creditors from discriminating against credit applicants on the basis of sex or marital status.

I have a copy of this agreement and understand and agree to the terms herein specified.

Rafael Ortega

2/14/80

SIGNATURE OF APPLICANT

DATE

SEE IMPORTANT INFORMATION ON PAGE 2 OF THIS APPLICATION

May I?

Writing Letters of Request

Here's the Idea   Frequently, you will write a business letter to request something from a company or organization. For example, you may need information to write a report or to plan a vacation, or you may want to order a certain product. **Letters of request** should contain the six parts of a business letter and should follow either the block or modified block form.

When you write a letter of request, follow two important guidelines. First, be specific. It is essential to provide all of the information needed in order to fill your request. To request information, state precisely what you need and for what purpose. To place an order, include details about the size, color, cost, or identification number of the product you want. Second, be sure that your letter is courteous. Remember, you are asking someone to help you.

Check It Out   Read the letter of requst on page 171.

- Is this letter of request courteous, specific, and to the point? Which form does this business letter have?

Try Your Skill   Write a letter to one of the following organizations, requesting the information mentioned.

1. The Bureau of Indian Affairs, 1951 Constitution Avenue N.W., Washington, D.C. 20001. Request information on the number of Indian reservations in Arizona for a paper on Apache Indians due next month.

2. American Youth Hostels, National Campus, Delaplane, Virginia 22025. Request information about getting a hostel membership card for a bike trip you are planning this summer.

```
25 Maple Terrace
Lansdale, Pennsylvania  19446
October 22, 1981


Public Relations
Wilson Brothers Bakery
Lansdale, Pennsylvania  19446


Dear Sir or Madam:


I understand that you give free guided tours
through your bakery to groups of twenty or more.
I am planning to bring a Cub Scout troop on your
tour.  I will need 25 tickets for any Saturday in
the month of December.  Please send the tickets
to the above address.


Very truly yours,

Nick Tuminello

Nick Tuminello
```

Keep This in Mind

Write a letter of request that is courteous, specific, and to the point. Use either the block or modified block form for this business letter.

Now Write Write a letter to a federal or state government agency requesting information on a topic that interests you. Be sure to ask for specific information, and supply all necessary information. Label your letter **May I?** Put it into your folder. You may want to make a copy of the letter and mail it.

Satisfaction Guaranteed

Writing Letters of Complaint

Here's the Idea When you have spent time and money ordering a product by mail, you hope to be satisfied with it. Similarly, the company from which you purchased that product has an interest in seeing that you are satisfied. However, if you are not satisfied with a product, you should write a **letter of complaint** to the company courteously explaining your problem.

When you write this kind of business letter, you must include all necessary information. Be sure to identify a product completely. State the specific name of the product, its size, color, and identification or catalog number. Mention when and where the item was ordered and the amount you paid for it. It is best to include a Xerox copy of the order form, your receipt, or both sides of the canceled check with your letter.

You must also identify the specific nature of your complaint. For example, is the item missing a part? Did an item arrive in damaged condition? State precisely how you want the problem to be handled. Are you returning the merchandise for a refund or credit? Do you want it replaced? If you are polite and to the point, most companies will make an effort to solve your problem.

Check It Out Read the letter of complaint on page 173.

- Does this letter of complaint contain specific information about the products and the problems? Is is courteous?

Try Your Skill Write a letter of complaint based on the following situation.

> You ordered a subscription to *Indoor Farming* from Halliday Publications, Incorporated at 1424 Wesley Street, St. Louis, Missouri 63190. The subscription cost $6.00, but you have been billed for $60.00.

28 Oak Road
Hartfort, Connecticut   06106
January 3, 1981

Kramer Clothes Catalog, Inc.
P.O. Box 140
Walden, North Dakota   58313

Dear Sir or Madam:

On October 4, 1980, I ordered two blue personalized T-shirts (catalog number R-246) and a
personalized sweatshirt (catalog number J-189)
from your fall catalog. I paid $20.85 for the
order: $5.95 for each T-shirt, and $6.95 for
the sweatshirt, plus $2.00 for postage and handling.

These items were intended as Christmas presents.
Your catalog states that you guarantee delivery
within six weeks. It has now been nearly eleven
weeks, and Christmas has passed. Under the circumstances, I would like to have the $20.85 refunded.

Sincerely,

Katie Montel

Katie Montel

Keep This in Mind

- Write a letter of complaint that contains specific information about a product, the problem with it, and how you want the problem to be handled.

Now Write   Write a letter of complaint based on a real product. Tell how you want the problem handled. Label your paper **Satisfaction Guaranteed**. Put it into your folder.

The Pen Is Mightier

Writing a Letter-to-the-Editor

Here's the Idea A newspaper is always eager to print responsible letters from its readers. The letters may support or dispute news articles or opinions expressed in the paper. The letters may also deal with current national issues. Writing a **letter-to-the-editor** can be an effective way to air your feelings on a subject and perhaps to influence public opinion.

When you write a letter-to-the-editor, you are writing a business letter. Thus, you must follow one of the two standard business forms and the related guidelines you have learned. In addition, remember that your letter may be published, becoming a matter of public record.

It is most important that you express your opinion in a reasonable, responsible way. You may be angry or upset about a particular action. However, to be convincing, you must state your opinion clearly and logically. You must also offer strong supporting evidence. You may find it helpful to remember the skills you learned in writing an explanatory paragraph or composition that states an opinion.

In writing a letter-to-the-editor, you must remember to keep the letter short. Many letters are not published because they are too lengthy to fit the space limitations of a newspaper. As a rule, a shorter letter has a better chance of being published.

Finally, you must always sign your full name and include your address. No responsible newspaper will publish an anonymous letter—no matter how well written it is. If a letter deals with personal information, however, you may request that your name be withheld if your letter is printed.

Newspapers, especially the larger ones, often have a policy stating a standard form for letters-to-the-editor. This policy may be stated on the editorial page, along with the address to which you should mail your letter. Read these instructions before you make a final copy of your letter.

Check It Out   Read this letter-to-the-editor.

---

44 Grove Street
Weston, Alabama   71654
January 15, 1981

Editor
Weston Weekly Post
Sheehan Road
Weston, Alabama   71654

Dear Sir:

I wish to urge the citizens of this town to vote
yes in the upcoming school tax referendum.

A no vote will mean that each taxpayer saves five
to ten dollars a year. However, a no vote also
means no foreign language program for junior high
students, no speech therapist for the high school,
no tennis or soccer teams, and two fewer school
nurses. At the elementary schools, a no vote means
no after-school gymnastics program and no after-
school dramatics or music program.

I urge all Weston voters to think: Are you going
to miss that five dollars as much as we students
will miss what it can buy?

Sincerely,

John McConnell

John McConnell

- Is this letter brief and well-organized?
- Does the letter state and support an opinion clearly?

Try Your Skill Imagine that your local newspaper has written an editorial supporting one of the following actions. Write a letter-to-the-editor either supporting or opposing the action.

1. eliminating a major community program, such as bus service, in order to save money
2. instituting the draft
3. raising the voting age to 25
4. abolishing the Olympic Games
5. instituting a national gas rationing program

Keep This in Mind

- Writing a letter-to-the-editor of a newspaper is an effective way to express your feelings publicly. State your opinion in a brief, well organized letter that is based on strong supporting evidence.

- For this business letter, also follow any specific guidelines set by the newspaper about an acceptable form. Always sign your letter, and include your full name and address.

Now Write Borrow or buy a recent issue of your local newspaper. Write a letter-to-the-editor in response to an article, editorial, or letter appearing in the issue. Express your feelings in a strong, well organized letter that is based on factual supporting evidence. Label your paper **The Pen Is Mightier** and put it into your folder.

Be Counted

Writing a Letter to an Elected Official

Here's the Idea   There will probably be times when you will want to write to an elected official. The United States has a form of government in which the power rests with the citizens entitled to vote and is exercised by their elected representatives. Thus, it is only natural that you would want to communicate with an official who represents you. In fact, it is your responsibility as a citizen to do so.

When would you want to write to an elected official? You might want to urge action on an issue or bill or to complain about a situation you want corrected. You might want to express your approval or disapproval of an official's performance. You might also want to apply for an appointment to a military academy, or to request help or information. Keep in mind that letters to elected officials will have more positive results if you write before an action is to be taken, than if you write to complain about it after the fact.

First, determine whether the issue you are dealing with is a city, state, or national issue. Then write to the appropriate officials. For a city, or municipal, problem, you should call your city hall to learn which of the city officials you should write to. For a state issue, write to your state representative or senator, or to the governor. Regarding a national, or federal, issue, it is most effective to write to your United States Senator or Representative, or to the President. You can find the names and addresses of these officials at the library.

When you write a letter to an elected official, you must clearly define the issue that concerns you. Are you writing to voice your questions about a nuclear power plant that is to be built in your area? Are you writing to express your support of a proposed change in your state's income tax? Whatever the issue, be sure to define it as factually as possible. You must also be specific in explaining what action you wish the official to take, if any.

177

For this kind of business letter, addresses and salutations differ somewhat. On the inside address and on the envelope, use *The Honorable* followed by the official's name and title. Write, for example, *The Honorable Jane Smith, U.S. Senator.* Use this form of address for all senators, representatives, governors, or mayors. Use *Mr.* or *Ms.* for all other city officials. Use *The President*, for the President of the United States. As a salutation, *Dear Sir* or *Dear Madam* is always acceptable. However, you may prefer a more specific greeting, like *Dear Senator Smith.* In all other parts of the letter, use the standard business letter form you have learned.

Check It Out   Read the letter on page 179.

- Does this letter concern a municipal, state, or federal issue? Is it written to an appropriate official? Does the letter clearly explain an issue and how the writer feels it should be handled? Does the letter include an appropriate salutation and inside address?

Try Your Skill   Write *Municipal, State,* or *Federal* to identify each of the following issues. Then find and write the name of a particular official to whom you yourself would write.

1. a state highway
2. the voting age
3. school athletics budget
4. defense funding
5. a broken street light
6. a national health plan
7. U.S. energy policy
8. the Equal Rights Amendment

Keep This in Mind

- In expressing your views on municipal, state, and federal issues, write to the appropriate elected officials. Be specific about the issue that concerns you and how you wish it to be handled. Include an appropriate salutation and address for the elected official.

```
          241 Taylor Avenue
          Hastings, Virginia   05432
          April 8, 1981


          Mr. Wayne Dobbs, Alderman
          City Hall
          1283 Main Street
          Hastings, Virginia   05432


          Dear Mr. Dobbs:


          This letter is in reference to the dangerous
          intersection at Taylor Avenue and Monroe Street
          in your district.  At present only a four-way
          stop sign directs traffic here.  In the past four
          months alone, there have been three serious
          accidents at this intersection.  These accidents
          resulted in one fatality, and six people have
          been hospitalized.


          The neighbors of this area would like to see a
          traffic light installed at this location.  The
          numerous phone calls we have made to the Division
          of Traffic have brought no response.  We would
          appreciate it if you as our elected representative
          could take a personal interest in this matter and
          see that some action is taken before anyone else
          is injured.


          Very truly yours,

          Andrea Mason


          Andrea Mason, President
          Taylor Avenue Neighborhood Association
```

Now Write   Write a letter to an elected official about an issue
that interests you. Be specific in expressing your viewpoint. Label
your paper **Be Counted** and put it into your folder. You may want
to make a copy of the letter and mail it.

Developing Dictionary Skills

Readout

Using a Dictionary Entry ·

Here's the Idea A dictionary is a reference book containing a list of words in a language and information about the words. It is probably the single most valuable reference you can use whenever you are reading or writing.

There are several kinds of dictionaries you may find helpful. Usually you will be able to find what you need in an abridged, or shortened, dictionary. Sometimes you may need an unabridged dictionary, which contains nearly all of the words in a language. In addition, there are some specialized dictionaries that include words related to a single subject only, such as medicine.

You will discover that most dictionaries vary in some ways. Every dictionary organizes information in its own way and uses its own symbols and abbreviations. Examine the front of a dictionary to find an explanation of its format. Become familiar with the dictionaries you use.

All dictionaries, however, list words in alphabetical order. Also, all dictionaries have two guide words in large, bold print at the top of each page to indicate the words listed on that page. The left guide word is the same as the first word on the page. The right guide word is the same as the last word on the page. To look for a word, flip through the dictionary until you find the page where the word comes alphabetically between the guide words.

Check It Out Examine the portion of the dictionary page at the top of page 183.

- How is each column of words listed? What special symbols are used? What words are new to you? What are the guide words? Would you find the word *mosaic* on this page?

mor·tar (môr′tər) *n.* [< OE. & OFr. < L. *mortarium*: for IE. base see MORBID] **1.** a very hard bowl in which substances are ground or pounded to a powder with a pestle **2.** a short-barreled cannon which hurls shells in a high curve **3.** a mixture of cement or lime with sand and water, used between bricks, etc., or as plaster —*vt.* **1.** to plaster together with mortar **2.** to attack with mortar shells

mor·tar·board (-bôrd′) *n.* **1.** a square board with a handle beneath, on which mortar is carried **2.** an academic cap with a square, flat top, worn at commencements, etc.

mort·gage (môr′gij) *n.* [< OFr. < *mort*, dead (see MORTAL) + *gage*, GAGE[1]] *Law* **1.** an agreement in which a person borrowing money gives the lender a claim to a certain piece of property as a pledge that the debt will be paid **2.** the deed, or legal paper, by which this pledge is made —*vt.* **-gaged, -gag·ing** **1.** *Law* to pledge (property) by a mortgage in order to borrow money *[they mortgaged their house to buy a new car]* **2.** to put a claim on; make risky *[he mortgaged his future by piling up debts]*

mort·ga·gee (môr′gə jē′) *n.* the lender to whom property is mortgaged

mort·ga·gor, mort·gag·er (môr′gi jər) *n.* the borrower who mortgages his property

mor·tice (môr′tis) *n., vt. alt. sp. of* MORTISE

☆**mor·ti·cian** (môr tish′ən) *n.* [< L. *mors*, death (see MORTAL) + -ICIAN] *same as* FUNERAL DIRECTOR

Mo·ses (mō′ziz) [LL. < Gr. < Heb. *mōsheh*, prob. < Egypt. *mes*, child] **1.** a masculine name **2.** *Bible* the leader who brought the Israelites out of slavery in Egypt and led them to the Promised Land, and who received the Ten Commandments

☆**mo·sey** (mō′zē) *vi.* [< *vamose*, var. of VAMOOSE] [Slang] **1.** to amble along **2.** to go away

Mos·lem (mäz′ləm, muz′-, mäs′-) *n.* [Ar. *muslim*, true believer < *aslama*, to resign oneself (to God)] a believer in the religion of Islam —*adj.* of Islam or the Moslems: also **Mos·lem′ic** (-lem′ik) —**Mos′lem·ism** *n.*

mosque (mäsk) *n.* [< MFr. < It. < Ar. *masjid* < *sajada*, to pray] a Moslem temple or place of worship

mos·qui·to (mə skēt′ō, -ə) *n., pl.* **-toes, -tos** [Sp. & Port., dim. of *mosca* < L. *musca*, a fly: for IE. base see MIDGE] a two-winged insect, the female of which has skin-piercing, bloodsucking mouthparts: some varieties transmit diseases, as malaria and yellow fever —**mos·qui′to·ey** (-ē) *adj.*

☆**mosquito net** (or **netting**) a fine mesh cloth or a curtain made of this for keeping out mosquitoes

moss (môs, mäs) *n.* [OE. *mos*, a swamp] **1.** a very small, green plant growing in velvety clusters on rocks, trees, moist ground, etc. **2.** any of various similar plants, as some lichens, algae, etc. —*vt.* to cover with a growth of moss —**moss′like′** *adj.*

moss agate agate with mosslike markings

☆**moss·back** (môs′bak′, mäs′-) *n.* [Colloq.] an old-fashioned or very conservative person

☆**moss pink** a hardy, perennial phlox forming sprawling mats with bristly, narrow leaves and white, pink, or lavender flowers

moss rose **1.** *same as* PORTULACA **2.** a variety of the cabbage rose with a roughened, mossy flower stalk and calyx

Try Your Skill

Look up the following words in a dictionary: *camera, empire, honor,* and *spiral.* Write a definition for each. Then examine the page on which each word is found. For each page, copy the guide words, any special symbols used, and three unfamiliar words.

Keep This in Mind

- A dictionary is a reference book that lists words alphabetically and explains each word. Become familiar with the dictionaries you use.

Now Write

When you are employed, you may hear the following words: *employer, foreman, labor union, manager, pension, promotion, seniority,* and *withholding tax.* Find each word in the dictionary and list the guide words for each page. Read each definition carefully. Then choose four of the words and use them in sentences. Label your paper **Readout** and put it into your folder.

A Grand Entry

Reading a Dictionary Entry

Here's the Idea   You refer to a dictionary generally to find the meaning of a word. However, a single dictionary entry contains a great deal of additional information to help you understand a word and use it correctly.

The **entry word** itself appears in bold print and is divided into syllables. The word *environment*, for example, is entered as **en · vi · ron · ment**. Check the entry word when you divide a word at the end of a line of writing.

The **pronunciation** of a word is shown in parentheses. Use the symbols and accent marks to help you sound out an unfamiliar word. The word *mortgage*, for example, is written as (môr gij). Refer to the explanation of symbols shown at the bottom of a page or at the front of the dictionary.

The **part of speech** of a word is indicated by an abbreviation in bold print. V*erb*, for example, may be abbreviated **vt.**, for *transitive verb*, or **vi.**, for *intransitive verb*. If a word can be used as more than one part of speech, the other parts of speech will be noted further along in an entry. Refer to the list of abbreviations at the front of the dictionary.

If a word has **special forms** or **endings**, these will be included next in the entry. The entry for the irregular verb *write*, for instance, includes the forms **wrote, written, writing**. Plural endings of some nouns are also given. For *cactus*, for instance, the two acceptable plural endings, **-tuses** and **-ti**, are shown.

The **origin**, or **history**, is given next, usually in brackets. Abbreviations, like *OE.* or *Sp.*, indicate the languages from which words came, like Old English or Spanish. Refer to the list of abbreviations given at the front of a dictionary.

Definitions are given next. The most common definition is often given first. If a word has a special meaning in a certain field, that meaning is indicated. One definition of *major* as a noun, says "*Educ.* a major field of study [her *major* is history]."

Sometimes a word may have a special meaning used in conversation and informal writing. This is termed a *colloquial* meaning and it is usually noted in the dictionary. For example, one definition of *ham* is "[Colloq.] an amateur radio operator." Slang—very informal, spoken language—is also indicated. For example, one definition of *cut* is "[Slang] to stop; discontinue." In many cases, the informal meanings are those that first appeared in the United States. These Americanisms, like the meanings given for *ham* and *cut*, are often noted in the dictionary by a special symbol, such as a star.

Finally, at the end of an entry, some dictionaries list **synonyms** and **antonyms**. For example, at the end of the entry for *kind*, the synonyms *kindly*, *benign*, and *benevolent* are explained, and the antonyms *unkind*, *unfeeling*, and *cruel* are listed.

Check It Out   Examine this dictionary entry.

fault (fôlt) *n.* [< OFr. *faulte*, ult. < L. *falsus*, FALSE] **1.** a thing that mars or makes something imperfect; flaw; defect **2.** *a)* a misdeed; offense *b)* an error; mistake **3.** responsibility for something wrong; blame *[it's my fault that he's late]* **4.** *Geol.* a fracture or zone of fractures in rock strata along with a shifting of the strata **5.** *Tennis, Squash,* etc. an error in service —*vt.* **1.** to find fault with; blame **2.** *Geol.* to cause a fault in —*vi.* **1.** to commit a fault in tennis, etc. **2.** *Geol.* to develop a fault —**at fault** guilty of error; deserving blame —**find fault (with)** to seek and point out faults (of) —**to a fault** too much; excessively

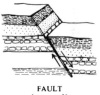

FAULT
(sense 4)

SYN.—**fault** refers to a definite imperfection in character, but not one which is strongly condemned *[her only fault is stubbornness]*; **failing** implies an even less serious shortcoming, usually one that many people have *[tardiness was one of his failings]*; **weakness** applies to a minor shortcoming that results from a lack of perfect self-control *[talking too much is his weakness]*; **foible** refers to a slight weakness that is regarded more as an amusing peculiarity than an actual defect in character *[eating desserts first is one of his foibles]*; **vice,** although it implies the doing of something morally wrong, does not suggest a serious moral weakness or shortcoming when used as a synonym for any of the preceding terms *[a little gambling is his only vice]* —**ANT.** virtue

· From what language did *fault* come? What parts of speech is *fault*? What special meanings are given? What is an antonym for *fault*?

Try Your Skill Read this entry and answer the questions.

reg·is·ter (rej′is tər) *n.* [< MFr. < ML. *registrum* < LL. < L. pp. of *regerere*, to record] **1.** *a)* a record or list of names, events, items, etc. *b)* a book in which this is kept [a hotel *register*] *c)* an entry in such a record **2.** registration; enrollment **3.** a device, as a meter or counter, for recording fares paid, money deposited, etc. [a cash *register*] ☆**4.** an opening into a room by which the amount of air passing, as from a furnace, can be controlled **5.** *Music* *a)* a part of a range of tones of the human voice or of an instrument having a specified quality *b)* an organ stop, or the tone quality it produces **6.** *Printing* exact placing of lines, pages, colors, etc. —*vt.* ☆**1.** to enter in or as in a record or list; enroll [to *register* a birth] **2.** to indicate as on a scale [a thermometer *registers* temperature] **3.** to show, as by a look on the face [to *register* surprise] **4.** to protect (mail) by paying a fee to have its delivery recorded at a post office **5.** *Printing* to cause to be in register —*vi.* **1.** to enter one's name, as in a hotel register, a list of eligible voters, etc. **2.** to enroll in a school, college, etc. **3.** to make an impression —**reg′is·tra·ble** (-trə b'l) *adj.* —**reg′is·trant** (-trənt) *n.*

1. From what language does *register* come?

2. As what parts of speech can *register* be used?

3. Name two specialized areas that use the term *register*.

4. Explain two ways in which a shop owner might use the term *register*.

5. What special meanings appear to be Americanisms?

6. Give the definition of *register* that fits its use in this sentence: Kim's face *registered* surprise when she saw the name on the letter.

Keep This in Mind

· A dictionary entry includes the meanings of a word and a great deal of other useful informaton. An entry may vary in different dictionaries.

Now Write On your paper list: *Entry word, Pronunciation, Parts of speech, Special forms, Origin, Definition* [*Colloq.*] and *Synonym and Antonym.* Using a dictionary, find and copy one example of each kind of information. Use a different entry to illustrate each kind of information. Label your paper **A Grand Entry** and put it into your folder.

More Ways Than One

Finding the Meaning of a Word

Here's the Idea   As you search for words in a dictionary, you will notice that many words have more than one meaning. Thus, whenever you look up a word, read through all of its meanings. Find the meaning that fits a particular context.

For instance, the simple word *break* has an extraordinary number of meanings. *Webster's New World Dictionary, Students Edition* lists thirty-four meanings for *break* as a verb. The same entry also includes thirteen meanings for *break* as a noun and twenty different meanings of *break* as it is used in phrases. In the following sentences, notice how the context helps you to determine the correct meaning.

1. The cowboy can *break* the wild horse in two weeks.
(In this context, *break* means "to tame an animal, as with force.")

2. We left home at the *break* of day.
(Here, *break* means "a beginning or appearance.")

3. Ann *broke* her fall by landing in the bushes.
(Here, *break* means "to reduce the force of by interrupting.")

4. I can't wait to *break* the good news to Dad.
(Here, *break* means "to make known; disclose.")

5. Meet me in the cafeteria during your *break*.
(Here, *break* means "an interruption of something regular.")

From these few examples, you can understand how many different meanings might be contained in a single entry.

There are some words, however, that seem to be repeated in more than one entry. For example, you will find the word *key* entered twice: *key*[1], a noun, means "an instrument, usually of metal, for moving the bolt of a lock and thus locking or unlocking something"; *key*[2], also a noun, means "a reef or low island." In each entry, *key* has a different origin. Such a word is called a *homograph*. Each entry is not a shade of meaning of the word; it is actually a different word. When you notice a word with more than one entry, read all entries to find the meaning you seek.

Check It Out   Examine these dictionary entries.

fair[1] (fer) *adj.* [OE. *fæger*] **1.** beautiful [a *fair* maiden] **2.** unblemished; clean [a *fair* name] **3.** light in color; blond [*fair* hair] **4.** clear and sunny [*fair* weather] **5.** easy to read; clear [a *fair* hand] **6.** just and honest; impartial; specif., free from discrimination based on race, religion, sex, etc. [*fair* employment practices; *fair* housing] **7.** according to the rules [a *fair* blow] **8.** likely; promising [in a *fair* way to benefit] **9.** pleasant and courteous, often falsely smooth [the traitor's *fair* words] **10.** favorable; helpful [a *fair* wind] **11.** of moderately good size **12.** neither very bad nor very good; average [a *fair* chance of winning] —*adv.* **1.** in a fair manner [play *fair*] **2.** straight; squarely [struck *fair* in the face] —**fair and square** [Colloq.] with justice and honesty —**fair to middling** [Colloq.] moderately good; passable —**fair′ish** *adj.* —**fair′ness** *n.*
SYN.—**fair** implies the treating of both or all sides alike, without showing preference for any side [a *fair* hearing]; **just** implies judgment according to a fixed standard of what is right or lawful [a *just* decision]; **impartial** and **unbiased** both stress being open-minded and free from prejudice for or against any side [an *impartial* referee; an *unbiased* account]; **dispassionate** implies the absence of strong feelings and, hence, suggests cool, reasoning judgment [a *dispassionate* critic]; **objective** implies the viewing of persons or things according to the facts as they really are [an *objective* study of the problems] Basic to all these synonyms is the idea of making judgments without being influenced by one's own feelings or interests —see also SYN. at BEAUTIFUL —**ANT. prejudiced, biased**
fair[2] (fer) *n.* [< OFr. < ML. < LL. < L. *feriae*, pl., festivals] **1.** orig., a gathering of people at regular times for barter and sale of goods **2.** a carnival where there is entertainment and things are sold, often for charity; bazaar ☆**3.** an exhibition, often competitive (**county fair, state fair**), of farm, household, and manufactured products, or of international displays (**world's fair**), with amusement areas and educational displays; exposition

· What is the origin of *fair*[1]? *fair*[2]?

· Which meaning of *fair*[1] is most familiar to you? *fair*[2]?

Try Your Skill   Read the following dictionary entries. Then, determine which meaning of *lean* fits the context of each sentence and write your answer.

lean[1] (lēn) *vi.* **leaned** or **leant**, **lean′ing** [OE. *hlinian*: for IE. base see CLIENT] **1.** to bend from an upright position; stand at a slant; incline [the old tree *leans* toward the barn] **2.** to bend the body so as to rest part of one's weight upon something [he *leaned* on the desk] **3.** to depend for advice, aid, etc.; rely (*on* or *upon*) [he still *leans* on his parents] **4.** to have a preference; tend (*toward* or *to* a certain opinion, attitude, etc.) —*vt.* to cause to lean [to *lean* a ladder against the house; to *lean* one's head back] —*n.* a leaning; inclination; slant —**lean′er** *n.*

lean[2] (lēn) *adj.* [OE. *hlæne*]   **1.** with little flesh or fat; thin; spare [a *lean* athlete]   **2.** containing little or no fat: said of meat   **3.** *a)* lacking in richness, profit, etc.; meager [a *lean* year for business]   *b)* characterized by being brief, direct, etc. [a *lean* style]   —*n.* meat containing little or no fat   —**lean'ly** *adv.* —**lean'ness** *n.*

SYN.—**lean** implies a healthy, natural absence of fat or fleshiness; **spare** suggests a muscular frame without any unnecessary flesh; **lanky** implies an awkward tallness and leanness, and, often, loose-jointedness; **skinny** and **scrawny** imply extreme thinness that is unattractive and that indicates a lack of strength and energy; **gaunt** implies a bony thinness such as that caused by a wasting away of the flesh from hunger or suffering —see also **SYN.** at THIN —**ANT.** fleshy, fat, stout

1. The roast beef was *lean* and tender.

2. The birches *leaned* over the road under the weight of the heavy snow.

3. During Ginny's illness, she *leaned* on her family for moral support and encouragement.

4. My Uncle Ed, who sells used cars, told me that this has been a *lean* year for his business.

5. The crowd continued to cheer Olympic speed skater Eric Heiden after he crossed the finish line and stood up, stretching his strong, *lean* body.

Keep This in Mind

· When you look up an unfamiliar word in the dictionary, determine which meaning fits the context.

· Sometimes a word has more than one entry, with a different meaning and origin for each.

Now Write   Use a dictionary to find one example of a word with many meanings and one example of a homograph. For each example, copy three definitions. Then write a sentence using each of the meanings you have written. Label your paper **More Ways Than One** and put it into your folder.

Developing Library Skills

Special Arrangements

Finding What You Need

Here's the Idea   A library is a treasury of information and ideas. There you will find factual sources dealing with a variety of subjects. There you will also find books and magazines dealing with a variety of imaginary experiences. To find what you need, you must first learn how your school or public library is organized.

All library books are classified into two general groups, fiction and nonfiction. **Fiction** books are arranged alphabetically according to the author's last name. For example, the novel *Ethan Frome*, written by Edith Wharton, would be filed under W.

Nonfiction books are arranged according to their subjects on a separate section of shelves. Many libraries use a system called the **Dewey Decimal System**. This system groups nonfiction books into ten numbered categories.

000-099	General Works	(encyclopedias, almanacs)
100-199	Philosophy	(ethics, psychology, occult)
200-299	Religion	(the Bible, mythology)
300-399	Social Science	(economics, law, education, government)
400-499	Language	(languages, grammar, dictionaries)
500-599	Science	(mathematics, biology, chemistry)
600-699	Useful Arts	(farming, cooking, sewing, television, business)
700-799	Fine Arts	(music, painting, dance, photography, sports)
800-899	Literature	(poetry, plays)
900-999	History	(biography, travel, geography)

On the spine of every nonfiction book is its **call number**. The call number, which includes the Dewey Decimal number and other useful information, identifies a particular book. Some libraries add the letter *B* to the call number of a biography or the letter *R* to the call number of a reference work like an encyclopedia.

Examine this model of a nonfiction book.

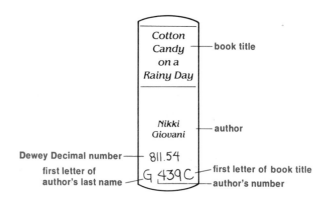

Check It Out Examine the books represented here.

The Great Gatsby

F. Scott Fitzgerald

Walking Tours of America

Louise Feinsot

917.304
WAL

All Creatures Wise and Wonderful

James Herriot

636.089
H435aw

Gone with the Wind

Margaret Mitchell

Nineteen Eighty-Four

George Orwell

WORKING

Studs Terkel

331.209
TER

Survive the Savage Sea

Dougal Robertson

910.09164
R545s

We Have Always Lived in the Castle

Shirley Jackson

- Which books are fiction and which are nonfiction?
- What is the general category of each nonfiction book?

Try Your Skill   Write the answers to the following questions.

1. Under what letter on the library shelves would you find the following fiction books?

Billy Budd by Herman Melville
Song of Solomon by Toni Morrison
The Time Machine by H. G. Wells
Catch-22 by Joseph Heller
The Crystal Cave by Mary Stewart

2. In which categories of the Dewey Decimal system would you find information on these subjects?

the history of television
a guide to low-cost travel in the U.S.
ESP
a play by William Shakespeare
the legal rights of consumers

Keep This in Mind

- In the library, fiction books are filed alphabetically by the author's last name.
- Nonfiction books may be classified in ten major categories of the Dewey Decimal System. Each nonfiction book has a call number.

Now Write   As your teacher directs, become familiar with the organization of your school or public library. Learn the locations of fiction and nonfiction books, reference books, magazines, and special collections.

On your visit to the library, find four fiction books and four nonfiction books that you might enjoy reading. In fact, you may want to check out one or more of these books. On your paper, write the titles, authors, and call numbers of the books you find. Label your paper **Special Arrangements**, and put it into your folder.

On File

Using the Card Catalog

Here's the Idea   In every library, you will find a file called the card catalog. The card catalog contains basic information about all the books in that library. In fact, each book is listed three times—by its author, by its title, and by its subject.

All three cards—author card, title card, and subject card—contain the same information. However, on each card the information is arranged under different headings. In this way, you are able to locate a book in one of several ways.

All three cards list the author, title, publisher, date of publication, and number of pages in the book. There is a notation if the book has illustrations or maps. There may also be a description of the book or a list of related books. In addition, all three cards list the call number of a nonfiction book in the upper left hand corner. This is the same number that appears on the spine of the book.

On an **author card**, the author's name is given at the top, last name first. Author cards are filed alphabetically by the author's last name. If there is more than one author, the card is filed by the name of the author whose name is shown first in the book.

On a **title card**, the title appears on the top line, with only the first word of the title capitalized. Title cards are filed alphabetically by the first word of the title. However, if A, An, or The appears as the first word in a title, look for the card under the first letter of the second word in the title.

On a **subject card**, the subject appears on the top line. The subject may be written in capital letters or in red. Subject cards are filed alphabetically by the first letter of the subject.

You will also notice some cards that say See or See also. These **cross reference cards** refer you to other subject headings that are related to the one you want.

Searching the card catalog will be quicker if you use the **guide cards**. These blank cards have tabs on which are written general subject headings. The headings help you to follow the alphabetical arrangement of the card catalog.

Check It Out   Examine the three sample cards on page 197.

- Under what letter would each card be filed? Where would you find more books by Daniel S. Halacy? Where would you find other books about alternative energy sources?

Try Your Skill   Suppose you are doing research on the subject of voting in the United States. Go to your school or public library and find a subject card, a title card, and an author card for books dealing with voting. Copy the important information as it appears on each card.

Keep This in Mind

- Every book in a library is listed in the card catalog on three separate cards—author, title, and subject. Each card shows the author, title, publisher, date of publication, number of pages, and other useful information. Cards for a nonfiction book also list its call number.

Now Write   Select an interesting subject that you can research at the library. Use the card catalog to find at least three nonfiction books about your subject. Copy the important information from the author, title, and subject cards. Label your paper **On File** and keep it in your folder. Also, choose the most interesting book you find, check it out of the library, and bring it to class.

333.7 **Halacy, Daniel Stephen**
H128e
 Earth, water, wind, and sun: our
energy alternatives / D. S. Halacy,
Jr. — New York : Harper & Row,
c1977.
 186 p. : ill.; 22 cm.

 Includes index.
 Bibliography: p. [179]-180.
 ISBN 0-06-011777-X : $8.95

title card

333.7 **Earth, water, wind, and sun**
H128e
 Earth, water, wind, and sun: our
energy alternatives / D. S. Halacy,
Jr. — New York : Harper & Row,
c1977.
 186 p. : ill.; 22 cm.

 Includes index.
 Bibliography: p. [179]-180.
 ISBN 0-06-011777-X : $8.95

subject card

333.7 **ENERGY**
H128e
 Earth, water, wind, and sun: our
energy alternatives / D. S. Halacy,
Jr. — New York : Harper & Row,
c1977.
 186 p. : ill.; 22 cm.

 Includes index.
 Bibliography: p. [179]-180.
 ISBN 0-06-011777-X : $8.95

To Know Better

Using an Encyclopedia

Here's the Idea You may not always need to read an entire book on a subject you want to know more about. Sometimes you only need to read a short article containing basic information. The place to find such articles is in an encyclopedia. An encyclopedia is a general reference work that contains a great deal of information on a wide variety of subjects. The articles are arranged in alphabetical order by subject from the first volume through the last. On the spine of each volume is either a single letter or a set of guide letters noting what is included.

In a large library, you will find several sets of encyclopedias, many at different reading levels. Be sure to choose one that you can read easily. Select a suitable encyclopedia for your work by skimming through several or by asking a librarian for assistance. You may select *The World Book Encyclopedia*, *Collier's Encyclopedia*, or the *Britannica Junior Encyclopaedia*, for example.

To find an article on a particular subject, you need to find the right heading. To do this, determine the key words of your topic. Often there will be more than one key word and more than one heading under which you might find information on your topic. For example, you might find information on pollution under "Environmental Pollution" or "Ecology." Select the appropriate volume and look under both headings. Guide words at the top of each page will help you find the headings quickly.

An encyclopedia article on an important subject is usually presented in parts, each with a subtitle. An article on "Environmental Pollution," for example, may include such parts as "Kinds of Pollution," "Causes of Pollution," "Controlling Pollution," and "History." Depending on the purpose of your research, you may need to read all of the article or only parts of it.

At the end of a major article you will find additional information to guide your research. For example, you may find lists of related articles in the encyclopedia, an outline of information on the subject, books for further reading, or a study guide.

Most encyclopedias also include an index, usually the first or last volume in a set. Use the index to locate related information that is presented in different articles. Some encyclopedias also publish yearbooks that contain up-to-date information about continually changing subjects.

Whenever you research a subject, always check more than one source of information. Check several encyclopedias, as well as other kinds of reference books. In addition to general encyclopedias, you may want to check some of the specialized encyclopedias that deal with one subject only. For example, you may need an encyclopedia that deals only with art or animals. If you discover different information in different sources, try to use the most recent or most reliable reference. Be sure that you identify every source you use.

Check It Out   Look at the encyclopedia shown below.

- In what volume, and under what key word, would you find information on American poets? causes of inflation? freedom of the press? the Nobel Prize? tropical climate? the novels of John Steinbeck? the rules for playing soccer? the Swiss Alps?

Try Your Skill   As your teacher directs, use an encyclopedia to answer the following questions.

1. Name three of the most heavily populated cities in the world.
2. What are the colors of roses?
3. What is the capital of the Netherlands?
4. In what year of the Civil War did the Battle of Gettysburg take place?
5. Where is the Taj Mahal?
6. Who was President of the United States during World War I?
7. Which native American Indian tribes have lived in Florida?
8. Who is the god of thunder in Norse mythology?
9. What musical instruments are commonly used in African music?
10. Name two important French directors of motion pictures.

Keep This in Mind

- An encyclopedia is a general reference work containing information on many different subjects. Articles are arranged alphabetically in numbered volumes. Examine a variety of encyclopedias, and select one that is suitable for you and the purpose of your research.

Now Write   Choose a subject that interests you, and look up that subject in two encyclopedias. List a few of the most important facts that you find in each, and compare them. Be sure to identify each source completely. List the names of the encyclopedias, numbers of the volumes, page numbers of the articles, and include several titles of other related articles or books mentioned. Also, name which encyclopedia you prefer and briefly explain your choice. Label your paper **To Know Better** and put it into your folder.

References on Request

Using Reference Works

Here's the Idea   Every library has a reference section with a collection of varied sources to help you research subjects in many different areas. Some reference works contain a range of general information, while others are more specialized. Few of these valuable references can be taken out of a library. In addition to dictionaries and encyclopedias, with which you are already familiar, there are several other standard references that you will find useful.

Atlases are books of maps. Many atlases also contain information about the earth's population, weather, and geologic structure. Among the most widely used atlases are the *National Geographic Atlas of the World, The International Atlas from Rand McNally*, and the *Atlas of World History*.

Almanacs and **yearbooks**, published each year, are the most useful sources of up-to-date facts and statistics. For example, in these references you will find information about current world events, governments, populations, products, and awards. You may want to use the *World Almanac and Book of Facts*, the *Information Please Almanac, Atlas, and Yearbook*, the *Statesman's Yearbook*, or the *Guiness Book of World Records*.

Biographical references contain information about important people. Useful reference works include the *Dictionary of American Biography, Current Biography, Who's Who, Twentieth Century Authors*, and *The Book of Presidents*.

A **vertical file** is the name of a library's collection of assorted pamphlets, catalogs, handbooks, and clippings. The collection is usually kept in a file cabinet, but its contents differ from library to library. It may include information about local events and schools, for example.

Magazines are valuable sources of information about a wide range of subjects, and a library may subscribe to any number of the nation's leading magazines. In order to locate specific information in magazines, you need to learn to use the *Readers' Guide to Periodical Literature*. The *Readers' Guide* contains the titles of articles, stories, and poems published in more than 100 major magazines. One hardcover volume of the *Readers' Guide* covers material published during a year. Several shorter, paperback volumes cover material for shorter time periods. Once you have learned to read its specially abbreviated format, you will find the *Readers' Guide* a valuable reference.

Become familiar with these standard references. Each contains an explanation of how its information is organized and what symbols and abbreviations are used. Often a single sample entry is presented. Before you use any reference work for the first time, examine these explanations.

Check It Out   Study this model of a section from the *Readers' Guide to Periodical Literature*.

FALCONS
New hope for the peregrine|restoration program in Rocky Moun-   title of article
tain National Park. K. Vanderwerf. il Nat Parks & Con Mag
53:10-15 Jl '79
Peregrine penthouse on Interior Department restores falcons to
Nation's Capital. il Nat Parks & Con Mag 53:25 S '79
FALCONS in art. See Birds in art
FALK, Joe, Jr
Tips for intensive gardens. Flower & Gard 22:25 Mr '78
FALK, Sydney W. and Schramm, D. N.
Did the solar system start with a bang? il Sky & Tel 58:18-22 |Jl '79| date of magazine
FALL. See Autumn
FALL vacations. See Vacations
FALLOUT shelters. See Atomic bomb shelters
FALLOWS, James   volume number
Washington: fat city. Atlantic |244|:|4+| Jl '79
FALWELL, Jerry   page number
Politicizing the word. L. I. Barrett. il por Time 114:62+ O 1 '79
FAMILY
Fractured family: following it into the future; excerpt from An
evangelical agenda—1984 and beyond. A. M. Nicholi, 2d. il por
Chr Today 23:10-15 My 25 '79
|See also| cross reference
Divorce
Fathers-in-law
FAMILY farms. See Farm ownership
FAMILY life
Life without television. |S. Amanda |il pors Parents 54:88+ Ag '79   author
Two careers, three kids, and her 2,000-mile commute. M. Craw-
ford. il por Ms 8:76-8 Ag '79
What happened when 5 families stopped watching TV? C. Trost
and E. Grzech. il |Good H |189:94+ Ag '79   name of magazine

- Read through one unmarked listing in this sample and explain all the information given. What other kinds of references are in the reference section of your school or public library?

Try Your Skill   Write the name of a reference work other than an encyclopedia that you might use to find the following information. If magazines would be the best source, write *Readers' Guide*.

1. Name five poems written by Langston Hughes.
2. What vocational schools and colleges are located in your area?
3. What countries share borders with Yugoslavia?
4. How were Presidents John Adams and John Quincy Adams related?
5. What is the average daily summer temperature in the Sahara Desert?
6. What is the current population of the United States?
7. Name two famous American composers.
8. Who are the present U.S. Senators representing New York?
9. What was Mark Twain's real name?
10. What recent national projects deal with wildlife conservation?

Keep This in Mind

- There are several kinds of useful specialized references. Learn to use those available in your library.

Now Write   Choose a well known person or place that interests you. Use several specialized references to research your subject. Skim each source and jot down several of the most interesting facts. Identify your sources by listing the titles, call numbers, and volume and page numbers of the sources you find most informative. Label your paper **References on Request** and put it into your folder.

The Research Report

Environmental Issues

Look Everywhere

Researching a Subject

Here's the Idea A report is similar to a composition; that is, a report is a group of paragraphs dealing with one subject. However, a report is always based on factual information that you must learn from sources outside your knowledge.

Suppose, for example, that you are assigned the subject of environmental issues to investigate and report on. This assignment identifies a general subject. You need to survey available information and select a specific aspect of the subject that interests you.

You understand that an environmental issue is one arising from the ways in which people's activities affect the land, air, water, and animal life. There are several critical environmental issues facing the United States today. The major concerns include problems of conservation and pollution. Such concerns affect everyone in some way.

For your report, you will need to choose an environmental issue for which you will be able to find enough information. Think about and jot down environmental concerns that interest you. Go to the library. Look through the card catalog for the subject cards *Environment* or *Ecology*. Look in the nonfiction section that contains books on environment. These would include books with Dewey Decimal System numbers in the 300's and 500's.

Search also throughout the reference section. Here you will find a variety of sources, including encyclopedias, for information on environmental issues. Magazines and the pamphlets found in the vertical file are also good sources of information to check, as are local and national newspapers.

Here is a sample list of sources you might check to find general information about environmental issues.

1. "Environmental Pollution" in *The World Book Encyclopedia*, Volume 6, pages 260b-261

2. *Clean Water for Us All*, U.S. Environmental Protection Agency, June, 1977

3. "Nature and Cities," by J. M. McCloskey in *Sierra* magazine, April, 1978, pages 14-16

4. "Preserving Wildlife—A Worldwide Struggle," U.S. *News and World Report* magazine, April 17, 1978, pages 62-65

5. "The Earth: Love It or ..." in the *Boston Herald Traveler*, March 1, 1972

After you have considered environmental issues in general, focus on a particular issue. Consider your interests and your particular environment. You will write your best report on an issue that affects you. You may also benefit from useful information that you will discover.

Make sure that the issue you choose to report on is not too broad to cover in a five-paragraph report. Within this specific length, you want to be able to cover a limited subject thoroughly.

Once you have chosen a particular environmental issue to investigate, search again in the sources already mentioned. If possible, talk to someone employed in the area you have chosen. You can also write to the U.S. Department of the Interior, Washington, D.C. Be sure to record each source of your information in your notebook. Record titles of books, encyclopedias, pamphlets, and magazine articles. Also write the volume and page number of the encyclopedias you may decide to use and the dates of the magazines.

Suppose that you decide to write a five-paragraph report on the role of zoos in wildlife conservation. The reading you do on the topic of zoos is really the beginning of your report.

Check It Out   On page 208, examine the list of sources you might find to write a report about the wildlife conservation efforts of zoos.

- What general library sources have you looked through?
- Is this a varied and specific list of sources with which to begin a report?

1. *Encyclopedia Americana,* Vol. 29 (1976), pp. 800-804

2. *Zoo Animals, People, Places,* a book by Bernard Livingston

3. *The Stationary Ark,* a book by Gerald Durrell

4. *U.S. News and World Report* magazine, Apr. 17, 1978, pp. 62-65

5. *Science Digest* magazine, (Sept., 1978), pp. 34-38

Try Your Skill   As practice for your report, choose one of these general areas of environmental issues to research in your library. Narrow the subject to a specific issue suitable for a brief report. Find and list four sources that would be helpful.

air pollution	wildlife conservation	recycling
water pollution	nuclear radiation	pesticides
soil pollution	noise pollution	urban renewal

Keep This in Mind

- With a general subject in mind, search through books, magazines, and other reference works to find a specific, limited subject for a report.

- With a specific subject chosen, begin research by examining sources. Keep a list of the sources.

Now Write   Choose an environmental issue to investigate for a report. Once you have a general idea of what you will write about, go to the library. To find a specific issue, check the reference shelves, the card catalog, the *Readers' Guide*, and the vertical file. If possible, talk to someone employed in the area you have chosen. Find at least four different kinds of sources in the library. Note the call numbers, the book titles, the magazine issues, or the vertical file references. Write all the information you have gathered and keep it in your folder.

Report Cards

Taking Notes

Here's the Idea To prepare a report, you must spend much of your time reading and gathering information. You will be able to complete these steps correctly once you learn about bibliography cards, note cards, and plagiarism.

Bibliography cards list sources of information. Use one 3x5 card for each source. Write out each card carefully. Usually, you will find the necessary information about a source within its first few pages. As you find and list sources, give each one a number. This number will identify a particular source, and will thereby help as you take notes.

Note cards state main ideas or facts related to your subject. Use a separate 3x5 note card for each fact, idea, or opinion. Add a heading or key phrase that states the main idea of the note. Be sure to label each note card with the source number you have given that source on its bibliography card. Include the exact page reference so that you can check a fact or quotation. The note itself should express one idea, which must be stated in your own words to avoid plagiarism.

Plagiarism is using someone else's words or ideas as your own. Plagiarism, a form of stealing, is a serious offense and can result in serious penalties. To avoid plagiarism, jot down information in your own words as much as possible and use short phrases. Check all facts, and identify statements of opinion. Use direct quotations only to express important or unusual information. Be sure to copy a statement exactly and to enclose it in quotation marks.

Check It Out Examine the sample cards on page 211.

- Which are bibliography cards? What information does each contain?

- Which is a note card? What is its source?
- Is the note card written in the words of a student?

Try Your Skill Read the following information. Make a bibliography card and a note card based on it.

"Pesticides and herbicides have, without doubt, allowed farmers to produce more crops and livestock than they could have done without these chemical aids. Insects destroy crops and affect the well-being and productivity of livestock. Weeds compete with crops for space, soil, and water. However, pesticides and herbicides also have undesirable effects on soils. They destroy beneficial soil organisms. Also, they are carried into waterways, where they contribute to the great pollution buildup that is prevalent all over the land."

from a book called *Shadow Over the Land*, by J. J. McCoy. The Seabury Press, New York, 1970, on pages 56 and 57, with library call number 628.5 Mcc

Keep This in Mind

- Make bibliography cards that identify all sources for your report.
- Write note cards containing specific information.
- Take notes in your own words. Avoid plagiarism, which is a serious offense.

Now Write In the last lesson, you listed at least four sources of information on a specific environmental issue, suitable for a five-paragraph report. Take that list and a stack of 3x5 note cards with you to your library. First, make bibliography cards for all suitable sources. Then, read through those sources and take notes. This process will take some time. Your teacher will want to check both sets of cards before you continue. Keep the cards together as your teacher directs.

Carpenter, Mary (1)

"Zoos: Last Hope To Preserve
Vanishing Species,"

Science Digest, Vol. 84

Sept., 1978   pp. 34-38   public library

Bridges, William (2)

"Zoological Gardens"

Encyclopedia Americana, Vol. 29

pp. 800-804   New York, copyright 1976

school
library

Durrell, Gerald. (3)

The Stationary Ark

New York, Simon and Schuster,

copyright 1976.

public library

590.744
D 965

---

preserve threatened species (3)

"In many cases, zoos will turn out to be
the last refuge of numerous species in a
human-being infested world."

page 147

Order, Please

Organizing Information

Here's the Idea   If you plan a report thoughtfully, you will be able to write the report much more easily. An essential step in planning is to organize the information you have gathered.

Begin by reading through your note cards. Separate them into several piles, each dealing with one general idea. Try to group the cards into four or five main ideas. If you find cards that do not belong with any others, you may want to omit these ideas from your report. At this point, however, save all the cards.

Next, read through the cards, one pile at a time. In what way are the cards in each pile related? State each main idea in a sentence. You should list only one idea for each group of cards.

For instance, if you were writing about the role of zoos in wildlife conservation you might find that all your information could be organized into four main ideas. You might have found facts about zoos of the past, facts about modern zoos, facts about what zoos can do to protect animals, and facts about what zoos can do to educate the public.

This organizational step requires careful thought. When you read all the cards that contained facts about what zoos can do to protect animals, for example, the information might at first have seemed too unrelated to be expressed by one main idea. The Bronx Zoo is breeding Andean condors, an endangered species. The National Zoo in Washington is studying the mating efforts of the giant pandas from China. Breeding programs for the rare tamarin exist at Chicago's Lincoln Park Zoo and at the Los Angeles Zoo. After some thought, however, you might be able to write this main idea: "Many modern zoos are working to conserve endangered species." This statement shows how a great deal of information is related. Follow a similar process in your report.

Check It Out   If you had organized information about zoos and wildlife conservation, you might have written this list of main ideas.

1. *In zoos of the past, animals were kept for various human purposes.*

2. *Modern zoos reflect an interest in animals for their own sake.*

3. *Many modern zoos are working to conserve endangered species.*

4. *Modern zoos are working to educate the public to support wildlife conservation efforts.*

· Is one main idea stated clearly in each sentence?

Try Your Skill   Organize the following environmental issues into five separate groups of four issues each. For each group, write one sentence that expresses the main idea of the environmental field represented by the various issues.

DDT	the blue whale	construction noise
paper recycling	traffic sounds	the California condor
open dumps	lindane	ocean dumping
incineration	plastics recycling	dieldrin
airport noise	compacting	the whooping crane
chlordane	glass recycling	metal recycling
very loud music	the Bengal tiger	

Keep This in Mind

· Organize your note cards into separate piles, grouping cards with the same main idea. Write one sentence stating the main idea of each group.

Now Write   Take out the note cards you have written for your report. Read them and organize them into four or five main groups. Think about the main idea of each group. Then make a list of sentences expressing the main idea of each group. Put the paper into your folder, and save the cards as your teacher directs.

Numbers and Letters

Making an Outline

Here's the Idea   After you have listed the main ideas for your report, make an outline. By making an outline, you will be organizing the ideas of your notes in a more detailed way. You will be deciding where each individual note card with its one idea fits into your report. In this way, you will be making a plan to follow when you write the report.

Before you write the outline itself, you need to arrange the main ideas you have listed in a logical order. Each main idea will become a main topic in your outline. The related facts on your note cards will become subtopics and details of the outline. Each main idea, subtopic, and detail will be stated in a word or phrase.

All outlines follow the same form, which you must follow whenever you make an outline. An outline begins with a title. Below that, first in importance, are the main ideas, shown by Roman numerals. Under main ideas, next in importance, are the subtopics, shown by capital letters. Under subtopics are the details, shown by Arabic numerals. If more specific details must be shown, small letters are used. In an outline, you must have no fewer than two main topics or subtopics.

Each part of the outline is indented from the one above. However, each symbol is in a straight line with the others like it. Each kind of symbol is followed by a period, although the words of the outline are not to be followed by periods. In a completed outline, the first word and all important words are capitalized in every line, as well as in the title.

Check It Out   Examine this outline that you might have written based on your notes about zoos and wildlife conservation.

- What ideas and details explain the role of zoos in wildlife conservation? Point out how the form for outlining has been followed correctly.

I. Introduction
   A. Effects of people on environment
   B. Attitudes towards animals measured by zoos
II. Zoos of the past
   A. Animals kept for human purposes
      1. Chinese Garden of Intelligence, for observation
      2. Egyptians, for prestige
      3. Romans, for sporting contests
      4. Europe in Middle Ages, for gifts
   B. Needs of animals not met
III. Modern zoos
   A. Interest in animals for themselves
      1. First zoos in U.S. in Philadelphia, New York, Chicago
      2. Reflected gains in scientific knowledge
   B. For entertainment and education also
   C. More understanding of animals
      1. New, natural exhibits
      2. More freedom for animals
IV. Commitment to conservation
   A. Zoo as "repository for vanishing species"
   B. Breeding in captivity
      1. 85% of all exhibited animals
      2. Formosan deer
      3. Animals saved from extinction
V. Educating the public
   A. Increase environmental awareness
   B. Teach about specific animals and problems
   C. Develop concerned citizens
      1. 115 million zoo visitors each year in U.S.
      2. To support wildlife conservation

Try Your Skill   Outline the information stated in the following paragraph from *The Wounded Earth* by Carl Marzani.

"The dictionary defines garbage as any waste parts of food— animal or vegetable—that are thrown away. In general usage the word includes trash, such as glass, paper, plastics, which is collected by the sanitation services. In the large cities, such as New York and Chicago, the sanitation services collect broken-down furniture, refrigerators, air conditioners, among other items. Increasingly, they also have to do something about old cars abandoned on the streets. Ecologists call all this solid waste. It costs us some three billion dollars a year to get rid of the two billion tons of waste produced every year—including seven million junked cars, twenty million tons of paper, forty-six billion cans. Fifteen percent of total solid waste is household trash and garbage, and it works out to three-and-one-half pounds a day per family."

Keep This in Mind

- Use your notes to write an outline of the ideas and details to be presented in your report. Follow the correct form for making an outline.

Now Write   Examine the list of main ideas you wrote in the last lesson for your own report on an environmental issue. Determine the most logical order for the ideas and number them to show that order.

Take out the note cards that you have grouped into separate main ideas. As you read the cards, decide on the order that would be the clearest. Work with the order of the cards until it seems right. Make an outline, using your list of main ideas and your note cards.

When your outline is written in its final form, arrange the cards in the order in which they appear in the outline. Keep your work together for the next step.

Put It in Writing

Writing the Introduction

Here's the Idea   Once you complete the outline for your report, much of what you do next will be familiar. Once you have completed researching a subject and organizing information, you are ready to begin writing. Writing a report is much like writing a composition. Each has three parts—an introduction, a body, and a conclusion—and the function of each part is similar. The introduction introduces the main idea of your subject. The body develops the main idea with supporting ideas and details. The conclusion summarizes the important information presented in the report.

However, there is an essential difference between a composition and a report. A report, unlike a composition, must never be written from the first-person point of view. You should not use the words *I, me,* or *my.* Your personal opinion has no place in a factual report.

When you write the introduction to a report, be sure to state what the report will be about. Sometimes you will want to present certain facts in the introduction. At other times you will want to keep the introduction brief and general. What you do for any report will depend on your subject and on your choice.

As you write your first draft, refer to your outline and your note cards. Use each of the main topics of your outline as a guide to writing the topic sentence of each paragraph. Use the subtopics of your outline and the facts from your note cards to develop each paragraph in a detailed way.

As you write, keep reading and reviewing your ideas. Are they clearly expressed? Are they organized logically? Is your writing detailed and interesting? Take time to think about how you can best express the information you have gathered.

Check It Out Here are the introduction and the first paragraph of the body of the report on zoos and wildlife conservation. They are shown as you might have written them after working on a first draft.

Human beings ~~have many effects on their environment~~, affect their environment in many ways that range from the most negative to the most positive. Throughout history, one ~~big~~ major way people have affected their environment is through their attitudes toward wildlife. Perhaps these attitudes, especially those toward animals, can best be ~~studied~~ measured by the ~~zoos that have been created~~ zoological gardens—or zoos that have been created.

The purposes of ~~zoological gardens~~ zoos have changed ~~a great deal~~ remarkably over the course of the last two thousand years. A Chinese ruler once created a Garden of Intelligence ~~for~~ that kept animals in ~~their~~ natural surroundings. Ancient Egyptian rulers kept animals ~~for~~ in order to glorify their own reputations. Romans kept animals for ~~sports~~ sporting contests. ~~In~~ In Europe in the Middle Ages, heads of state ~~had~~ kept collections of exotic animals to give as gifts. Generally, in ~~In~~ zoos of the past, the needs of animals were not understood. Many animals died, ~~and were~~ only to be replaced by others trapped in the wild.

- How does this first draft use the information shown in the outline?
- What main idea is presented in the introduction?

Try Your Skill Using the information from this outline, write an introductory paragraph for a report on recycling.

I. Advantages of recycling aluminum cans
  A. Environmental cost of producing new cans
     1. About 15,000 kilowatt-hours of electricity to produce one ton of aluminum from bauxite ore
     2. About three tons of mineral wastes for each ton of aluminum produced
     3. About one million tons of aluminum thrown away each year
  B. Environmental savings from recycling old cans
     1. About 450 kilowatt-hours of electricity to obtain one ton of aluminum through recycling
     2. Almost no mineral wastes
     3. Fewer problems with solid waste disposal

Keep This in Mind

- Use your outline and note cards to write the first draft of a report.
- A report, like a composition, has an introduction, a body, and a conclusion. In an introduction, be sure to state your topic clearly.

Now Write Take out your outline and note cards and review them. Think about whether to introduce the environmental issue you have researched in a general or a detailed way. Decide how to state the main idea of your information about this issue.

Using both your outline and your note cards, write the introduction to your report. Try to present your ideas clearly. Your first draft, however, need not be perfect. When you have finished the introduction, put all your work back into your folder.

The Mainspring

Writing the Body and Conclusion

Here's the Idea The main part of your research is presented in the body of a report. When you write the body, follow your outline. The topic sentence of each paragraph in the body will correspond to a main topic in your outline. The note cards will supply the details. Use those details, specific examples, and quotations that will add the most to your report.

Be sure to use quotation marks when you use the words of another writer. When you prepare your final copy, you will give that writer credit in the correct way.

A report, like a composition, should come to a logical ending. A report should have a clear conclusion in which you tie ideas together naturally. You may include additional facts about the topic. However, your most important purpose is to summarize the information presented in the report.

As you complete your first draft, continue the process of writing, reviewing what you have written, and rewriting. Do you like what you have written? Is it interesting and accurate? Is there a beginning, a middle, and an end to the development of your idea? Take the time to review your report and work on it thoughtfully.

Check It Out On the next page is the rest of the body and the conclusion of the report on zoos and wildlife conservation. They are shown as you might have written them after working on a first draft.

- Compare this first draft with the outline for the report. What details, examples, or direct quotations are used to develop the body?
- Does the conclusion sum up the information presented in the report?

A In contrast, the

∧ ~~The~~ purposes of modern zoos have arisen from an interest in animals, ~~themselves~~ *for their own sake*. In the United States, the first zoos reflected this interest. They were opened in Philadelphia, Chicago, and New York, *beginning* in the 1860's. Entertainment and education were major functions of these zoos, *, and remain so today.* ∧ However, gains in scientific knowledge

are reflected in striking

∧ ~~created~~ changes, *being made* in the ways, *that* zoos exhibit animals.

S ~~Stone~~ *barred,* ~~B~~ cages are being replaced with, *natural, living* environments that allow animals greater freedom. Lions, for example, may live in an open area surrounded by a deep moat; birds may live in a tree-filled, climate-controlled building.

Many modern

are   *committed to*

∧ ~~Modern~~ zoos, now, ~~have~~ a policy of conserving animal species. About eighty-five percent of exhibited animals are being born in captivity. William G. Conway, *, director of The Bronx zoo,* expects that this trend will continue. He has said, "The zoo of the future is an environmental park. It should be, among other things, a repository for vanishing species." *In fact, at* ∧ At the

same

time that the government of Taiwan declared the Formosan deer extinct, the Bronx Zoo had

fifty   *several*

~~50~~ ∧ of them. It is generally agreed that, other

including the Père David deer and the Hawaiian Goose,

animals, would also be extinct if it were not for zoos. "Although the broad purpose of a zoo's existence is still to entertain and educate the public, breeding previously wild species in captivity will be the major thrust over the next ten years".

Modern zoos also educate the public about animals.
(to the needs of)
Zoos increase environmental awareness by exhibiting animals in their natural surroundings. Many zoos teach the public directly about specific animals by presenting various special programs. Through educational programs, these visitors will become aware of public laws and policies that affect wildlife. A knowledgeable public will support more humane laws dealing with wildlife conservation. Human beings and animals can benefit only by sharing their surroundings.

"Each year over 115 million visitors come to the 130 zoos in the United States — more than the combined attendance at all U.S. professional basketball, football, and baseball games."

Try Your Skill   As practice for your own report, the **Try Your Skill** exercises in this section have asked you to consider many ideas about environmental issues. Review these exercises. Then write a conclusion, one paragraph that summarizes the information you have learned about environmental issues.

Keep This in Mind

- Use the ideas, details, examples, and direct quotations from your outline and note cards to develop the body of a report.
- Write a conclusion that summarizes the information presented in the report.

Now Write   Take what you have written thus far for your own report about an environmental issue. Review your outline and your notes, and write the body and conclusion of your report. Keep your writing lively, clear, and direct. Make sure you use quotation marks if you use other writers' words. When you are finished writing, put your work into your folder.

The Last Word

Completing the Report

Here's the Idea   When you revise the draft of a report, rewrite any sentences that are not clear. Check for correct grammar, spelling, capitalization, and punctuation. Make all necessary corrections before you copy your report neatly. You are now ready to write footnotes and a bibliography.

A **footnote** gives credit to a writer whose words or ideas you used. A direct quotation requires a footnote, which is usually written on a separate page at the end of the report. The material to be footnoted is followed with a number that is written slightly above a line like this:[1]. The numbers should run in order and should match the numbers on the footnote page.

To prepare your footnotes, find each quotation you have used. Locate the note card with the source number that refers you to a bibliography card. That bibliography card should contain all the information you need.

The first line of a footnote should be indented. Each footnote should include the author's first and last names, in that order; the title of the source; the volume number, if applicable; the date, if the reference is a magazine; and the page number. If you have two or more consecutive notes from the same source, use the abbreviation *Ibid.* after the first footnote. *Ibid.* stands for a Latin word meaning "in the same place" and is used instead of repeating the same information. *Ibid.* should be followed by a page number, if it differs from the previous page reference.

Finally, prepare your **bibliography**, which is a complete list of sources you used. A bibliography usually appears on a separate, final page. Each entry contains the information from your bibliography cards, except for the source number and library location. The form for a bibliography entry differs slightly for books, magazines, and encyclopedias. The beginning of an entry is not indented, although all lines after the first one are indented. Entries in a bibliography are arranged alphabetically by the last name of the author. If no author is given, use the first main word of the title to determine the order. Page numbers are given if less than the entire work was used as a source of information.

Check It Out   Study the form of the footnotes and bibliography for a report on zoos and wildlife conservation.

Bibliography

Bridges, William. "Zoological Gardens," *Encyclopedia Americana*, Vol. 29 (1976), pp. 800-804.

Carpenter, Mary. "Zoos: Last Hope To Preserve Vanishing Species," *Science Digest*, Vol. 84 (Sept., 1978), pp. 34-38.

Durrell, Gerald. *The Stationary Ark*. New York: Simon and Schuster, 1976.

Livingston, Bernard. *Zoo Animals, People, Places*. New York: Arbor House, 1976, pp. 263-282.

Footnotes

¹William Bridges, "Zoological Gardens," *Encyclopedia Americana*, Vol. 29. (1976), p. 800.

²Bernard Livingston, *Zoo Animals, People, Places*, p. 263

³Mary Carpenter, "Zoos: Last Hope To Preserve Vanishing Species," *Science Digest*, Vol. 84 (Sept., 1978), p. 34.

⁴*Ibid.*, p. 38

- Identify the information listed for each footnote.
- Identify the information given in each bibliography entry.

Try Your Skill   Read the following passage about pollution and the description of its source. Write a footnote and a bibliography entry based on this information. Use the correct form.

"Few modern families can grow their own apples, produce their own milk, fell their own timber, reprocess their own sewage, or do any of the many other things that would help to cut down waste and reduce pollution. What we can do, however, is continually to press for and support the social changes that will help to bring about environmental improvement. As individuals, we can resist the temptation to equate the quality of our own domestic lives with the quantity of our showy, nonessential possessions. 'Putting things in the wrong place,' is, after all, one possible definition of pollution, even if it does not tell the whole story."

from page 125 of a book titled *Earth in Danger: Pollution* by Ian Breach, published in 1976 by Doubleday & Company, Inc., in Garden City, New York

Keep This in Mind

· Use footnotes to give credit to writers whose words or ideas you include in a report.

· Prepare a bibliography to show your sources.

Now Write   Review your complete report. Make any corrections necessary. Also write a good title.

Insert the numbers for your footnotes into the first draft of your report. Find the information you need for your footnotes on your source cards. Copy it in the correct form on a separate paper labeled *Footnotes*. Write a bibliography entry for each source you used. Copy the entries in alphabetical order onto a separate sheet of paper labeled *Bibliography*. Use the proper form.

Neatly copy your report in final form.

For help in preparing the final copy of your report, see **Handbook Section 16, The Correct Form for Writing**.

Also, examine the final copy of the report on the role of zoos in wildlife conservation shown on the following pages.

Sarah Hoyle

English 401

March 8, 1981

Wildlife Conservation

Human beings affect their environment in many
ways that range from the most negative to the most
positive. Throughout history, one major way people
have affected their environment is through their
attitudes toward wildlife. Perhaps these attitudes,
especially those toward animals, can best be
measured by the zoological gardens--or zoos--that
have been created.

The purposes of zoos have changed remarkably
over the course of the last two thousand years. A
Chinese ruler once created a Garden of Intelligence
that kept animals in natural surroundings. Ancient
Egyptian rulers kept wild animals in order to glorify
their own reputations. Romans kept animals for
sporting contests. In Europe in the Middle Ages,
heads of state kept collections of exotic animals
to give as gifts.[1] Generally, in zoos of the past,
the needs of animals were not understood. Many
animals died, only to be replaced by others trapped
in the wild.

In contrast, the purposes of modern zoos have arisen from an interest in animals for their own sake. In the United States, the first zoos reflected this interest. They were opened in Philadelphia, Chicago, and New York, beginning in the 1860's. Entertainment and education were major functions of these zoos, and remain so today. However, gains in scientific knowledge are reflected in striking changes being made in the ways that zoos exhibit animals. Barred, stone cages are being replaced with natural, living environments that allow animals greater freedom. Lions, for example, may live in an open area surrounded by a deep moat; birds may live in a tree-filled, climate-controlled building.

Many modern zoos are now committed to a policy of conserving animal species. About eighty-five percent of exhibited animals are being born in captivity. William G. Conway, director of the Bronx Zoo, expects that this trend will continue. He has said, "The zoo of the future is an environmental park. It should be, among other things, a repository for vanishing species."[2] In fact, at the same time that the government of Taiwan declared the Formosan deer extinct, the Bronx Zoo had fifty of them. It is generally agreed that several other animals, including the Père David deer and the Hawaiian goose, would be extinct if it were not for zoos. "Although the broad purpose of a zoo's existence is still to entertain and educate the public, breeding previously wild species in captivity will be the major thrust over the next ten years."[3]

Modern zoos also educate the public to the needs of animals. Zoos increase environmental awareness by exhibiting animals in their natural surroundings. Many zoos teach the public directly about specific animals by presenting various special programs. "Every year over 115 million visitors come to the 130 zoos in the United States--more than the combined attendance at all U.S. professional basketball, football, and baseball games."[4] Through educational programs, these visitors will become aware of public laws and policies that affect wildlife. A knowledgeable public will support more humane laws dealing with wildlife conservation. Human beings and animals can benefit only by sharing their surroundings.

Footnotes

[1]William Bridges, "Zoological Gardens,"
Encyclopedia Americana, Volume 29 (1976), page 800.

[2]Bernard Livingston, Zoo Animals, People
Places, page 263.

[3]Mary Carpenter, "Zoos: Last Hope To Preserve
Vanishing Species," Science Digest, Volume 84
(September, 1978), page 34.

[4]Ibid., page 38.

Bibliography

Bridges, William. "Zoological Gardens," Encyclopedia
    Americana, Volume 29 (1976), pages 800-804.

Carpenter, Mary. "Zoos: Last Hope to Preserve
    Vanishing Species," Science Digest, Volume
    84 (September, 1978), pages 34-38.

Durrell, Gerald. The Stationary Ark. New York:
    Simon and Schuster, 1976.

Livingston, Bernard. Zoo Animals, People, Places.
    New York: Arbor House, 1976, pages 263-282.

Thinking Clearly

The Truth

Distinguishing Between Facts and Opinions

Here's the Idea   Every day you send and receive messages by speaking, listening, reading, and writing. To communicate effectively, you must think clearly and reason well. To think clearly means to recognize the truth and to understand the ways that truth may be misrepresented.

Clear thinking begins by recognizing what is a statement of fact and what is a statement of opinion. Statements of **fact** can be proven true or false. Statements of **opinion** cannot. For example, if you state that the governor vetoed a proposal to subsidize housing for the elderly, you have presented a statement of fact. Someone can either prove it or disprove it. If you state that the governor is not interested in the problems of the elderly, you have presented an opinion. There is no way to prove your statement. You may be able to support it with reasons or facts, but you cannot prove it.

People who make statements of fact are often required to have proof that their statements are true. For example, news reporters must be prepared to verify, or prove, the statements they make in their reports. Advertisers also must be prepared to verify the claims they make in advertisements. You may want to verify such statements yourself before you take a certain action or buy a certain product.

There are two methods for verifying a statement of fact. First, test the statement for yourself. If a co-worker states, "You're listed for the night shift next week," you can check the truth of the statement yourself by looking at the list. Second, consult a reliable source. If someone states, "The polls show that the mayor is expected to win re-election," you will probably have to check a newspaper to verify the statement.

The one sure way to distinguish between a fact and an opinion is to apply a simple test. A statement of fact can be proven true or false. A statement of opinion cannot.

Check It Out   Consider the following pairs of statements.

> **Fact**   The majority of Americans learn the news from television.
>
> **Opinion**   Television newscasters aren't as good as newspaper reporters.

> **Fact**   Lorraine Denton admitted that she did not know how she could avoid proposing a tax increase.
>
> **Opinion**   Lorraine Denton is the only honest candidate in the race.

> **Fact**   Front-wheel-drive cars put more weight over the driving wheels than rear-wheel-drive cars do.
>
> **Opinion**   Front-wheel-drive cars are safer than rear-wheel-drive cars.

· Which statements could be proven true or false? What reliable source could you use to check each statement of fact?

Try Your Skill   Consider each of the ten statements below. Write whether each is a fact or an opinion. For each fact, name a source you could use to prove the statement true or false.

1. Today's temperature is minus ten degrees Fahrenheit.
2. The weather this winter has been terrible.
3. Senator Holmes never answered the letter I sent her.
4. Senator Holmes doesn't care what the voters in her district think.
5. Doctors are more interested in making money than they are in healing the sick.
6. Dr. Rosso charged me fifty dollars to treat an eye infection.
7. My supervisor hasn't given me any overtime in two weeks.
8. My supervisor is trying to get me to quit.
9. Hooper would be a better governor than Baxter would.
10. Hooper has said that the state should eliminate sales taxes.

Keep This in Mind

• A statement of fact can be proved. An opinion cannot. Use your own observation or a reliable source to test whether a statement or fact is either true or false.

Now Write Look through several issues of a local newspaper to find a current issue that is important within your community. Write, or find, three statements of opinion about the issue. Write, or find, three statements of fact related to the issue. For each statement of fact, write what you would do to verify the statement. Be sure you identify the sources of any statements you find. Label your paper **The Truth** and put it into your folder.

Is That So?

Expressing Opinions

Here's the Idea   To be a clear thinker, you need to be able to express statements of opinion as well as to recognize them. You can express an opinion in any of three ways. You can make a judgment. You can make a statement of obligation. You can make a prediction.

One way to state an opinion is to make a **judgment**, an expression of your own taste and values. For example, if an advertiser claims that a breakfast cereal is made without added sugar, that is a statement of fact. It may be true or false. However, if the advertiser claims, "It's a delicious cereal," that is a judgment. The difference lies in the word *delicious*, a judgment word.

The meanings of judgment words differ among people, depending on their backgrounds and values. After all, a "delicious" lunch for one person is a spinach salad, while for another it is a hamburger and French fries. Because of the use of a judgment word, there is no way to prove the statement true or false. Other common judgment words include *good*, *bad*, *beautiful*, *ugly*, *right*, *wrong*, *valuable*, and *worthless*.

A second way to express an opinion is to make a **statement of obligation**. The key words in statements of obligation are *should*, *ought to*, *must*, and similar terms. "Property owners should support the tax bill." "You must arrive before nine o'clock." Both of these are statements of obligation. When expressed as commands, they sound like factual statements. However, they are not. Like judgments, they cannot be proven true or false.

A third way to express an opinion is to make a **prediction**. "You will love each of the eighteen hits on this great album" and "I start work on Monday" are both predictions. The statements seem factual. However, the expected response may not result, and the expected event may not take place. Until situations have actually occurred, you cannot prove such statements true or false.

Should you eliminate all judgments, obligations, and predictions from your speaking and writing? That is not necessary. Be sure, however, that the opinions you express are sound. A sound opinion is one that is supported by reasons or facts, or one that can be traced to a reliable source. Be sure also that you recognize opinions expressed by others and that you consider them carefully.

Check It Out   Read each of these statements of opinion.

1. You ought to test-drive a Mammoth before you buy any other car.
2. Mirror-All gives your floors their brightest shine.
3. Everyone should have a career.
4. Painfree will cure your tension headache within minutes.
5. The Mayor took her toughest stand on the budget in a meeting before the City Council today.

   • Which is a judgment? Which is a statement of obligation?
     Which is a prediction? Which statements might be sound?

Try Your Skill   Below are eight statements of opinion. Decide whether each is a judgment, a statement of obligation, or a prediction. Which might be traced to a reliable source?

1. Wasting fuel is irresponsible and unpatriotic.
2. Each of us should avoid unnecessary travel.
3. Energy supplies will continue to shrink over the next decade.
4. If you pay taxes in this state, you owe it to yourself to support Senator Klein's bill.
5. Property taxes have a vicious stranglehold on the homeowners in this state.
6. Buy a Speedster, the sportiest car in America.
7. A national health insurance program should be developed.
8. As President, Stuart Smith will lead this country to peace and prosperity.

Keep This in Mind

· An opinion may be a judgment, a statement of obligation, or a prediction. A sound opinion is one that can be supported by reason or facts, or one that can be traced to a reliable source.

Now Write   Look through a magazine or newspaper to find statements of opinion. Be aware of opinions in articles as well as in advertisements. Find and copy statements of opinion of each type. After each statement, tell whether it could be supported by facts. Label your paper **Is That So?** Keep it in your folder.

The Whole Truth

Avoiding Generalizations

Here's the Idea   "Politicians take bribes!" "Assembly line workers are careless!" These are examples of one of the most common errors in reasoning—generalizing. **Generalizations** are broad statements based on a number of instances. It is true that a few politicians have been found guilty of taking bribes, and that a few assembly line workers are careless. However, by attributing the faults of a few to a complete group, you have committed the error of generalizing. To be a clear thinker, you must avoid making generalizations.

To avoid making generalizations, use "absolute" words with care. Limit a statement to a specific person or situation, or qualify your statements with less sweeping words. For example, avoid using absolutes like *all, each, every, everyone*. Instead, use *most, many, much*. In place of *none, no, no one*, or *nobody*, use *few* or *some*. In place of *always*, say *usually, often*, or *sometimes*. In place of *never*, use *seldom* or *rarely*. Be careful of making absolute statements that misrepresent the truth.

Some generalizations are harmless. For example, the statement "Every time I wash the car it rains" is a simple exaggeration that emphasizes someone's feelings. On the other hand, some generalizations are harmful and can be misused. Consider the statement, "Welfare spending is responsible for the rising cost of living." This kind of statement could be misused to influence support for a political candidate or a piece of legislation. It is not only a generalization, but a dangerous one.

The most dangerous generalization is the stereotype. A **stereotype** is a generalization used against races, religions, nationalities, minority groups, or professions. Stereotypes may be expressed, for example, by ethnic jokes, racial slurs, or remarks that degrade women or police officers. A stereotype is harmful to those at whom it is aimed. It also reflects the limited, prejudiced attitudes of the speaker or writer. Try to eliminate all stereotypes from your thinking. Reject stereotyped views of others.

Check It Out   Consider the following statements.

1. Students today cannot read as well as they used to.
2. The crime rate is rising everywhere.
3. Americans are always friendly.
4. Every time I say something, you contradict me.
5. Lucille never finishes any of the projects she starts.
6. Wealthy people are selfish.

- Which statements are generalizations? Which are stereotypes? Which statements are harmful?

Try Your Skill   Explain why each of the following generalizations is harmful or harmless. Then rewrite each statement by qualifying it.

1. Women are smarter than men.
2. Handicapped people have to lead restricted lives.
3. High school dropouts are responsible for vandalism.
4. Artists are moody.
5. Young, inexperienced drivers cause accidents.
6. Fat people are jolly.

Keep This in Mind

- A generalization is a broad statement based on a number of instances. The most harmful generalization is the stereotype. Avoid making generalizations and reject stereotypes.

Now Write   Be aware of generalizations expressed on television and radio and in newspapers and magazines. On your paper, write three generalizations you have heard recently. Below each, write your opinion on the same subject. Then, using one of your opinions as a topic sentence, write a paragraph to support the opinion. Develop the paragraph using facts and figures. Label your paper **The Whole Truth** and put it into your folder.

Group Discussion

What's the Problem?

Defining the Discussion

Here's the Idea   When problems arise, people talk them over. Sometimes it is helpful to set up study groups to research the problem and talk it over. By sharing knowledge, people are able to enlarge their understanding of the problem.

A discussion group is often formed to meet the needs of a community or business organization. Each person who joins a group should have a genuine interest in the problem. Small groups can have better discussions than large ones.

Once a group has been set up, its first task is to narrow the field for discussion. The next step is to state the problem in the form of a question. After stating the problem, a group decides on the purpose of its discussion. The purpose will be either to explore the issue or to recommend a solution to the problem.

Suppose, for example, that you are appointed to a committee to work on ways to improve the parks in your town. The subject of park development is too large for one group to handle. Your group decides to limit its discussion to the question of bicycle paths and rentals. You state the problem as follows: What can our park district do to improve the facilities for bicycle riding?

Then your group sets the purpose of its first discussion. At its first discussion, a group begins to investigate the problem. Your group, for example, may need to ask important questions about bicycle paths. How much land is available? What would be the approximate cost? Since there is no pressure to come to a decision, the group agrees to explore the issue. In a later discussion the purpose will be to recommend a solution to the problem.

Check It Out   Consider the following situation.

> The school population in your community has decreased. The budget can no longer support three elementary schools. The school board has suggested closing one school. You have agreed to serve on a committee to investigate which school should be closed.

· What do you think the purpose of your first discussion should be? State the problem for discussion in the form of a question.

Try Your Skill   Suppose you are faced with the following problem:

> On the border of your town, there is a major shopping center. In order to get to it, people must cross a set of railroad tracks. During the past two years, there have been several serious accidents at the crossing. It seems clear that gates should be installed. A town meeting has been called to discuss this issue, and you are going to attend.

Write three specific questions that will help focus on the problem and encourage discussion. In class, compare your questions with those of your classmates. Which ones would provoke the most interesting discussion? Why?

Keep This in Mind

· Keep discussion groups small, and be sure that each person has a genuine interest in the problem. Narrow the topic. State the problem in the form of a specific question. Establish the purpose of your first discussion.

Now Speak   In each part of this section, you will be working toward participating in a group discussion. Follow these first steps to set up your group.

1. Divide into groups of four to six people.
2. Choose a topic that will interest each person in your group. Your topic should be related to a school or community issue.
3. Narrow your topic.
4. State your problem in the form of a question.
5. Decide on the purpose of your first discussion.

Are You Ready?

Gathering Information

Here's the Idea Once you have set up a group, you must research the problem. Begin by analyzing the situation. Ask yourself these questions: What do most people in the community seem to think about this issue? How do the people in my group feel? Has anyone revealed any strong opinions or prejudices? What is my attitude towards the problem for discussion?

Your next step is to review what you know about the subject. Write your opinions and your supporting evidence. Decide which areas you need to study most thoroughly.

As you review your knowledge, think of resources you can use to up-date your information. You will need to learn about recent changes. Perhaps you will want to interview key people in your community, such as the mayor, a city commissioner, a school board member, or the chief of police. Find out what resources are available at your public library or at city hall. For example, suppose you need to read the minutes of the last city council meeting. Where would you find them?

When you have up-dated your information, review your opinion. What new ideas or evidence have you discovered? Have you changed your mind? At this point you may want to adjust your opinion.

Finally, think about what effect your ideas and opinions will have on other people in your group. On which points will you need to be the most persuasive? On which points are you most willing to be flexible? Be prepared to listen to the ideas of others.

Check It Out Consider this situation.

The City Council has proposed to replace the streetlights in Jack's neighborhood. The project will cost the city $20,000. Many people believe that the present streetlights are satisfactory. They are opposed to spending more money. However, Jack thinks that the present lighting presents a safety hazard to people after dark. He had joined a study group that will research the question of safety.

· How should Jack begin his research? Name two community resources that might help Jack up-date his information.

Try Your Skill   Suppose that your city is considering building a nuclear power plant as an alternative energy source. The question of safety has been raised. Many people in the community want to learn more about the issue.

One source of current information is the library. As your teacher directs, use your school or public library to find out more about nuclear power plants. List five sources of available information. In class discussion, compare your sources with those that your classmates have found.

Keep This in Mind

· Review what you know about a subject. Use available community resources to bring your information up-to-date. Reconsider your own opinion, and decide what you most want to learn from others.

Now Speak   Research the problem your group will discuss. Begin by asking yourself these questions: Which community leaders might give me current information? What library resources will help me?

Use a variety of resources. Jot down important findings on note cards. Up-date your information. Finally, explore your own attitude toward the problem.

Tuning In

Listening To Learn

Here's the Idea In order for a discussion group to accomplish its goal, everyone must listen intelligently. Keep your mind on what is being said. Use the following guidelines to help you develop good listening skills as a member of a group discussion.

1. Be sure that everyone in a group can hear. Establish a quiet setting before you begin. During a discussion, eliminate interference. If there is interference, tell the member of the group who is speaking that you cannot hear.

2. Concentrate on the message of each member of the group who speaks. Don't focus on the way people look or how they speak. If you are too critical, you may miss an important point.

3. Stay calm. Often discussions involve controversial issues. A member of the group may say something that will cause you to react strongly. Try not to get upset. Keep your mind on the question for discussion.

4. Assume that everyone has something important to say. Even if someone's contribution does not interest you, listen closely. What seems unimportant at first may be helpful to you later on.

5. Keep your mind active. You have to be involved in order to listen intelligently. Some of the material presented in a discussion may be difficult to understand. Jot down questions you may need to ask.

6. Review what has been said. Ask yourself whether or not you can accept evidence that has been presented. Use pauses in a discussion to evaluate what you have heard.

Check It Out Complete the following activity.

At the direction of your teacher, choose a speaking situation in your school to observe. For example, observe an assembly or a meeting. Watch a discussion group in action. Write your observations about the group's listening skills. Include as many details as you can.

- Were the speakers also good listeners? Why or why not? Explain your evaluation in terms of the guidelines discussed in this lesson.

Try Your Skill   Arrange yourselves in groups of five to eight students. Using any textbook, find a passage about a factual subject. Select a fairly complex passage containing numbers, dates, names, or statistics. Have one person read the material, without interruption, at a normal speaking rate. Have the other members of a group take notes on the main ideas of the passage. When the reader finishes, compare notes. Discuss errors or omissions. Suggest ways to improve your listening skills.

Keep This in Mind

- Concentrate when you listen. Do not allow yourself to become distracted. Stay calm. Review what is said.

Now Speak   Using information that you have gathered for your group discussion, choose the area that interests you most. Organize this material into a two- or three-minute talk. Write down three questions about the material you will cover. Be sure the answers can be included in your talk. Practice your talk several times.

Present your talk to someone else. Your listener should be someone from another discussion group. After your talk, ask your listener the questions you have prepared. How well did she or he listen? Which guidelines were most difficult to follow?

Now switch roles and test your own ability to listen carefully.

On Speaking Terms

Making Your Contribution

Here's the Idea When you take part in a discussion, you are responsible for sharing your ideas with the group. You should also help the group work in an orderly, cooperative way. There are several ways in which you can contribute to a group discussion.

1. Present your ideas clearly. Support your statements with facts or examples. Be firm, but show that you are ready to consider the opinions of others.

2. Listen for confusion. Be ready to clarify what you have said or to ask about what someone else has said. Sometimes you can do this by asking a question that will bring out additional information.

3. Help to keep the discussion moving. Watch for signs that participants are losing interest. Usually, you can stimulate the discussion by introducing a new idea.

4. Keep harmony in the group. Be open-minded and willing to compromise. You can also help to patch up differences among others. Try to keep the discussion running smoothly.

5. Encourage everyone to contribute. Often one person may try to dominate a group. Someone else may not want to contribute at all. Try to equalize the group by getting everyone to talk. It is always important, however, to be tactful.

6. Help bring the discussion to a close. Think about the goals the group has set. Have you reached them, or do you need to meet again? You should keep in mind that all problems do not have solutions. Your purpose may have been to explore rather than to solve a problem.

Check It Out   Complete the following activity.

As your teacher directs, observe a public discussion, perhaps at a P.T.A. meeting or at a community college. Note how the participants behave as group members. Write down your observations.

- Did the discussion group accomplish its goals? Why or why not? Explain your evaluation in terms of the guidelines discussed in this lesson.

Try Your Skill   Consider the following situation.

The incidence of street crime in your neighborhood has increased by ten percent in the past year. A group of concerned citizens is investigating the problem. As part of your research, you want to find out what attitudes people have about crime.

Arrange to interview someone you know, such as a friend or a family member, on the subject of street crime. Write five or six questions that you think will provoke discussion. Take notes on what the person says to you. Be ready to discuss your interview in class.

Keep This in Mind

- Be a responsible member of a discussion group. Present your ideas clearly. Stimulate the discussion and encourage the group to work together. When the discussion is over, help bring it to a logical conclusion.

Now Speak   As your teacher directs, hold your group discussion. Follow the guidelines you have learned about listening intelligently and participating actively as a member of a discussion group.

Write Again

The more practice you have, the more comfortable you become with writing. The preceding lessons have taught you many writing skills. In the following eleven pages you will find additional practice in improving those skills. As you finish each lesson, your teacher may assign one of these additional exercises. Give them your best effort.

Developing an Effective Vocabulary

Part 1 **Close Encounters** In a newspaper, find three examples of definition, restatement, example, comparison, or contrast used as context clues. Copy each, and circle the word that the clue helps to define.

Part 2 **A Hint of an Idea** Write several sentences giving information that would help a careful reader infer the meaning of the word *shy*.

Part 3 **Up Front** In a magazine or newspaper, find five words that contain prefixes. List the words and circle the prefixes.

Part 4 **Afterwards** In a textbook, find five words that contain suffixes. List the words and circle the suffixes.

Part 5 **The Centerpiece** Look up the words *flexor*, *gratis*, *digress*, and *abruptness* in a dictionary. Use your knowledge of roots to restate each definition in your own words. Use two of the words in sentences.

Part 6 **On the Mark** In a dictionary, find two synonyms for the word *serious*. Use each in a written sentence that shows its precise meaning.

Part 7 **Extrasensory Description** List sensory words that describe a store that you like. Be specific and try to use every sense.

Part 8 **Some Critical Points** Write several sentences evaluating qualities of a restaurant you enjoy. Use precise words to convey as much objective information as you can.

Writing Effective Sentences

Part 1 **Direct Action** Write one sentence describing an award. Write another explaining why such an award is important. Write a third telling how someone won the award.

Part 2 **Point-Blank** Write three brief sentences about books. Rewrite each, adding one related detail that will make the sentence more interesting or more specific.

Part 3 **No-Show** Write one sentence giving an unsupported opinion about a well known person. Write a second sentence in which an idea about the person is repeated. Then rewrite each empty sentence to improve it.

Part 4 **Battle of the Bulge** Write two padded sentences explaining why you were late for some appointment. Rewrite each, eliminating unnecessary words or revising as needed.

Part 5 **Think Small** Write two overloaded sentences about a friend. Make each contain at least three ideas. Then improve the sentences by breaking each into several shorter sentences.

Part 6 **Balance of Power** Imagine that you are listing your qualifications for a job. Write two sentences containing similar parts that are not parallel. Then rewrite the sentences, making the parts parallel.

Part 7 **Variations on a Theme** Write two sentences, each describing yourself. Then write a variation of each.

Analyzing the Paragraph Section 3

Part 1 **Make a Stand** In a newspaper, find a paragraph about a current problem. Decide what the main idea is, and write it.

Part 2 **In Unison** Write one sentence expressing your opinion of television. Then write five sentences related to this idea.

Part 3 **What's the Point?** How do you feel about cities? Write two good topic sentences for paragraphs about cities. Write sentences that could be developed further.

Part 4 **Multiple Choice** Write three topic sentences related to sports. Write one that could best be developed by details, one that could be developed by examples, and one that could be developed by facts and figures.

Part 5   **The Name of the Game**   Write a topic suitable for a narrative paragraph, another for a descriptive paragraph, and another for an explanatory paragraph. Label each.

Writing a Paragraph

Part 1   **A Limited Edition**   Narrow the general topic "entertainment" by answering *who, what, when, where, why,* and *how* questions. Write the specific topic.

Part 2   **Set Your Sights**   Think of a form of entertainment you enjoy. Write a direct and interesting topic sentence about it.

Part 3   **Selective Service**   Write a paragraph about your favorite form of entertainment. Use details, examples, or facts and figures to develop your idea.

Part 4   **The Bottom Line**   Write a paragraph about a movie or play you attended. Write an ending sentence that sums up the main idea in a strong, interesting way.

Section 5   # A Writer's Choices

Part 1   **Who's Watching?**   Imagine that you work in a hospital. The fire alarm sounds. What happens? Write three paragraphs that tell about it, using the three different points of view.

Part 2   **One or the Other**   Write two paragraphs—narrative, descriptive, or explanatory—about nature. Write one paragraph about a real experience, using facts. Write one paragraph about an imaginary experience, using details.

Part 3   **What's in a Word?**   Write a paragraph describing a concert or show you enjoyed. Write a second paragraph describing a concert or show you disliked. Underline the words that help you express your feelings.

Part 4 **Identity Crisis** Suppose that you are writing a story about your life. Write three possible titles for the story.

The Narrative Paragraph

Part 1 **In the Beginning** Think about what you might do to apply for a job. List your actions in chronological order. Using transitions, write a paragraph about an actual experience.

Part 2 **In Any Event** Write a narrative paragraph about a real or imagined accident. Develop vivid details by asking yourself *who, what, when, where, why,* and *how* questions.

The Descriptive Paragraph

Part 1 **Impressions** Think of how your town changes in winter. Make a list of sensory details that you remember. Then write a descriptive paragraph using the list.

Part 2 **Direction Finders** Think of a real or imaginary beach. List the important sensory details and organize them using spatial order. Then write a paragraph of description.

The Explanatory Paragraph

Part 1 **How About That?** Suppose you have to wrap a fragile gift for the mail. Make a list of the steps you would follow. Using clear transitions, write an explanatory paragraph that explains the process.

Part 2 **I Believe** Write an explanatory paragraph that states your opinion about the military draft. Support it with three reasons or facts. Use transitions to show order of importance.

Part 3   **A Definite Answer**   Write an explanatory paragraph that defines a rewarding job. Use details or facts and figures to develop your definition.

Analyzing the Composition

Part 1   **Group Dynamics**   Think about the skills you have learned in the past several years. Write five topics that would be suitable for compositions.

Part 2   **A Threesome**   Under the headings *Introduction*, *Body*, and *Conclusion*, write notes that tell what you would include in each part of a composition about a special friend.

Part 3   **For Every Purpose**   Choose a holiday as a general topic. In a few sentences, write what you would include in a narrative composition, a descriptive composition, and an explanatory composition.

The Narrative Composition

Part 1   **In the Event of**   Plan the introduction, body, and conclusion of a narrative composition about a person forced to make an important choice. In your notes, list details about people, places, and events related to a real or imaginary situation.

Part 2   **Be a Troubleshooter**   Think about someone facing an important decision. Consider the situation from different points of view. Choose one, and write an introduction to a narrative about the situation. Then write two or three paragraphs developing the body of the narrative.

Part 3   **So to Speak**   Write a dialogue between someone making an important decision and someone who believes the decision is wrong. Follow the rules for punctuation of quotations.

Part 4   **A Final Offer**   Write a conclusion resolving the conflict faced by someone who has made a difficult choice. Then write a title for the composition.

The Descriptive Composition

Part 1 **Behind the Scenes** Use a quiet place, like a library or a forest, as the topic for a descriptive composition. Write and organize pre-writing notes.

Part 2 **Full of Life** Observe or recall a quiet place. List as many sensory details as you can. Use the details to write the introduction and body of a description of the place.

Part 3 **In the Shape of** Decide what spatial order and transitions you would use to write a description of a quiet place. Then write a conclusion and a title for the composition.

The Explanatory Composition
Explaining a Process
Section 13

Part 1 **How So?** Make a list of five processes that involve using common machines. Write possible titles for compositions on these skills.

Part 2 **One, Two, Three** Choose a process that involves using a machine and list details for each step involved. Write the body of an explanatory composition, giving a step-by-step explanation.

Part 3 **In Connection with** Think of a process that requires the help of some machine. List the steps in the process and add transitions that make the order clear. Then write an introduction and a conclusion.

The Explanatory Composition
Stating an Opinion
Section 14

Part 1 **Look at It This Way** What do you think about a law that would require all passengers in a car to wear seatbelts? Plan an explanatory composition that states your opinion. In your pre-writing notes, include reasons or facts that support your opinion.

Part 2   **And Here's Why**   List three reasons or facts to support your opinion of a law that would require passengers in a car to wear seatbelts. Arrange the evidence in order of importance. Write the body of your explanatory composition.

Part 3   **A Sure Thing**   Review your opinion of a law that would require passengers in a car to wear seatbelts. Add transitions that show the reasons and their order of importance. Write an introduction that presents your opinion. Write a conclusion that sums up your argument.

Section 15   The Explanatory Composition
Stating a Definition

Part 1   **What in the World?**   Think of a form of transportation that you could define in an explanatory composition. Make detailed notes for the introduction, the body, and the conclusion.

Part 2   **Class Consciousness**   Write a definition of a form of transportation, such as a subway or motorcycle. Name your subject, its class, and its special characteristics. Use your definition as part of an introduction to an explanatory composition.

Part 3   **On the Whole**   Think of a form of transportation you enjoy using. Use facts and figures or personal details to develop a definition of it in the body of an explanatory composition. Then write a conclusion in which you summarize your main idea.

Section 16   Letters, Applications, and Résumés

Part 1   **Dear Friend**   Write a personal letter expressing your sympathy to a friend whose grandmother has died recently. Label each part of the letter.

Part 2 **First Class** Draw a rectangle to represent an envelope. Address it as if it were a letter you were going to send to a friend.

Part 3 **Office Hours** Write to the chamber of commerce of your town requesting information about tourist attractions and historical sites in your area. Use the modified block form for this letter.

Part 4 **Schoolwork** Write a letter to a community college asking about evening courses in accounting. Include specific information about yourself.

Part 5 **Working Papers** Write a letter to a day care center seeking part-time employment. Include all necessary details.

Part 6 **The Subject Is You** Think of a job in your community for which you are well qualified. Prepare a résumé with that job as your objective.

Part 7 **In Good Form** Ask for a job application at a local supermarket or department store. Fill it in completely and honestly.

Part 8 **Take the Credit** Ask a local bank for a credit application for a used-car loan. Fill in the application carefully and completely.

Part 9 **May I?** Write a letter to the Consumer Information Center, Pueblo, Colorado 81009, asking for a list of publications on auto repair.

Part 10 **Satisfaction Guaranteed** Write a letter of complaint to a clothing company about a pair of shoes you bought by mail. Invent details about a problem and how you want it to be handled.

Part 11 **The Pen Is Mightier** Read the letters-to-the-editor in a recent issue of your local newspaper. Then write a letter-to-the-editor yourself, taking a position on one of the same topics.

Part 12 **Be Counted** Write to an elected official evaluating his or her performance in that position. Be specific in your comments.

Section 17 **Developing Dictionary Skills**

Part 1 **Readout** In your dictionary, find the word *friend*. Write the guide words for the page. Copy five words from the page that are new to you, and use them in sentences.

Part 2 **A Grand Entry** Find the word *work* in a dictionary. Copy the pronunciation, language of origin, parts of speech, four meanings, a synonym, and an antonym.

Part 3 **More Ways Than One** Look up the word *light* in a dictionary. Copy four different meanings. Write a sentence of your own for each one.

Section 18 **Developing Library Skills**

Part 1 **Special Arrangements** Think of a career in sports or entertainment. Use your school or public library to find at least three nonfiction books about this kind of work. Write their titles, authors, and call numbers.

Part 2 **On File** In your library, find a title card, author card, and subject card for books about careers in a sports or entertainment field that interests you. Copy the important information from the cards.

Part 3 **To Know Better** Find an encyclopedia article about a sport or a type of entertainment. List the name of the encyclopedia, the volume number, and letters, the guide words on the page, and the names of related articles or books.

Part 4 **References on Request** Write the titles of two reference books with information about a career in sports or entertainment. Use the *Readers' Guide* to find the name of a magazine with an article about that career.

The Research Report

Part 1 **Look Everywhere** As a subject, choose some source of energy. Narrow the subject and find three sources of information about it. List detailed information about your sources.

Part 2 **Report Cards** Choose a book, a magazine article, and an encyclopedia article about one energy source. Make a model bibliography card for each. Make a note card from one source.

Part 3 **Order, Please** Choose a book, magazine article, or encyclopedia article about one source of energy. From it, choose three related facts and write them. State the main idea of the facts in one sentence.

Part 4 **Numbers and Letters** Find a magazine article about some source of energy. Write the first two main ideas in the article. Under each main idea, write the facts or details. Finally, write your notes in outline form.

Part 5 **Put It in Writing** As the population grows, so will the nation's energy requirements. Write the introduction to a report on a present or future energy source, including this observation.

Part 6 **The Mainspring** In a book or magazine article about an energy source, find several interesting facts or figures, and one direct quotation. Copy them and write a statement about them that could be used as a conclusion.

Part 7 **The Last Word** Find a magazine article about a present or future energy source, and copy two brief quotations. Write footnotes for the quotations. Then, make a bibliography entry for the article.

Thinking Clearly

Part 1 **The Truth** Read the front page of a recent newspaper. Copy three statements of fact and one statement of opinion.

Part 2 **Is That So?**   Look through a magazine to find statements of opinion. Copy a judgment, a statement of obligation, and a prediction. Underline any that seem to be sound opinions.

Part 3 **The Whole Truth**   Try to find two generalizations in a magazine about health, beauty, or decorating. Copy and explain any that are stereotypes.

Section 21 Group Discussion

Part 1 **What's the Problem?**   Your community is trying to encourage more people to register to vote. Write two specific questions you could ask that would encourage discussion of the situation.

Part 2 **Are You Ready?**   You are investigating present and proposed programs for older citizens. List three possible sources of information about programs currently in operation, their costs, and their value.

Part 3 **Tuning In**   Listen to two different newscasts about the same topic, one on radio and one on television. Take notes from each. Then write the important points that they have in common.

Part 4 **On Speaking Terms**   Observe and listen to a group discussion on radio or television. Write two ways in which the moderator or host helped the discussion. Explain your opinion of the value of the discussion.

Handbook

A detailed Table of Contents for the Handbook appears in the front of this book.

The Sentence and Its Parts

Sentences are structures. They are made up of various parts. These parts can be put together to create good, clear sentences. The arrangement of the parts of a sentence is important, just as the choice of words is.

In this section you will study the different parts of sentences. You will learn how to put these parts together to build clear, effective sentences.

Part 1   The Sentence

In conversation, you might use only parts of sentences. For example, you sometimes reply to questions with a word or two:

See you later. Not Again! Right.

However, in writing, complete sentences are important. With them, your ideas are clear and understandable.

A sentence is a group of words that expresses a complete thought. A sentence makes sense because it is a whole idea, not just part of one.

Look at these sentences:

> Diana opened a checking account.
> Air controllers use radar.
> During the crisis, people panicked.

If part of an idea is missing from a sentence, a sentence fragment results. A **sentence fragment** is a group of words that does not express a complete thought. These, for example, are sentence fragments:

> Opened a checking account. (Who opened an account?)
> Air controllers. (What about air controllers?)
> During the crisis. (What happened?)

Exercise A For each group of words that is a sentence, write *S* on your paper. For each sentence fragment, write *F*.

1. A seat on the bus.
2. Accepts only exact fare.
3. Craig lounged in front of the TV.
4. Palm trees line the avenue.
5. Randy works at a beauty salon.
6. An axle and the two rear tires.
7. On the dashboard of the Toyota.
8. Has green and orange stripes.
9. Artists painted a mural on the walls.
10. Six flights of stairs.

Exercise B Follow the directions for Exercise A.

1. Snowplows cleared the major highways.
2. Low-interest loans from the bank.

3. Checked the oil and the water.
4. The best brand of peanut butter.
5. This store advertised for clerks.
6. Keith returned Carlotta's letter.
7. Finally got a driver's license.
8. Four lanes of traffic.
9. At the nearest grocery store.
10. This practice is not fair to the consumer.

Part 2 The Subject and the Predicate

All sentences have two basic parts: the subject and the predicate. The **subject** tells *who* or *what* the sentence is about. The predicate tells something about the subject.

Subject	Predicate
(Who or What)	*(What is said about the subject)*
The defendant	pleaded with the judge.
The race car drivers	awaited their signals.
A jazz band	played outside.

Each sentence above expresses a complete thought.

Remember the parts of a sentence in this way. Think of the sentence as telling who did something or what happened. The subject tells *who* or *what*. The predicate tells *did* or *happened*.

Who or What	Did or Happened
A group of reporters	interviewed the mayor.
The huge trailer	barely cleared the bridge.
That hot-air balloon	dropped sharply.

The subject of the sentence tells *who* or *what* did something, or what the sentence is about.

The predicate of the sentence tells what is done or what happens.

Head two columns *Subject* and *Predicate*. Write the proper words from each sentence in the columns.

1. The Garcia family lives down the hall.
2. Hundreds of people gathered in the town square.
3. Evan quickly gulped down four hamburgers.
4. All the scenery was made by the cast.
5. The west side street fair attracted large crowds.
6. Jerry's brother works the night shift at G.M.
7. That old record is a 78 r.p.m.
8. This restaurant's service is very fast.
9. Police cars sped to the scene of the break-in.
10. Most employees receive a bonus each December.

Exercise B Follow the directions for Exercise A.

1. The Sunday newspaper weighs ten pounds.
2. A letter without postage is returned to the sender.
3. Trisha was a bridesmaid in her sister's wedding.
4. A misty waterfall tumbled down the mountainside.
5. Christy waited nervously by the phone.
6. The primary elections show voters' preferences.
7. The value of gold rose sharply last week.
8. All the clerks added up their receipts for the day.
9. That dingy old hotel was once a glamorous resort.
10. Cam Stevens caught a seventy-yard pass.

Part 3 The Verb and the Simple Subject

There are a few words in every sentence that are more important than the rest. These essential words form the basic framework of the sentence. Look at these examples:

Subject	Predicate
The **defendant**	**pleaded** with the jury.
The race car **drivers**	**awaited** their signal.
A small **band**	**played** outside.

All the words in the subject part of the sentence are called the **complete subject.** Within the complete subject is a key word, the **simple subject.** In the last example above, *a small band* is the complete subject. *Band* is the simple subject.

The **complete predicate** is all the words that tell something about the subject. The key word within the complete predicate is the **simple predicate** or **verb.**

In the sentence about the band, the complete predicate is *played outside.* The key word is *played.*

The key word in the subject of a sentence is called the simple subject. We will refer to it as the subject.

The key word in the predicate is the simple predicate. The simple predicate is the **verb.** Hereafter, we will refer to the simple predicate as the *verb.*

Finding the Verb and the Subject

The verb and the subject are the essential words in any sentence. Other words only tell more about these key words. Locate these key words in any sentence by first finding the verb. It shows action or a state of being. Then ask *who* or *what* before the verb. That answer will give you the subject of the verb.

Ralph Nader responded in a TV editorial.
Verb: responded
Who responded? Ralph Nader
The subject is *Ralph Nader.*

The automobile in the museum display ran on steam.
Verb: ran
What ran? automobile
The subject is *automobile.*

Diagraming Subjects and Verbs

Any sentence can be diagramed to show its parts. A sentence diagram shows how the parts fit together.

A sentence diagram shows the importance of the subject and the verb. These key parts are placed on a horizontal main line.

They are separated by a vertical line that crosses the main line. The subject appears before the verb. Later you will learn how every other word in the sentence has its own place in the diagram, too.

Within the diagram, only words capitalized in the sentence are capitalized. No punctuation is used.

These two diagrams show subjects and verbs:

Amy stubbornly insisted.

The operator helped us.

Exercise A Label two columns *Verb* and *Subject*. Number your paper from 1 to 10. For each sentence, write the verb and its subject.

1. Jeff routinely compares prices at different stores.
2. During the avalanche, huge rocks rolled downhill.
3. That mitt in the closet is Danielle's.
4. Many stations program soft rock music.
5. Two fire trucks pulled out of the station.
6. This garage holds 800 cars.
7. Unfortunately, Tom lost his temper.
8. This year a biologist won the Nobel Prize.
9. The shortstop relayed the ball for a double play.
10. The corner bookstore sells only paperbacks.

Exercise B Follow the directions for Exercise A.

1. Luckily, Maureen saved her ticket stub.

2. Josh rarely sleeps late on Saturdays.
3. Finally, the paramedics arrived.
4. A team of doctors operated for four hours.
5. Twenty people came to Rick's party.
6. Kyle fiercely defended the goal.
7. Proudly, Jenny displayed her trophy.
8. Just before dawn, the blizzard struck.
9. Many small cars get good gas mileage.
10. In speeches today, the candidates discussed the issues.

Part 4   The Parts of a Verb

While many verbs consist of one word, others consist of several words. A verb is often composed of a **main verb** and one or more **helping verbs.**

Helping Verbs +	Main Verb =	Verb
has	sent	has sent
will	leave	will leave
must	see	must see
could have	heard	could have heard

In naming the verb in any sentence, you must name all the words that make up the verb.

These words are frequently used as helping verbs:

am	are	have	will	may
is	be	do	would	might
was	has	does	can	shall
were	had	did	could	should

Separated Parts of a Verb

In some sentences, you will find words inserted between the parts of the verb. These words are not included in the verb. Look at the following sentences. The parts of the verb are in bold print.

Darrel **has** never **seen** a Mel Brooks movie.
The warehouse **was** recently **converted** to shops.
That amendment **has** not **been passed**.

Some verbs are joined with other words to make contractions. To name a verb that appears in a contraction, pick out only the verb. The word *not* and its contraction *n't* are never verb parts.

Bob **could**n't **swallow** the oyster. (*Could swallow* is the verb.)
The singer **did**n't **know** the lyrics. (*Did know* is the verb.)

Exercise A   List the verbs in the following sentences.

1. Most people would never camp during the winter.
2. Old silent movies are sometimes shown on TV.
3. The plastic lenses in your glasses won't break easily.
4. Three players were recently elected to the Baseball Hall of Fame.
5. Some apes are being taught sign language.
6. Production of electric cars may soon begin.
7. Those cars are illegally parked.
8. Susan couldn't find a pay phone.
9. You shouldn't have brought gifts.
10. The author will probably appear on talk shows.

Exercise B   Follow the directions for Exercise A.

1. Alice would surely have noticed any rust on the car.
2. An earthquake had suddenly struck San Francisco.
3. The basketball tournament will surely be cancelled.
4. Because of an injury, Bailey couldn't play.
5. Income tax forms must be mailed by April 15.
6. The police can't explain the strange footprints.
7. Your backpack will never hold all that food.
8. Jeremy didn't have enough money for tolls.
9. Carrie has recently enlisted in the Navy.
10. Linda has already seen this double feature.

Part 5 Sentences in Unusual Order

In most sentences, the subject comes before the verb. Sometimes, though, part or all of the verb comes before the subject of a sentence.

To find the subject of a sentence, first find the verb. Then ask *who* or *what* before it. That answer will be the subject.

Sentences Beginning with *There*

The verb often comes before the subject in sentences beginning with *there*.

There may be used in two different ways. It may be used to explain the verb and tell where something is.

> There are your photos. (*Photos* is the subject; *are* is the verb. *There* tells where your photos are.)
> There is the entrance. (*Entrance* is the subject; *is* is the verb. *There* tells where the exit is.)

Sometimes *there* is used simply as an introductory word to help get the sentence started.

> There is no cure for a cold. (*Cure* is the subject; *is* is the verb.)
> There are four candidates. (*Candidates* is the subject. *Are* is the verb.)

To diagram a sentence starting with *there*, you must know if *there* tells *where* or is an introductory word. If *there* tells *where*, it belongs on a slanted line below the verb. If *there* is an introductory word, it is placed above the subject on a parallel line.

> There is the control panel.

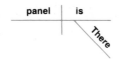

There has been a big response.

There	
response	has been

Exercise A Write the subject and the verb in each sentence. Tell whether *there* is used to tell *where* or as an introductory word.

1. There is the owner's manual.
2. There are too many ruts in this road.
3. There has been a big response.
4. There went your last chance.
5. There are several kinds of billiards.
6. There is the cap for the radiator.
7. There is the editorial page.
8. There goes the last runner.
9. There is a chance of rain tomorrow.
10. There is the entrance for employees.

Exercise B Follow the directions for Exercise A.

1. There must be a theater in this town.
2. There are programmers for each station.
3. There will be a discount on certain items.
4. There goes a Yamaha cycle.
5. There are 100 centimeters in a meter.
6. There goes my whole paycheck!
7. There is the last tangerine.
8. There is the boundary line.
9. There will be a rematch.
10. There are many types of health foods.

Other Sentences with Unusual Word Order

Besides sentences beginning with *there*, there are other kinds of sentences with unusual word order. These are some of them:

1. Sentences beginning with *here*

> Here come the paramedics. (*Paramedics* is the subject. *Come* is the verb.)
>
> Here is the leak in the tire. (*Leak* is the subject. *Is* is the verb.)

The word *here*, unlike *there*, always tells *where* about the verb.

2. Questions

> Do you use the metric system? (*You* is the subject; *do use* is the verb.)
>
> Can Wendy keep her deadline? (*Wendy* is the subject; *can keep* is the verb.)

3. Sentences starting with phrases or other descriptions

> Inside the drawer were our candles. (*Candles* is the subject; *were* is the verb.)
>
> Steadily came the signal. (*Signal* is the subject; *came* is the verb.)

To find the subject in a sentence with unusual word order, first find the verb. Then ask *who* or *what*.

> Here is a shortcut.
> *Verb:* is
> *Who or what is?* shortcut
> *Subject:* shortcut

To diagram a sentence with unusual word order, use the usual format. The verb and the subject still belong on the horizontal main line with the subject written before the verb.

> From the bleachers came hisses.

hisses	came

Sentences Giving Commands

Most sentences that give commands do not state the subject. Because commands are always given to the person spoken to, the subject is *you*. Although *you* is not stated, we say that it is understood.

> Check the sports page. (*You* is the subject of *check*.)
> Play your favorite albums. (*You* is the subject of *play*.)

The sentence diagram for a command shows the subject *you* in parentheses.

> Watch for landmarks.

(you)	Watch

Exercise A Label two columns *Subject* and *Verb*. Number your paper from 1 to 10. Write the subject and verb for each sentence.

1. Count your change.
2. Here is the teller's window.
3. Guess again.
4. Have you recorded the concert?
5. Does the subway stop here?
6. Across the lake whisked the iceboat.
7. Can you swim?
8. Out of the debate came a proposal.
9. Park closer to the curb.
10. Here is the briefcase.

Exercise B Follow the directions for Exercise A.

1. Tell me your idea.
2. Here is a calendar for 1956.
3. Send a telegram.
4. Does your brother work at the hospital?
5. Over the dunes bounced a jeep.
6. Here are the spark plugs.
7. Inside the van was a studio.
8. Did Gail laugh into the microphone?
9. Was the film shown in slow motion?
10. Ask for the manager.

Part 6   The Objects of Verbs

In many sentences, the verb does not need another word to complete its meaning. The action the verb describes is complete.

> The Who *performed*.   These jeans *have shrunk*.
> Chris was *pitching*.   The jet *will land*.

However, other verbs do not express complete meanings by themselves. Additional words must complete their meaning in the sentence.

> A trailer carried_____. (Carried what?)
> The mayor signed_____. (Signed what?)

The Direct Object

> A trailer carried two *horses*.
> The mayor signed the *bill*.

As shown above, one kind of word that completes the action of a verb is called the **direct object**. The direct object receives the action of a verb. In the sentences above, *horses* receives the action of *carried*. *Bill* receives the action of *signed*.

At times, the direct object may tell the *result* of an action.

> Marco makes great *tacos*.
> Nicole finished her *report*.

To find the direct object, first find the subject and verb. Then ask *whom* or *what* after the verb.

> The agency hired Barbara.
>   *Verb:* hired
>   *Hired whom?* Barbara
>   *Direct object:* Barbara

> This machine makes snow.
>   *Verb:* makes
>   *Makes what?* snow
>   *Direct object:* snow

When a verb has a direct object, it is called a **transitive verb.** When a verb does not have a direct object, it is called an **intransitive verb**. Look at how these verbs differ:

> The raft *disappeared*. (*Disappeared* is intransitive. It has no direct object.)
> This center *recycles* newspapers. (*Recycles* is transitive. It has a direct object, *newspapers*.)

The same verb may be transitive in one sentence and intransitive in another.

> Intransitive: Rick cooked.
> Transitive: Rick cooked spaghetti.

Transitive or Intransitive?

Are the verbs in the following sentences transitive or intransitive?

> Leona *watched* closely.
> Leona *watched* from the back row.
> Leona *watched* the playoffs.

In the first two examples, the verb *watched* has no direct object. *Watched* is intransitive in those sentences. In the third sentence, however, if you ask *whom* or *what* after the verb, you find that *playoffs* is the direct object. *Watched* is a transitive verb in that sentence.

> Leona watched the playoffs.
> *Verb:* watched
> *Watched what?* playoffs
> *Direct object:* playoffs

Exercise A Write the direct object of each verb.

1. The ballplayers have signed their contracts.
2. Derek dealt the cards.

3. My friends attended a rally.
4. We need more wood for the fire.
5. Lynn will exchange her sweater.
6. Quickly, the lawyers selected a jury.
7. Don't the Steelers have a good record?
8. Ellen has found a part-time job.
9. Three prisoners plotted their escape.
10. Has Congress considered the new bill?

Exercise B   Decide whether the verb in each sentence is *Transitive* or *Intransitive*.

1. McDonald's opened a new restaurant here.
2. The bank increased its interest rate.
3. Gas prices have risen recently.
4. Last weekend the new arcade opened.
5. Sandy left the game early.
6. Shawn left soon afterward.
7. Cindy has changed the tire.
8. Dad's ideas have certainly changed.
9. Top officials will meet tomorrow.
10. You will meet lobbyists outside.

The Indirect Object

Along with direct objects, some sentences also have indirect objects of the verb. Sometimes indirect objects tell *to whom* or *to what* about the verb. At other times they tell *for whom* or *for what* about a verb.

> The bank gave **Aaron** a *loan*. (gave *to* Aaron)
> David left the **waiter** a *tip*. (left *for* the waiter)
> The director gave the **crew** a *break*. (gave *to* the crew)

The words in bold type in the sentences above are the indirect objects. The words in italics are the direct objects.

Only sentences with direct objects can have indirect objects. Indirect objects appear between the verb and direct object. The words *to* and *for* are not used with an indirect object.

> Sarah handed her *sister* the phone. (*Sister* is the indirect object of *handed*.)
>
> Sarah handed the phone to her *sister*. (*Sister* is not an indirect object.)

To diagram a direct object, place it on the main line after the verb. The vertical line between the verb and object does not go below the main line.

> Emily made a sweater.

Emily	made	sweater

An indirect object belongs on a horizontal line attached below the verb.

> Emily made her friend a sweater.

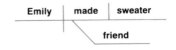

Exercise A Label three columns *Verb, Indirect Object,* and *Direct Object*. For each sentence below, write those parts. Not all sentences will have all three parts.

> Example: The clerk gave Kelly her receipt.

Verb	Indirect Object	Direct Object
gave	Kelly	receipt

1. The salesperson showed Tim a stereo.
2. Adam gave Marla a velour shirt.
3. Carlos lifts weights every day.
4. The candidate showed the audience some charts.

5. Melissa Manchester gave Daniel her autograph.
6. The prisoner was serving a light sentence.
7. The director gave Deena a part in the film.
8. Coupons can save consumers money.
9. Our educational TV station has no commercials.
10. Mr. Gage gave the employees their assignments.

Exercise B   Follow the directions for Exercise A.

1. Bill's car needs new brakes.
2. Rachel gave the machine a kick.
3. Ms. Rogers left her secretary a message.
4. Johnson fumbled the ball.
5. Police must read suspects their rights.
6. Kate ate lunch in the park.
7. Both parties held conventions in Miami.
8. Jon tossed Ricardo the ball.
9. Todd always wears dark clothes.
10. The officer handed Jamie a ticket.

Part 7   Linking Verbs with Predicate Words

Instead of expressing action, some verbs tell of a state of being. Such verbs link the subject of a sentence with a word or group of words in the predicate. Since they link the subject with some other word or words, they are often called **linking verbs**.

> Bo *is* the lead-off hitter.   The road *must be* slick.
> The meeting *was* secret.   The winners *were* the Knicks.

The most frequently used linking verb is *to be*. *To be* can have many forms. This list will help you to become familiar with them:

be	been	is	was
being	am	are	were

Helping verbs are sometimes used with the verbs *be*, *being*, and *been*. Here are examples:

might be	are being	has been
can be	were being	should have been
will be	is being	may have been

The words linked to the subject by linking verbs like *to be* are called **predicate words**. The three kinds of predicate words are **predicate nouns, predicate pronouns,** and **predicate adjectives**. They always tell something about the subject.

The main dish is *veal*. (predicate noun)

This is *she*. (predicate pronoun)

Laws are *necessary*. (predicate adjective)

The linking verbs *is* and *are* join the subjects and predicate words in the above sentences.

Here are some other common linking verbs:

appear	seem	sound	grow
feel	look	taste	become

The above linking verbs, like *be*, have various forms (*sounded, became, seems*). They can be used with helping verbs, as in *had tasted, would seem, might have looked*.

John *looks* pale.

The judge *seemed* fair.

This record *has become* a hit.

For a sentence diagram, place a predicate word after the verb on the main line. A slanted line above the main line separates the verb from the predicate word. That line, like the predicate word, points back toward the subject.

Art Buchwald is a columnist.

Art Buchwald | is \ **columnist**

These pretzels seem stale.

| pretzels | seem \ | stale |

Direct Object or Predicate Word?

Two kinds of words can complete verbs. A verb may have a direct object, or it may have a predicate word. How can you tell the difference between a predicate word and a direct object?

The verb is the clue. Determine if the verb is an action verb. If so, the word following it that tells *whom* or *what* is a direct object.

A barge blocked the *river*. (*Blocked* is an action verb. *River* is its direct object.)

This machine shreds *paper*. (*Shreds* is an action verb. *Paper* is its direct object.)

In contrast, the verb may be a linking verb. If so, the word following it that tells about the subject is a predicate word.

Megan is an identical *twin*. (*Is* is a linking verb. *Twin* is a predicate word.)

Those wax figures look *real*. (*Look* is a linking verb. *Real* is a predicate word.)

Look at the following sentences:

Nathan is a blood *donor*.
Nathan needs a blood *donor*.

The first sentence has a linking verb, *is*. The word *donor* follows the linking verb and tells about the subject. It is a predicate word. The second sentence has an action verb, *needs*. In this sentence, *donor* tells *whom* about the action verb. It is a direct object.

Exercise A Label three columns *Subject, Linking Verb,* and *Predicate Word*. Find these parts in the sentences below and place them in the proper columns.

1. Kurt Vonnegut is the author.
2. Wendy is good at ice hockey.
3. Some diets have become fads.
4. Christina's native language is Swedish.
5. The governor has become seriously ill.
6. Jesse Owens was an Olympic athlete.
7. The eye chart looks blurry.
8. Susan seems uncomfortable.
9. Moon boots look very warm.
10. Ruth Streeter was the first female major in the Marines.

Exercise B Make four columns on your paper. Head the columns *Subject, Verb, Direct Object,* and *Predicate Word.* Find these parts in the sentences below and place them in the correct columns.

1. Rivera hit a grounder to left field.
2. Donna rents a small apartment downtown.
3. Inflation has become a problem for everyone.
4. Sunspots are dark regions on the sun.
5. With a long vacation ahead of him, Tim grew lazy.
6. Pam devoured the butterscotch sundae.
7. Our fudge has become a liquid.
8. The Illini cut the Buckeyes' lead.
9. Brad won a prize in the lottery.
10. Nuclear power has become a controversial issue.

Part 8 Compound Sentence Parts

Sentence parts can be *compound,* which means "having two or more parts."

All of the sentence parts described so far in this section can be compound—subjects, verbs, direct objects, indirect objects, and predicate words.

A conjunction (*and, or, but*) joins the two parts in a compound form. In a compound form of three or more parts, the conjunction usually comes between the last two parts.

Diagraming Compound Subjects

To diagram compound subjects, split the subject line. The conjunction belongs on a dotted line connecting the subjects.

Clowns, mimes, and dancers performed at the street fair.

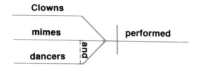

Diagraming Compound Verbs

To diagram compound verbs, split the verb line in the same way.

The leaders met and signed the treaty.

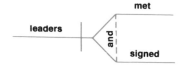

Diagraming Compound Objects

To diagram compound direct objects or indirect objects, split the object line.

The Mets have six wins and four losses. (compound direct object)

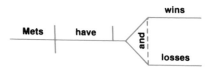

Ed told Amy and Debbie a terrible joke. (compound indirect object)

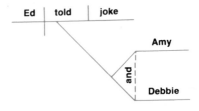

Diagraming Compound Predicate Words

To diagram compound predicate words, split the predicate word line.

Ingredients in chili are meat, tomatoes, and beans.

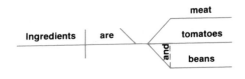

Exercise A   As your teacher directs, show the compound parts in the following sentences. Tell whether they are compound subjects, verbs, objects, or predicate words.

1. Ramon and Laura got the best work schedules.
2. The car skidded and then slid around.
3. Was the stoplight red or yellow?
4. Both TV and radio broadcast the President's speech.
5. Traditional holiday foods are ham, duck, and turkey.
6. Dan's German shepherd looks huge but friendly.
7. The fire sputtered and finally died out.
8. Paco added mushrooms and cheese to the salad.
9. Randy served tacos, tostadas, and enchiladas.
10. The team practiced free throws and layups.

Exercise B For each of the following sentences, make the part noted in parentheses compound. Write the new sentences.

1. Becky gave her collie a bath. (*indirect object*)
2. The parachutist floated to earth. (*verb*)
3. Kim can fix the projector. (*direct object*)
4. The pitcher warmed up. (*subject*)
5. Does the car have radial tires? (*direct object*)
6. The Cardinals are in the National League. (*subject*)
7. That steep driveway looks slippery. (*predicate word*)
8. Carefully, we washed the fragile glasses. (*verb*)
9. Show Vanessa the safety deposit box. (*indirect object*)
10. In Washington, the protestors were mostly students. (*predicate word*)

Part 9 The Four Kinds of Sentences

You use different kinds of sentences for different reasons. You may want to state something, or you may want to ask a question. Sometimes you may want to give a command. At other times, you may want to express strong feeling. For each of these times, you use a different kind of sentence.

A **declarative sentence** is used to make a statement. It ends with a period (.).

> Wings gave a benefit performance.
> Critics praised that director.

An **interrogative sentence** asks a question. It ends with a question mark (?).

> Do you like disco music?   Is the snake loose?

An **imperative sentence** gives a command. It usually ends with a period.

> Enjoy yourselves.   Change the channel, please.

An **exclamatory sentence** shows strong emotion. It ends with an exclamation point (!).

What an upset that was!   It's so dark in here!

Exercise A For each of these sentences, write *Declarative, Interrogative, Imperative,* or *Exclamatory* on your paper to show what kind each is. Add the proper punctuation mark.

1. Are the car windows rolled up
2. Who scored the field goal
3. Carrie waded through flooded streets
4. Do you have an ID card
5. Compare these two brands
6. What a dull match that was
7. Soon the cameras were pointing at me
8. Last year the company went bankrupt
9. Don't forget your hat and gloves
10. How thoughtful you are

Exercise B Follow the directions for Exercise A.

1. Are you influenced by ads
2. Last night Pete called a hotline
3. How did you make those braids
4. Keep your comments to yourself
5. Which jockey is riding Silver Streak
6. I'm so scared
7. Hold the line, please
8. At the end of the film, everyone was crying
9. What terrific pastry Lutz's Bakery has
10. We must reserve seats in advance

Part 10 Sentence Patterns

The various sentence parts can be shaped into sentences in an endless number of ways. Most sentences, however, follow certain basic **sentence patterns**. The five patterns that follow are the most common ones.

Pattern One

Pattern One is the most basic type of sentence. It has a subject and a verb. The subject is usually a noun or pronoun. In this chart, N stands for the noun (or pronoun) in the complete subject. V stands for the verb in the complete predicate.

N	V
The amendment	passed.
The union	is striking.
I	understand completely.

Pattern Two

Pattern Two sentences have a noun (or pronoun) following the verb. This noun is a direct object.

N	V	N
The referee	made	a bad call.
Mariya	has	an unusual name.
Barry Brothers	held	an auction.

Pattern Three

In this pattern, two nouns follow the verb. The first noun (or pronoun) is an *indirect object*. The second is a *direct object*.

N	V	N	N
The woman	handed	me	my ticket.
Jennifer	showed	the guard	her badge.
Manilow	gave	the old song	a new twist.

Pattern Four

In a Pattern Four sentence, the verb is a *linking verb* (LV). Following the linking verb is a *predicate noun* (or pronoun).

N	LV	N
My brother	became	plant supervisor.
Gonzalez	is	an outfielder.
Those clogs	are	hers.

Pattern Five

A linking verb is followed by a *predicate adjective (Adj)* in this pattern.

N	LV	Adj
The last lap	will seem	easy.
That shirt	is	too expensive.
Foxboro Stadium	must be	full.

Exercise A Tell which sentence pattern is used in each sentence.

1. The bookcase toppled over.
2. Leslie is wearing her roommate's jacket.
3. Mark gave the Datsun a tune-up.
4. The octane level is too low.
5. This gas tank holds twenty gallons.
6. The coach showed films of the last game.
7. The American family has changed.
8. Those stories are rumors.
9. The scouts are watching Darnell.
10. The pecan pie is delicious.

Exercise B Follow the directions for Exercise A.

1. The horses are rounding the final bend.
2. Tomahawk is lagging behind.
3. Tony seems restless.
4. Jamie saw a bullfight in Mexico.
5. The matador was a young boy.
6. The musical was a flop.
7. Mr. Ridolfi gave me a job application.
8. Gena taught the understudy her lines.
9. That explosion sounds close.
10. All the trains are running late.

REVIEW The Sentence and Its Parts

The Parts of a Sentence   Write the subject and verb for each of the following sentences. If there is a direct object, indirect object, or predicate word in any sentence, write that part, too. Label each part.

1. One of the skaters has injured his knee.
2. There is the clinic.
3. How does a videotape recorder work?
4. Then came the applause.
5. Inside the machine is a tiny computer.
6. The new security system hasn't been installed yet.
7. On most radio stations, does the disc jockey choose the songs?
8. Here comes a northbound bus.
9. Underground homes are saving energy.
10. Have the Oscars been awarded yet this year?
11. Five good films are the nominees.
12. There are many single parents.
13. Mary Ann has shown Len the error in his checkbook.
14. Smith Brothers pays its workers a good wage.
15. The officer completed her inspection.

Kinds of Sentences   Decide whether each sentence is *Declarative, Interrogative, Imperative,* or *Exclamatory.* Write your answer. Also write what end punctuation mark should be used for each.

16. Each jet must follow a flight pattern
17. Did Bart nick his chin with the razor
18. Make a copy of this memo, please
19. Has Consumers' Union rated motorcycles
20. How dismal this weather is

Using Complete Sentences

You use sentences to communicate ideas and feelings. If a sentence is well written, it will express your ideas clearly and completely.

Occasionally, though, people put words together carelessly. Then the message is confusing.

One cause of confusion is leaving out part of a sentence. The remaining group of words is a **sentence fragment**. Another problem is created when two or more sentences are written as one. This group of words is called a **run-on sentence.**

Both of these writing errors weaken communication. In this section you will learn how to avoid them.

Part 1 Recognizing Sentence Fragments

If a group of words is only part of a sentence, it is called a **sentence fragment**. A sentence fragment does not express a complete thought.

Since something is missing from the sentence, a fragment is quite confusing. Frequently, the subject is left out. If so, the reader wonders *who* or *what* the sentence is about. Otherwise, the verb may be left out. Then the reader wonders *what happened?* or *what about it?*

> Fragment: Opened the box slowly. (Who or what opened? The subject is missing.)
>
> Sentence: I opened the box slowly.
>
> Fragment: The producer at the control panel. (What happened? The verb is missing.)
>
> Sentence: The producer fell asleep at the control panel.

Fragments Due to Incomplete Thoughts

Fragments can occur when a writer is in a hurry. He or she jots down only bits of ideas. These ideas are incomplete. The writer's pen doesn't keep up with his or her flow of thoughts.

These pieces of ideas might make sense to the writer. To a reader, however, they will probably seem unclear.

Here is an example of a series of fragments:

> New TV shows. Introduced in the fall each year.
> Never finish the season. Cancelled due to low ratings.
> Or get different time slots.

These complete sentences show what the writer meant:

> Many new TV shows are introduced in the fall each year. Many of them, however, never finish the season. Due to low ratings, they are cancelled by the networks. Other new shows with poor ratings get different time slots.

Fragments Due to Incorrect Punctuation

Every sentence ends with a punctuation mark. That mark may be a period, a question mark, or an exclamation point. Sometimes a writer uses one of these punctuation marks too soon. The idea is incomplete. A sentence fragment results.

Fragment: The gossip columnist for the newspaper. Made many enemies.

Sentence: The gossip columnist for the newspaper made many enemies.

Fragment: With four speakers. This stereo system has great sound.

Sentence: With four speakers, this stereo system has great sound.

Fragment: The President named Clark. To a Cabinet post.

Sentence: The President named Clark to a Cabinet post.

Exercise A For each group of words that is a sentence, write *S* on your paper. For each sentence fragment, write *F*. Add words to change the fragments into sentences.

1. A victory for the Celtics
2. That truck is carrying an overweight load
3. Denim jeans usually fade
4. Had a strange nickname
5. About the First Amendment
6. Brad takes vitamins
7. At a local health-food store
8. Works as a social service aide
9. Late in the third quarter
10. Many new cars have front-wheel drive

Exercise B Follow the directions for Exercise A.

1. The most outstanding player on the court
2. A ferry boat on the river
3. Bargain-hunters head for auctions

4. Raced on their motorcycles
5. Warm coffee cake every morning
6. The Black Hawks won in a powerplay
7. Eric ate nothing but eggs
8. Plunged into the icy waters
9. Adult evening classes are offered
10. Organized a garage sale

Part 2 Recognizing Run-on Sentences

A **run-on sentence** is two or more sentences written incorrectly as one.

A run-on is confusing. The reader keeps going without knowing where the first idea ends and the second one begins. To recognize the end of each complete thought, the reader needs a period or other punctuation mark. These are some examples:

Run-on: Scott works at a photo studio he develops film.
Correct: Scott works at a photo studio. He develops film.

Run-on: Voting age was once 21 now it is 18.
Correct: Voting age was once 21. Now it is 18.

A common error is using a comma instead of a period. Again, the result is a run-on.

Run-on: On TV, prime time begins at 7:30 P.M., it ends at 10 P.M.
Correct: On TV, prime time begins at 7:30 P.M. It ends at 10 P.M.

Run-on: Some cars use leaded gas, others need unleaded.
Correct: Some cars use leaded gas. Others need unleaded.

Exercise A Correct the following run-on sentences.

1. A film board rates movies, the ratings are G, PG, R, and X.

2. Jordan is a candidate for the state legislature her platform is lower taxes.

3. Households are becoming smaller, one-child families are more common.

4. This grocery store has generic brands, they are economical.

5. There are many kinds of RV's, vans, campers, and trailers are three.

6. Last year, our town had a record snowfall it exceeded fifty inches.

7. Shana keeps a diary she writes in it daily.

8. A ground crew checked the plane, then the plane took off.

9. Emily gave up she couldn't win the argument.

10. Do you play a team sport which one do you like best?

Exercise B Follow the directions for Exercise A.

1. Cora charged the car's battery, she used jumper cables.

2. The population of the city has fallen people are moving to the suburbs.

3. Gregory blushed he was embarrassed.

4. Cable TV has many types of programs, it requires a monthly fee.

5. There are three major commercial networks they are ABC, NBC, and CBS.

6. The temperature was 20 degrees the wind made it seem even colder.

7. A plane crashed into the lake, firefighters rescued the four passengers.

8. Foster Beach is closed the waves are too high.

9. Voter turnout was low, Stevens won easily.

10. The wilderness school offers backpacking trips, students spend time alone in the wilderness.

REVIEW Using Complete Sentences

Sentences, Sentence Fragments, and Run-on Sentences
Number your paper from 1 to 20. Identify each of the following groups
of words as a *Fragment, Sentence,* or *Run-on*.

1. Were formerly called the Oilers
2. Do people dream in color
3. Records are still more popular than tapes
4. Anita and Ron, together with their families
5. The President appoints Supreme Court Justices
6. Many people wear glasses, others wear contact lenses
7. On fourth down with twenty yards to go
8. An outdoor job rather than a desk job
9. Dental X-rays show cavities
10. Rescue workers used a helicopter they dropped rafts
11. A third-floor apartment with many windows
12. Likes ice cream with root beer
13. The Cubs beat the Pirates the Braves edged out the Dodgers
14. Has gone on a camping trip
15. TV news gives brief reports newspapers give more details
16. Radio announcers must have pleasant voices
17. George reads lips he is deaf
18. This car has a diesel engine
19. The train takes a scenic route it runs along the Grand
Canyon
20. First aid for burns is ice water and ointment

Using Nouns

Clear, effective sentences result from knowing how words work.

The words used in sentences fall into certain groups or classes. You can talk and write without knowing these labels. Skilled speakers and writers, however, understand the different classes of words.

In this section you will learn about one important group of words: nouns.

Part 1   What Is a Noun?

You use words to name people, places, and things around you. Whenever you name something, you are using a noun.

A noun is a word used to name a person, place, or thing.

Nouns name things that can be seen, such as foods, clothes, machines, and animals. In addition, they name things you cannot see, like thoughts, emotions, and beliefs.

Persons:	librarian, Tracy Austin, singer, pilot
Places:	valley, Detroit, hallway, beach
Things:	book, honesty, ribbon, love

Exercise   Make three columns on a sheet of paper. Label them *Names of Persons, Names of Places,* and *Names of Things.* Find the nouns in the following paragraph. List each one in the proper column.

> In the middle of the nineteenth century, gold was discovered in California. Soon afterward, the Gold Rush began. Many people picked up pans and headed for the West. These miners were seeking instant wealth. As a result, many people settled in California.

Proper Nouns and Common Nouns

In the following sentence, notice how these two italicized nouns differ.

> One *driver, Peter Holmes,* lost control.

Driver, the first noun, is a general word. It refers to many people. It is a **common noun**. A common noun is a general name.

The second noun, *Peter Holmes,* refers to only one person. It is a proper noun. A **proper noun** is a specific name.

A common noun is the name of a whole group of persons, places, or things. It is the name that is common to the group.

A proper noun is the name of a particular person, place, or thing. Proper nouns are capitalized.

Look at the following examples of common nouns and proper nouns. As you can see, some nouns are made up of more than one word.

Common Nouns	Proper Nouns
island	Jamaica
restaurant	Villa Rosa
athlete	Muhammed Ali
cereal	Total
congresswoman	Elizabeth Holtzman
street	Delaware Avenue

Exercise A Make two columns on your paper. Label one column *Common Nouns* and the other *Proper Nouns*. Place each of the following nouns in the correct column. Capitalize all proper nouns.

1. actress, jane fonda, james earl jones
2. month, time, july, thursday, september
3. river, lake huron, stream, ohio river
4. stevie wonder, pianist, musician, herbie hancock
5. motorbike, harley-davidson, yamaha, motorcycle
6. department store, montgomery ward, macy's
7. mount whitney, appalachian mountains, peak, hills
8. nurse, mercy hospital, emergency room, hospital
9. team, baseball, atlanta braves, dave kingman
10. japan, canada, greece, country, nation

Exercise B Write five sentences of your own, using at least one proper noun in each sentence.

Part 2 How a Noun Is Used

Using Nouns as Subjects

Frequently, a noun is used as the subject of a sentence. As you learned in **Section 1**, the subject tells *whom* or *what* is being talked about.

> This *job* provides many kinds of benefits. (The noun *job* is the subject of the verb *provides*.)

Damage from the fire is covered by insurance. (The noun *damage* is the subject of the verb *is covered*. As you can see, the subject is not next to the verb.)

Two or more nouns may form a compound subject.

Strange *lights* and eerie *noises* frightened us. (Both the nouns *lights* and *noises* are the subject of the verb *frightened*.)

The *union* and *management* could not agree. (The two nouns *union* and *management* are the subject of the verb *could agree*.)

Exercise A   Write the nouns used as the subjects.

1. A hypnotist cured Amy of sleeplessness.
2. Alcohol from grain is used in gasohol.
3. Hundreds of people competed in a contest.
4. Death Valley has the lowest elevation in the country.
5. Molly went to the police academy.
6. Many species of animals are becoming extinct.
7. The hostages remained inside.
8. In the future, all foods will be dated for freshness.
9. Busloads of fans arrived at the stadium.
10. After the dance, Phil and Marsha helped with cleanup.

Exercise B   Follow the directions for Exercise A.

1. On most days, a seaplane takes off from this lake.
2. The city of Honolulu has clean air.
3. The detective wore a bulletproof vest.
4. Gilda Radner and Bill Murray are comedians.
5. During the dry spell, water was scarce.
6. At the half, Wisconsin trailed by twelve points.
7. The Federal Aviation Administration regulates airlines.
8. With a thud, the gymnast landed on the mat.
9. When will the race start?
10. Donna Summer and ShaNaNa are on "Midnight Special."

Using Nouns as Direct Objects

Instead of being a subject, a noun may be a direct object. The direct object completes the action of a verb. It answers *whom* or *what* about the verb.

> Trade schools train *students* in carpentry. (The noun *students* tells *whom* about the verb *train*.)
>
> The trial drew heavy *publicity*. (The noun *publicity* tells *what* about the verb *drew*.)
>
> A crew repaired the *boiler* and the leaky *pipes*. (Both the nouns *boiler* and *pipes* are direct objects. They tell *what* about the verb *repaired*.)

Exercise A   Write the nouns used as direct objects.

1. Dori sold her car through a want-ad.
2. This table will need two coats of paint.
3. On the train, we played Scrabble and Boggle.
4. In case of fire, ring this alarm.
5. Most soap operas have loyal fans.
6. Dennis pays his bills twice a month.
7. The laundromat has ten washers and four dryers.
8. The real estate agent made a large commission.
9. On that snowy day I got a sunburn.
10. The climber dug his ax into the mountainside.

Exercise B   Follow the directions for Exercise A.

1. Different colors reflect different moods.
2. Does chicken soup cure colds?
3. Telephone linemen must climb tall poles.
4. This river has clear, clean water.
5. Marlene donated time and money to the campaign.
6. The *Farmer's Almanac* predicts a severe winter.
7. Turn off your radio and headlights.
8. A mime uses only gestures and expression.
9. One reporter asked touchy questions.
10. Lauren sanded the doors and woodwork.

Using Nouns as Indirect Objects

Sometimes a noun is used as an indirect object. An indirect object tells *to whom* or *for whom* or *to what* or *for what* about the verb.

> The Nineteenth Amendment gave *women* the vote. (*Women* is the indirect object. It tells *to whom* about the verb *gave*.)

> This tollway charges *cars* and *trucks* different tolls. (The nouns *cars* and *trucks* are the compound indirect object, telling *to what* about the verb *charges*.)

Only sentences with direct objects have indirect objects. The indirect object appears before the direct object.

Subject	Verb	Indirect Object	Direct Object
Dominic	sent	the bank	his application.
The rules	allow	each player	two guesses.

The word *to* or *for* is never used with an indirect object.

Exercise A Find the nouns used as indirect objects.

1. Jeff sent Linda a card.
2. The United States loans many countries money.
3. The club served friends and family a vegetarian meal.
4. The secretary bought her boss lunch.
5. Karen tossed her brother the Frisbee.
6. Ms. Scott gave each employee a raise.
7. I saved Bill a seat on the bus.
8. Some people tell therapists their problems.
9. Orlando sent the company a letter of complaint.
10. The store sold Carrie and Jenny a radio.

Exercise B Follow the directions for Exercise A.

1. The magician handed Tony the ace of spades.
2. Foster parents give children temporary homes.
3. The stars show sailors the way.

4. Lee found her brother and his wife an apartment.
5. The cashier gave Barry incorrect change.
6. One good movie can bring an actor fame.
7. The man at the carnival gave Vicky a second chance.
8. The nurse handed Cody and Jessica magazines.
9. The trucker wouldn't give Jack a ride.
10. This meeting has given Meg some good ideas.

Using Nouns as Predicate Words

At times, a noun in the predicate part of a sentence is linked to the subject. That noun is a predicate noun. It always follows a linking verb. The predicate noun and the subject mean the same thing.

Video games are costly *gifts*.

Two symptoms of the flu are *fever* and *aches*.

In the above sentences, the nouns *gifts*, *fever*, and *aches* are all predicate nouns.

Exercise A Find the nouns used as predicate nouns.

1. During the winter, snow tires may be a necessity.
2. Alaska is the largest state.
3. Bennie's Diner is a good place for a snack.
4. Martin Luther King, Jr. was a leader in civil rights.
5. In 1979 Jane Byrne became the mayor of Chicago.
6. New Year's Eve is a time for celebration.
7. My favorite talk show hosts are Johnny Carson and Phil Donahue.
8. The second-largest urban area is Mexico City.
9. Bonnie's suggestion is a good idea.
10. Is the capital of Canada Ottawa?

Exercise B Follow the directions for Exercise A.

1. In Britain, the Prime Minister is Margaret Thatcher.

2. The copperhead and the rattlesnake are poisonous snakes.

3. Kung fu is a form of self-defense.

4. Woody Allen once was a writer for TV shows.

5. Ann Meyer is a fine basketball player.

6. Holistic medicine is a recent concept in health care.

7. Harry Reasoner is an interviewer on the program "60 Minutes."

8. My favorite desserts are strudel and ice cream.

9. O'Hare is the world's busiest airport.

10. That braided hairstyle has become a fad.

Part 3   Making Nouns Plural

A noun that names one thing is singular. A noun that names more than one thing is plural.

These rules will show you how to form the plurals of nouns:

1. To form the plural of most nouns, just add s:

bottles   rings   planes   baskets

2. When the singular noun ends in s, sh, ch, x, or z, add es:

glasses   flashes   ranches   foxes

3. When the singular noun ends in o, add s:

solos   radios   rodeos   pianos   altos

For a few words ending in o, add es:

potatoes   heroes   echoes   cargoes   tomatoes

4. If a singular noun ends in y with a consonant before it, change the y to i and add es:

lady—ladies   family—families   hobby—hobbies

When a vowel (*a, e, i, o, u*) comes before the *y*, do not change the *y* to *i*. Just add *s*:

> way—ways   valley—valleys   boy—boys

5. For some nouns ending in *f*, add *s* to make the plural:

> chiefs   griefs   roofs   proofs

For many nouns ending in *f* or *fe*, change the *f* to *v* and add *s* or *es*. Since there is no rule to follow, you will have to memorize such words. Here are some examples:

> leaf—leaves   half—halves   life—lives
> wife—wives   elf—elves   self—selves

6. The plural of some nouns is the same as the singular. These must be memorized.

> deer   sheep   moose   salmon   trout

7. Some nouns form their plurals in special ways. They, too, must be memorized.

> tooth—teeth   ox—oxen   man—men
> mouse—mice   foot—feet   woman—women
> child—children   die—dice   goose—geese

Dictionaries show the plural of a word if it is formed in an unusual way. Here is a dictionary's entry for the noun *spy*. Its plural, *spies*, is shown.

spy (spī) *vt.* **spied, spy′ing** [< OFr. < OHG. *spehōn*, to examine < IE. base *spek-*, to watch closely, from which also comes L. *specere*, to see] to catch sight of; see [I *spied* her in the distance] —*vi.* **1.** to watch closely and secretly; act as a spy **2.** to look carefully —*n., pl.* **spies 1.** a person who keeps close and secret watch on another or others **2.** a person hired by a government to get secret information about the affairs, esp. military affairs, of another government, as of an enemy in wartime —**spy out** to discover or seek to discover by looking carefully

If you have a question about plurals, use a dictionary.

Exercise A Write the plural of each of these nouns. Then use your dictionary to see if you are right.

1. shelf	6. calf	11. belief	16. city
2. knife	7. horse	12. studio	17. envelope
3. ox	8. sheep	13. eyelash	18. library
4. church	9. scout	14. cavity	19. roof
5. tray	10. potato	15. tax	20. foot

Exercise B Write each sentence. Correct the errors in plural forms of nouns.

1. The sheriffs and their deputys investigate robberys.
2. We bought radishs and tomatos at the roadside stand.
3. Workmans used knifes to prune branchs from the trees.
4. Each of the boxs contained twenty foots of rope.
5. These companys reported losses last year.
6. Four womans and four mens trained as astronautes.
7. The codes use buzzs, rings, and beeps.
8. Those crews work for various Hollywood studioes.
9. Judith takes photoes at all the wrestling matchs.
10. On one of the bathroom shelfs are Grandpa's false tooths.

Part 4   Making Nouns Possessive

A noun can show possession or ownership.

    child's toy   Sally's car   horse's saddle

The possessive of a noun can show that something is part of a person.

    Jerry's knee   Jill's happiness   boy's smile

The above nouns show ownership with 's. Words like *child's*, *Sally's* and *Jerry's* are possessive nouns.

While people and animals usually possess things, sometimes things are also used in the possessive. There is *a week's time*, a *restaurant's menu*, or *your life's work*, for example.

How To Form Possessives

Here are three rules for forming the possessive of nouns.

1. If the noun is singular, add an apostrophe (') and s.

Chris	Chris's glasses
Florida	Florida's weather
Ms. Healy	Ms. Healy's job

2. If the noun is plural but does not end in s, add an apostrophe and s.

children—children's songs   men—men's clothes

3. If the noun is plural and ends in s, add only the apostrophe.

workers—workers' pay   Cohens—Cohens' driveway

Exercise A   Write the possessive form of each of these nouns.

1. year	8. editor	15. hostess
2. David	9. Harris	16. ranch
3. Senate	10. manager	17. woman
4. Sandy	11. city	18. July
5. skater	12. chairperson	19. Rick Fields
6. player	13. committee	20. zoo
7. Katie	14. Les	

Exercise B   Follow the directions for Exercise A.

1. drivers	8. months	15. children
2. tourists	9. geese	16. fish
3. Bakers	10. coaches	17. linemen
4. people	11. engineers	18. Thompsons
5. dreamers	12. photographers	19. divers
6. Jets	13. cities	20. cooks
7. goalies	14. shoppers	

REVIEW Using Nouns

Recognizing Nouns List the nouns in each of the following sentences. Be sure to capitalize each proper noun that you list.

1. From the center of the court, williams sank a basket.
2. The convention was held during april in houston.
3. On the sixteenth day at sea, the skipper sighted the island of oahu.
4. Mark russell is a teacher at whitney young high school.
5. The bookseller searched for books about mexico.

Nouns Used in Sentences Decide how each italicized noun is used. Write *Subject, Direct Object, Indirect Object,* or *Predicate Noun*.

6. Customs agents inspect *luggage*.
7. *Roberta* tacked shingles onto the roof.
8. Finally, Amanda told her *friend* the truth.
9. A soundproof *booth* overlooks the recording studio.
10. The only officer on board was an *ensign*.

Forming Plurals Write the plural form of each noun.

11. hero	16. glass	21. bath
12. splash	17. pulley	22. man
13. chef	18. loaf	23. proof
14. deer	19. solo	24. tooth
15. punch	20. ally	25. luxury

Forming Possessives Write the possessive form of each noun.

26. Barry	30. city	34. secretary
27. readers	31. nephew	35. class
28. member	32. children	
29. officials	33. Hollis	

Using Pronouns

While nouns are valuable for naming people, places, and things, they can be overused. Sentences like this one show how awkward it is to use only nouns:

> When Rita started Rita's job, Rita worked nights.

Instead, you can substitute pronouns for some of the nouns. Then you can say:

> When Rita started *her* job, *she* worked nights.

You can see that the words *her* and *she* take the place of the noun *Rita*. These pronouns convey the same meaning clearly and concisely.

Part 1 Personal Pronouns

A pronoun is a word used in place of a noun. A pronoun is a useful word. It may be used in three situations:

1. It may refer to the person speaking.

   I went fishing.   *We* argued.

2. It may refer to the person spoken to.

   You like *your* co-workers, don't *you*?

3. It may refer to other people, places, or things.

   He stopped *them* in the doorway.   *She* left *her* post.

As you can tell from the examples above, a pronoun often refers to a person. Therefore, the most frequently used pronouns are called **personal pronouns.**

Personal pronouns have many variations. Just like the nouns they replace, personal pronouns may be singular or plural. Look at the following chart to see how personal pronouns change from singular to plural.

Singular:	I	me	my, mine
	you	you	your, yours
	he, she, it	him, her, it	his, her, hers, its
Plural:	we	us	our, ours
	you	you	your, yours
	they	them	their, theirs

The chart shows that most plural pronouns are totally different from their singular forms. Notice these examples:

Singular	Plural
I laughed.	*We* laughed.
Leave *it* alone.	Leave *them* alone.
She forgot.	*They* forgot.

Write the pronouns used in place of nouns. After each pronoun, write the noun or nouns it stands for.

1. Beth chipped her front tooth.
2. Curtis sealed the envelope and stamped it.
3. The game has lost its appeal for Kim.
4. Leon filed his notes.
5. Mr. Walker, do you have an account here?
6. "I voted before work," said Pamela.
7. The fishermen wore their licenses on their jackets.
8. When Ken finally arrived, he apologized.
9. You should not jump-start a frozen battery, Gene.
10. Claire said she had no insurance yet.

Exercise B Follow the directions for Exercise A.

1. The workers felt cheated. They walked out.
2. Do some doctors joke while they operate?
3. "Is that your car?" the policewoman asked Lee.
4. The city condemned the building and had it torn down.
5. Rick told Nina, "I enjoy my job."
6. Ms. Corelli said to her students, "We have several problems to solve."
7. Bats rarely bite, but many people are afraid of them.
8. The deaf students watched their interpreter.
9. Carrie heard a noise, and it frightened her.
10. Ted had made up his mind, but then he changed it.

Part 2   Forms of Pronouns

Pronouns can be used in all the ways that nouns are used. Like nouns, personal pronouns can be subjects, objects, predicate words, and possessives.

Exercise   The following sentences use different forms of pronouns correctly. Read each sentence aloud.

1. Red and gold are *their* colors.
2. The sugar doughnut is *mine*.
3. *He* veered to the left.
4. The best lineman is *he*.
5. The tallest player is *she*.
6. Connie and *she* tied for first place.
7. The next apartment is *theirs*.
8. The students filled out *their* schedules.
9. Is that *your* telephone?
10. Is that bike *yours*?
11. Give *her* another chance.
12. Mack and *he* said the decision was *theirs*.
13. Lori and *they* dug the car out of the snow.
14. The rain delayed Natalie and *them*.
15. Monica and *she* were talking with Luke and *me*.

A personal pronoun changes forms, however, as its use in a sentence changes. Look at these sentences:

> *He* swims every day. (*He* is the subject.)
> Nothing stops *him*. (*Him* is the direct object.)
> *His* strength has increased. (*His* is possessive.)

In the sentences above, all three pronouns refer to the same person. The forms, though, are different.

The three forms of personal pronouns are **subject form, object form,** and **possessive form.** This chart shows the forms for all the personal pronouns.

	Subject	Object	Possessive
Singular:	I	me	my, mine
	you	you	your, yours
	he, she, it	her, him, it	his, her, hers, its
Plural:	we	us	our, ours
	you	you	your, yours
	they	them	their, theirs

The Subject Form of Pronouns

Subject Pronouns

I	we
you	you
he, she, it	they

When a personal pronoun is the subject of a sentence, its subject form is used. Here are some examples.

We jumped hurdles.   *He* ran a mile.
They formed a carpool.   *She* has poison ivy.

You probably have little trouble using pronouns as subjects. Problems may occur, though, with the predicate pronoun. Predicate pronouns are pronouns that are linked to the subject. They follow linking verbs, just as predicate nouns do.

That was *he* on the phone. (*He* is a predicate pronoun used after the linking verb *was*.)

It must be *they*. (*They* is a predicate pronoun used after the linking verb *must be*.)

As you see, the subject forms of pronouns are used for predicate pronouns. Because that form may not sound natural at first, you may sometimes be confused about which form to use. In that case, try reversing the subject and the predicate pronoun. The sentence should still sound correct.

The hero was *he*.
He was the hero.

These sentences, too, correctly use the subject form for predicate pronouns:

Is that *she*?
It was *I* who called.
Your best friend is *he*.

Remember to use the subject form for both subjects and predicate pronouns.

The Object Form of Pronouns

Object Pronouns

me	us
you	you
him, her, it	them

For an object, the object form of a personal pronoun is correct.

The three kinds of objects are direct objects, indirect objects, and objects of prepositions.

These sentences use the object form of the pronoun for direct objects:

> The assistant manager hired *her*.   The Bears traded *him*.
> The noise awakened *them*.   Dora warned *me*.

In these sentences, the object form is used for indirect objects:

> Dennis handed *me* a note.   I wished *them* success.
> Jane gave *him* directions.   Sue told *us* her predictions.

Besides direct and indirect objects, the other kind of object is the object of a preposition. A preposition is a short connecting word like *by*, *with*, or *from*. A pronoun that follows such a word is the object. For information about prepositions see **Handbook Section 7**.

The following sentences use the object form for objects of prepositions.

> Their patients depend on *them*.
> Come with *me* to the sneak preview.
> Ben Vereen stars with *him* in a new series.
> Connie sat next to *her* on the subway.

The Possessive Form of Pronouns

Possessive Pronouns

my, mine	our, ours
your, yours	your, yours
his, her, hers, its	their, theirs

A possessive pronoun shows belonging or ownership. Some possessive pronouns are used alone. Then the possessive pronoun is used like a noun. It is a subject, object, or predicate word. Here are some examples:

> *Yours* is blue. (subject)
> Doug borrowed *hers*. (direct object)
> Roger gave *his* a shine. (indirect object)
> Some campers left without *theirs*. (object of preposition)
> This backpack is *mine*. (predicate pronoun)

At other times, possessive pronouns are not used by themselves. Rather, they are used to describe nouns. Notice how these possessive pronouns tell about nouns:

> The company opened *its* new branch office.
> Jessica tallied *her* score on the pinball machine.
> Brad put *his* last dime into the parking meter.
> The girls ate *their* lunches in the park.

Exercise A   Choose the correct pronoun from the two given in parentheses. Write it. Read the sentence to yourself.

1. The mail was all for (she, her).
2. The manager gave (they, them) a discount.
3. That idea was (your, yours).
4. Cassie talked (I, me) into the job.
5. Maybe (she, her) has forgotten.
6. Of course (he, him) reads the fine print.
7. The lawyer is (she, her).
8. It was not (I, me).
9. Our first choice is (he, him).
10. Somebody followed (he, him) home.

Exercise B   Follow the directions for Exercise A.

1. Did (she, her) see you?
2. That career appeals to (she, her).
3. The only volunteers were (they, them).
4. The man in charge of refreshments is (he, him).

5. Wasn't the call for (I, me)?
6. The actual inventor of the gadget was (I, me).
7. Maybe the bus driver can tell (we, us).
8. Wasn't the Marine (he, him)?
9. Is this wallet (her, hers) or Pat's?
10. The paramedic gave (she, her) oxygen.

Exercise C The personal pronouns in the following sentences are in italics. Write each pronoun and label it *Subject Form*, *Object Form*, or *Possessive Form*.

1. *She* shook sand from the towel.
2. The pollwatcher is *she*.
3. Finally *I* understood.
4. Della parked *her* car in the alley.
5. James served *us* some chili.
6. The jacket with the emblem is *mine*.
7. *My* interview is tomorrow.
8. Does *he* need an interpreter?
9. Did *they* buy tickets?
10. Are *we* early?

Part 3 Using Pronouns in Compound Constructions

Compound sentence parts, or compound constructions in a sentence have more than one part. The parts are joined by a word like *and*, *or*, or *nor*, as in *Carla and I*. A pronoun may be one or both of these parts.

For compound constructions, you will have to decide which pronoun form to use. These sentences use pronouns correctly as compound parts:

> *Yvonne* and *I* visited Denver. (*Yvonne* and *I* are both subjects. The subject form *I* is used.)

> Steve poured *her* and *me* some coffee. (*Her* and *me* are indirect objects. The object forms are used.)

Just between *you* and *me*, I'm scared. (*You* and *me* are objects of the preposition *between*. The object forms are used.)

There is a way to avoid problems with compound parts. Just think of each part separately. For instance, in the first example above, omit the *Yvonne and*. Should the sentence read *I visited Denver* or *Me visited Denver*? As you see, the pronoun *I* is correct:

Here is another example:

> Lynn is helping Evan and (I, me).
> Lynn is helping *me*.

Exercise A   Choose the right pronoun from the two given.

1. Teresa and (he, him) packed the cooler.
2. Karla frowned at Craig and (they, them).
3. Mick and (she, her) washed the lab utensils.
4. The candidate shook hands with Marta and (I, me).
5. My boss and (I, me) both have a hearing problem.
6. Ms. Shore and (they, them) share the kitchen.
7. (We, Us) and our neighbors divided the expense.
8. The most careful workers are Carlos and (she, her).
9. The saddest faces belonged to Annie and (I, me).
10. Just between you and (I, me), I have never driven on an expressway before.

Exercise B   Follow the directions for Exercise A.

1. Chet and (they, them) rented a meeting hall.
2. Do you and (she, her) play tennis?
3. That team has lost to both Phillips and (we, us).
4. The contenders are Clancy and (I, me).
5. (They, Them) and the CIA both do overseas work.
6. Somebody with a bad cold sat behind Tish and (I, me).
7. The coach can't decide between Ben and (he, him).
8. The band and (he, him) practiced daily.
9. Magda and (I, me) took the auto maintenance course.
10. The other tenants and (we, us) are signing a petition.

Part 4 Antecedents of Pronouns

A pronoun is used in place of a noun. The noun it replaces is called the pronoun's **antecedent**. A pronoun refers to its antecedent.

> Jeremy missed *his* friends. (*His* takes the place of the noun *Jeremy*. *Jeremy* is its antecedent.)
>
> The stagehands waited for *their* cues. (*Their* refers to the noun *stagehands*. *Stagehands* is the antecedent.)

Usually, the antecedent appears before the pronoun. The antecedent may be either in the same sentence or in the preceding sentence, as in this example:

> The firefighters chopped a hole in the roof. *They* used axes. (*They* refers to *firefighters*.)

Pronouns may be the antecedents of other pronouns:

> I choose *my* own hours. (*I* is the antecedent of *my*.)

In one important way, a pronoun must be like its antecedent. The pronoun must have the same number as its antecedent. If the antecedent is plural, then the pronoun must be plural.

A pronoun must agree with its antecedent in number.

> The ranger grabbed *her* binoculars.
> (*Ranger* is singular; *her* is singular.)
>
> Drivers have *their* own pit crews.
> (*Drivers* is plural; *their* is plural.)
>
> Andrew Wyeth exhibited *his* paintings.
> (*Andrew Wyeth* is singular; *his* is singular.)

Exercise A In these sentences the personal pronouns are italicized. Write each pronoun and its antecedent.

1. The waiter picked up the tip and pocketed *it*.
2. Jeff, which books do *you* need?

3. Sloths hang upside down by *their* hook-like claws.

4. At first Ray wouldn't wear *his* glasses in public.

5. The cashier in the express line closed *her* register.

6. All workers on duty must wear *their* badges.

7. Some overactive children have high levels of lead in *their* blood.

8. "I lost *my* transfer," said Cindy.

9. "*We* left *our* hardest job until last," said Kit and Bill.

10. Glenn cut out the pieces of the pattern and pinned *them* together.

Exercise B   Follow the directions for Exercise A.

1. Sue, train *your* foxhound not to chase rabbits.

2. Do *you* have to work overtime, Lee?

3. Most students bring *their* own lunches.

4. The fans in the bleachers waved *their* hats.

5. Mark overheard the conversation and worried about *it*.

6. Suddenly Bev got *her* second wind.

7. Chip painted *his* car with a glass finish.

8. "*I* have never ridden in a sidecar," said Maggie.

9. "Pam and *I* have brought *our* enlistment papers," said Alice.

10. Gladys started the argument, and Angie ended *it*.

Part 5   Compound Personal Pronouns

A **compound personal pronoun** is a pronoun with *self* or *-selves* added. These are the compound personal pronouns.

myself	ourselves
yourself	yourselves
himself, herself, itself	themselves

Compound personal pronouns are used for emphasis as in these sentences:

> The children planned the menu *themselves*.

> Mr. Mendez *himself* apologized.

> We chopped the firewood *ourselves*.

Exercise A Write a compound personal pronoun for each sentence. After it, write its antecedent.

1. Mel treated (pronoun) to a pizza.
2. Tina blames (pronoun) for everything that goes wrong.
3. Some people expect too little of (pronoun).
4. We served (pronoun) at the reception.
5. What do you want for (pronoun), Jenny?
6. The computer (pronoun) can correct some mistakes.
7. Steve doesn't like to shop by (pronoun).
8. The lamp will turn (pronoun) off in ten minutes.
9. The diplomats (pronoun) were held hostage.
10. The dentist (pronoun) took the X-rays.

Exercise B Follow the directions for Exercise A.

1. Even the chief (pronoun) pitched in.
2. Puzzled, the parakeet watched (pronoun) in the mirror.
3. Harry weighs (pronoun) every morning.
4. The wrestlers prepared (pronoun) for the match.
5. Don't wear (pronoun) out, Georgia.
6. I (pronoun) took that message.
7. Gwen and I can do the work by (pronoun).
8. Have you students heard (pronoun) on tape?
9. That window couldn't have opened (pronoun).
10. The fans yelled (pronoun) hoarse.

Part 6 Demonstrative Pronouns

The pronouns *this, that, these,* and *those* point out people or things. They are called **demonstrative pronouns.**

This and *these* point to people or things that are close in space or time. The pronouns *that* and *those* point to people or things that are farther away.

This is a drive-in.	*These* are the correct answers.
That was her maiden name.	*Those* were my first words.

Exercise   On your paper, write the correct demonstrative pronoun for each blank.

1. _____ was a close game last night.
2. _____ is my locker right here.
3. _____ is Ms. Prieto across the street.
4. _____ were exciting days to be alive.
5. _____ was my sister I was sitting with.
6. _____ are my skates I'm carrying.
7. _____ was the hardest test I had ever taken.
8. _____ is Leon's birthday we're celebrating, not yours.
9. _____ are more expensive than these.
10. _____ are more expensive than those.

Part 7 Interrogative Pronouns

The pronouns *who, whom, whose, which,* and *what* are used to ask questions. They are called interrogative pronouns.

Who rang the alarm?	*Which* are the best seats?
Whom did you meet?	*What* is your advice?
Whose is this?	

Exercise   Write all the pronouns in these sentences. After each pronoun, write *Demonstrative* or *Interrogative* to show what kind it is.

1. That was a good question.
2. Who checks air pollution levels?
3. Which is the best?
4. Is this the winning ticket?
5. To whom was the memo sent?
6. Who is the manager?
7. Whose are these keys?
8. To whom should Jim give these?
9. Those over there should be returned.
10. What are these for?

Part 8   Indefinite Pronouns

One type of pronoun does not refer to a definite person or thing. Such pronouns are called **indefinite pronouns.**

Here are some indefinite pronouns. All of them are singular.

another	each	everything	one
anybody	either	neither	somebody
anyone	everybody	nobody	someone
anything	everyone	no one	

Since they are singular, the pronouns above are used only with the singular possessive pronouns *his*, *her*, and *its*.

> *Everyone* has *his* own interests.
> *Each* of the delegates showed *his* pass.
> *Each* of the delegates showed *his* or *her* pass.

In the last example, notice that the phrase *his or her* is used instead of *his*. That phrase points out that the indefinite pronoun may refer to either a male or a female. Many people prefer such a phrase.

Although most indefinite pronouns are singular, some are plural. They refer to more than one person or thing. The following indefinite pronouns are plural. They are used with the plural possessive *their*. Look at these examples:

> both   many   few   several

Both of my brothers brought *their* dates.
Few of the tenants have paid *their* rent.
Many of the patients leave *their* rooms.
Several of the oil companies have raised *their* prices.

Depending on their meaning in a sentence, a few indefinite pronouns can be either singular or plural. Look at these examples:

some   none   all   any   most

Most of the movie was better than *its* ending.
Most of the rebels hated *their* country's dictator.
All of this food has sugar in *it*.
All of the rock groups have *their* fans.

Exercise A   Write each indefinite pronoun.

1. Everybody was watching the Superbowl.
2. Few of the students are from Cuba.
3. We saw nobody we knew.
4. The reporter interviewed several of the Steelers.
5. Have you met any of her relatives?
6. Finally someone heard my shouts.
7. Have all of the raffle tickets been sold?
8. Neither of those cars has snow tires.
9. I'll try some of the potato salad.
10. Ken got that watch from one of his aunts.

Exercise B   Choose the right pronoun from the two given.

1. Everything was in (its, their) place.
2. Each of the sorters is good at (his or her, their) job.
3. Many of the drivers use (his or her, their) own cars.
4. Everyone offered to share what (he or she, they) had.
5. One of the clinics has extended (its, their) hours.
6. Neither of the boxers was pulling (his, their) punches.
7. All of the schools must keep (its, their) costs down.
8. Some of them have changed (his or her, their) shifts.

9. Some of the food looked as if (it, they) had been out in the sun too long.

10. Nobody can do everything by (himself or herself, themselves).

Exercise C For each sentence write the indefinite pronoun and the correct verb from the two given.

1. One of your friends (is, are) here.
2. (Has, Have) anything happened?
3. Somebody always (times, time) the commercials.
4. Either of these albums (is, are) suitable.
5. Neither of the men (hears, hear) well.
6. Some of the voters (is, are) undecided.
7. None of the work (is, are) dull.
8. Both of the taxis (looks, look) empty.
9. Everyone (remembers, remember) that wedding.
10. Each of these skirts (needs, need) to be drycleaned.

Part 9 Special Problems with Pronouns

Contractions and Possessive Pronouns

Sometimes certain contractions are confused with possessive pronouns.

A contraction is created by joining two words. An apostrophe shows where one or more letters are left out when the words are joined.

you're = you + are   it's = it + is
they're = they + are   who's = who + is

The above contractions sound like the possessive pronouns *your, their, its,* and *whose.* Although the words are spelled differently, they may be confused.

Incorrect:	*Your* changing *you're* mind, aren't you?
Correct:	*You're* changing *your* mind, aren't you?

To decide which word is correct, replace the contraction with the words it stands for. If the sentence sounds right, then the contraction is correct.

Incorrect:	Call me when its time to leave.
Correct:	Call me when it's (it is) time to leave.

Exercise A Choose the right word from the two given.

1. (Their, They're) looking for trouble.
2. The dancers were snapping (their, they're) fingers.
3. (Whose, Who's) your new neighbor?
4. (Whose, Who's) the jockey?
5. (Your, You're) the referee.
6. (Whose, Who's) window overlooks the alley?
7. (Their, They're) playing a good defensive game.
8. (Their, They're) uncle will meet the children after school.
9. (Your, You're) sure about that, aren't you?
10. The steel workers were all wearing (their, they're) goggles.

Exercise B Write the words each contraction below stands for.

1. Who's in charge here?
2. She's filed for unemployment compensation.
3. They're all getting a raise.
4. He'd never seen a play before.
5. They'll call me.
6. I'm busy right now.
7. You're next.
8. We'd travelled by Greyhound before.
9. Something's burning!
10. We've got our baggage claims.

Who and Whom

The pronouns *who* and *whom* cause problems for many people. *Who* is used as the subject of a sentence. *Who* sounds natural in most questions.

> *Who* moved the picture?   *Who* is on a diet?

Whom is harder to get used to. *Whom* is used as an object.

> *Whom* did Dick Cavett interview?
> (direct object of the verb *did interview*)
>
> For *whom* will you vote?
> (object of the preposition *for*)

Exercise A   Choose the right pronoun from the two given.

1. (Who, Whom) was his stepmother?
2. (Who, Whom) did you ask?
3. (Who, Whom) knows how to use an airbrush?
4. (Who, Whom) is carrying the ball?
5. (Who, Whom) was that song dedicated to?
6. (Who, Whom) won the first round?
7. (Who, Whom) did you get a ride with?
8. (Who, Whom) signed the check?
9. (Who, Whom) did you speak with last time?
10. (Who, Whom) spoke with you last time?

Exercise B   Follow the directions for Exercise A.

1. (Who, Whom) tackled Evans?
2. (Who, Whom) did Frank tackle?
3. (Who, Whom) would do a thing like that?
4. (Who, Whom) did you see at the party?
5. (Who, Whom) will that Great Dane obey?
6. (Who, Whom) trained that dog?
7. About (who, whom) were you talking?
8. (Who, Whom) does she like?
9. With (who, whom) does he feel comfortable?
10. Behind (who, whom) was she standing?

We and Us with Nouns

The pronouns *we* and *us* are often used with nouns, as in the phrases *we girls* and *us Americans*. Such phrases may sometimes cause problems.

To decide whether to use *we* or *us*, omit the noun. First say the sentence with *we*, and then with *us*. You will then probably be able to choose the correct pronoun.

Problem:	(We, Us) players work out daily.
Correct:	We work out daily.
Correct:	We players work out daily.
Problem:	There is a new theater for (we, us) young people.
Correct:	There is a new theater for us.
Correct:	There is a new theater for us young people.

Them and Those

Them and *those* are sometimes confused. To use the words correctly, remember that *them* is always a pronoun. It takes the place of a noun.

Finally, someone noticed *them*. (In this sentence, *them* is used as the direct object.)

Them is never used to tell about a noun. *Those* should be used.

Incorrect:	Have you seen *them* stock cars?
Correct:	Have you seen *those* stock cars?

Exercise A   Choose the correct pronoun from the two given.

1. Is that one of (them, those) water filters?
2. (We, Us) recruits cannot live off base.
3. Of course (we, us) trainees get paid.
4. Loretta was accepted by one of (them, those) training programs.
5. (Them, Those) elephant seals often weigh two tons.

6. Slide rules have been replaced by (them, those) calculators.

7. The orientation session is for (we, us) new students.

8. (We, Us) Puerto Rican students will translate for you.

9. Barbados is one of (them, those) new nations.

10. Do you like (them, those) pepperoni pizzas?

Exercise B   Follow the directions for Exercise A.

1. (Them, Those) X-ray technicians wear lead aprons.

2. (We, Us) sheet metal workers serve a long apprenticeship.

3. Sitting this close to (them, those) poison ivy plants is unwise.

4. Listen to (them, those) sirens.

5. Ms. Sobecki congratulated (we, us) finalists.

6. What is delaying (them, those) ambulances?

7. (We, Us) volunteers are proud of ourselves.

8. Recently I went to one of (them, those) appliance shows.

9. (We, Us) pedestrians aren't using any energy but our own.

10. (Them, Those) crash helmets have saved some lives.

REVIEW Using Pronouns

Using Pronouns Correctly   Number your paper from 1 to 20. Choose the correct pronoun from those given in parentheses.

1. (She, Her) checked the blueprints for errors.
2. Did (we, us) have any choice?
3. Could (he, him) have left already?
4. The news surprised (I, me).
5. The last contestant was (I, me).
6. Ask (you, your) doctor to sign this form.
7. The bowlers recorded (they, their) own scores.
8. I sold (he, him) the last ticket.
9. Norma and (I, me) took down the storm windows.
10. Between you and (I, me), I will vote for Thomas.
11. The fugitives finally turned (themself, themselves) in.
12. You security guards must protect (yourself, yourselves), too.
13. (This, That, Those) is the post office across the street.
14. (This, That, These) are sunflower seeds I'm eating.
15. Everyone brought (his or her, their) own lunch.
16. (We, Us) waitresses can't wear (them, those) tight shoes.
17. Few of the packages had lost (its, their) labels.
18. (It's, Its) going to rain.
19. (Who, Whom) is the scout watching?
20. Someone left (his or her, their) book.

Using Verbs

There is one kind of word that every sentence must have. It is the verb. The verb brings a sentence to life. Without a verb, a sentence would not exist.

In **Handbook Section 1** you found out how to recognize verbs. In this section you will discover more about verbs and how they are used.

Part 1   What Is a Verb?

A verb tells of an action or a state of being.

Action Verbs

Some verbs indicate action, even if the action is unseen.

Christy *listens*.   The Philies *lost*.
A shark *surfaced*.   The crew *waited*.

An action verb tells that something is happening, has happened, or will happen.

Linking Verbs

Some verbs simply tell that something exists. Such verbs express a state of being rather than action.

My watch *is* wrong.　　These footprints *are* a clue.
This room *seems* stuffy.　　The chocolate *tastes* bitter.

These verbs are called **linking verbs**. They link the subject with some other word or words in the sentence.
The most common linking verbs are these:

be (am, are, is, was,	look	smell	seem
were, been, being)	appear	taste	sound
become	feel	grow	

Certain linking verbs can also be used as action verbs.

Linking Verb	Action Verb
The call *sounded* urgent.	Someone *sounded* the alarm.
My sister and I *look* alike.	Observers *look* through a telescope.

After you have found the verb in a sentence, see how it is used. Decide whether it expresses action or simply links the subject with a word in the predicate.

Transitive and Intransitive Verbs

In many sentences an action verb expresses an idea by itself. In other sentences a direct object completes the action of the verb. As you have learned, the direct object answers *whom* or *what* after the verb.
A verb that has a direct object is a **transitive verb**.

The FBI agent *opened* the *letter*.
(The direct object *letter* completes the meaning of the verb *opened*.)

WNTH *broadcasts* humorous *plays*.
(The direct object *plays* completes the meaning of the verb *broadcasts*.)

A verb that does not have a direct object is a different verb. It is an **intransitive verb**.

> The cars *collided*.
>> (The verb *collided* has no direct object.)
>
> My wallet *sank* into the mud.
>> (The verb *sank* has no direct object.)

Some action verbs are always transitive or always intransitive. Other verbs can be either. A single verb may be transitive in one sentence and intransitive in another. Compare these examples:

Transitive Verb	Intransitive Verb
I *noticed* your haircut.	No one *noticed*.
The band *ended* its concert.	The movie *ended* happily.
The horse *kicked* its trainer.	The baby *kicked* furiously.

Exercise A   Write the verb in each sentence. After each verb write *Action* or *Linking* to show what kind it is.

1. Molly removed the old paint.
2. A virus causes plantar warts.
3. The prairie dog village covered four acres.
4. Monday was my birthday.
5. He is sleepy.
6. The Cherokees became angry.
7. The water looked deep.
8. Joan looked in the closet.
9. Harvey tasted the sauce.
10. The sauce tasted too salty.

Exercise B   Follow the directions for Exercise A.

1. We watched the pressure gauge.
2. Water is expensive in southern California.
3. The sky grew dark.
4. Darrell grew herbs on the windowsill.
5. The radiators feel cold.

6. The nurse felt Jan's swollen wrist.
7. Did you see that Harley-Davidson?
8. Are you an officer?
9. Mitch sounded glum.
10. Debbie sounded the fire alarm.

Exercise C Write the action verb in each sentence. After it write *Transitive* or *Intransitive* to show what kind it is.

1. The plane lost an engine.
2. The brakes squealed.
3. A beached whale's weight can crush its lungs.
4. Something glittered at the bottom of the pool.
5. We played electronic football.
6. Scrub the pan with steel wool.
7. Don't worry about anything.
8. Has the snow stopped?
9. Did anyone help you?
10. Ted bought an ant farm for his niece.

Part 2 Parts of a Verb

Verbs often have more than one part. They may be made up of a **main verb** plus one or more **helping verbs**.

The most common helping verbs are forms of *be, have,* and *do*. They may also be used as main verbs. Notice their forms:

> be—am, is, are, was, were, been, be
> have—has, have, had
> do—does, do, did

Used as Main Verb	Used as Helping Verb
Sue *is* sorry.	Sue *is* talking on the phone.
Bill *has* many friends.	Bill *has* worked as a stuntman.
You *did* me a favor.	You *did* win the election.

These are other frequently used helping verbs:

can	will	shall	may	must
could	would	should	might	

Helping verbs combine with the main verb to become parts of the verb.

Helping Verb(s) + Main Verb = Verb

must	allow	must allow
should have	known	should have known
had	skated	had skated
will be	arriving	will be arriving

At times the parts of the verb are separated. The words that come between them are not part of the verb. For example:

> *Do* you *want* more syrup on your pancakes?
> Eric *has* just recently *begun* junior college.

Exercise A   Make two columns. Label them *Helping Verb* and *Main Verb*. Write the parts of the verbs in the proper columns.

1. The fish were biting.
2. The ice had melted.
3. Nan will draw a map.
4. I might make some vegetable soup.
5. Somebody should have told the shop steward.
6. Nobody could run that fast.
7. Cesar had not been listening to the radio.
8. That class has been cancelled.
9. Can you help me?
10. May I see that newspaper?

Exercise B   Follow the directions for Exercise A.

1. You should have used transistor batteries.
2. Martin has been telling us about his car.
3. I am teaching myself.
4. Wilma might have noticed something.

5. Their overalls were spattered with paint.
6. Did all the doctors agree?
7. Marilyn was whistling a happy tune.
8. Has the pork been cooked long enough?
9. When was the phone disconnected?
10. Would anyone else have agreed to such a plan?

Part 3 Tenses of a Verb

Verbs indicate time. They tell when an action or state of being occurs. By changing form, verbs can show past time, present time, or future time.

Changes in the form of verbs to show time are called **tenses**. Forms usually change in one of these ways:

1. Different spellings
   cry   cried   spin   spun   pull   pulled

2. Use of helping verbs
   will work   has talked   has dried

This list shows examples of the six main tenses for the verbs *dance* and *stop*.

Present Tense	I dance.	She stops.
Past Tense	I danced.	She stopped.
Future Tense	I will dance.	She will stop.
Present Perfect Tense	I have danced.	She has stopped.
Past Perfect Tense	I had danced.	She had stopped.
Future Perfect Tense	I will have danced.	She will have stopped.

Simple Tenses

The **present tense** shows time in the present. The form of the present tense is usually the same as the name of the verb. With singular subjects, add -*s* to the verb.

I *swim*.   Leslie *swims*.   My brother *swims*.

The **past tense** shows past time. To form the past tense of most verbs, add -*d* or -*ed*.

> She *worked*.   Bob *cooked*.   They *acted*.

A number of verbs form the past tense in unusual ways.

> Kevin *drove*.   The choir *sang*.   The room *shook*.

The **future tense** indicates time in the future. To form this tense, use *shall* or *will* with the verb.

> The players *will rest*.   Don *will know*.
> I *shall demand* an answer.

The three tenses described above are called the **simple tenses**.

Perfect Tenses

You use **perfect tenses** when you refer to two different times, one earlier than the other. The helping verbs *has*, *have*, and *had* are used to form the perfect tenses.

The **present perfect tense** tells of something occurring in some indefinite time before the present. The helping verb *has* or *have* is used in present perfect tense.

> Kim and Ann *have met*.   Bo *has placed* in the finals.
> The judge *has decided*.   We *have baked* muffins.

The **past perfect tense** tells of a time that occurred before another time in the past. The helping verb *had* is used.

> Megan *had guessed* our names even before she *met* us.
> Rod *had brought* the albums that Neil *played*.

The **future perfect tense** tells of some time in the future occurring *before* a different time in the future.

> By the time Sally is twenty, she *will have finished* nurse's training.
> The waves *will have worn* away this land before the sea wall can be built.

Exercise A Find the verbs. Tell the tense of each.

1. Ruth was the captain.
2. Steve plays hockey.
3. We buy our groceries there.
4. Every day there are 150,000 more people on earth.
5. Terry pitched the ball.
6. By then we will have graduated.
7. Lisa will adjust the stereo.
8. The band had already left.
9. She has accepted the nomination.
10. Dave had a good suggestion.

Exercise B Write a sentence for each of the verbs below.

1. gulp (past)
2. stroll (present)
3. salute (past)
4. watch (future)
5. close (past perfect)
6. dance (present perfect)
7. sing (present)
8. delay (future)
9. finish (future perfect)
10. talk (past perfect)

Part 4 Principal Parts of a Verb

The **principal parts** of a verb are its three basic forms. By combining these forms with various helping verbs, you can make all tenses. The principal parts of a verb are the **present tense**, the **past tense**, and the **past participle**. You will usually find them listed in that order.

The past tense and past participle of most verbs are formed by adding -*d* or -*ed* to the present form. These verbs are called **regular verbs**. They form their past tense and past participle in regular ways.

Present	Past	Past Participle
walk	walked	(have) walked
play	played	(have) played
move	moved	(have) moved

Certain regular verbs change their spelling when the *-d* or *-ed* is added. The following verbs are examples.

Present	Past	Past Participle
pay	paid	(have) paid
rip	ripped	(have) ripped
carry	carried	(have) carried
flip	flipped	(have) flipped

The past participle is used for perfect tenses. It must always be used with a helping verb.

The mourners *had cried*.   Dale *has lost* weight.
My jeans *have faded*.   The Cubs *have rallied*.

Exercise   Make three columns on your paper. Label them *Present*, *Past*, and *Past Participle*. List the principal parts of these verbs in the proper columns.

1. dress	6. type	11. invite
2. march	7. hurry	12. groan
3. crash	8. play	13. hope
4. start	9. greet	14. whisper
5. save	10. stamp	15. name

Part 5   Irregular Verbs

You have learned the principal parts for regular verbs. However, many verbs do not follow the regular pattern of adding *-d* or *-ed* to form the past tense and past participle. Such verbs are called **irregular verbs**. Here are some examples.

Present	Past	Past Participle
fall	fell	(have) fallen
make	made	(have) made
buy	bought	(have) bought
read	read	(have) read
go	went	(have) gone

As you can see, irregular verbs have one or more different forms.

Use a dictionary if you need to know the principal parts of a verb. If the dictionary doesn't list parts, then the verb is regular. For irregular verbs, the dictionary will list the irregular forms. It will give two forms if both the past and past participle are the same, as in *meet, met*, for instance. If all principal parts are different, it will give three forms, as with *take, took, taken*.

Using Irregular Verbs

You can be sure of the forms of an irregular verb in one of two ways. You can check the parts of a verb in the dictionary. Otherwise, you will have to learn the principal parts of commonly used irregular verbs.

Once you know the principal parts, use them correctly. Use the past participle with *have* and *be* helping verbs. The past participle is used for present perfect and past perfect tenses. The past form is not used with helping verbs.

Although irregular verbs may seem confusing, they may seem simpler when you study the following five patterns.

Group 1 Certain irregular verbs keep the same form for all three principal parts. Verbs like this are easy to remember.

Present	Past	Past Participle
burst	burst	(have) burst
cost	cost	(have) cost
cut	cut	(have) cut
let	let	(have) let
put	put	(have) put
set	set	(have) set

These sentences use irregular verbs from this group.

Every morning, we *let* the dog out. (present)
That new coat *cost* Gary half of his paycheck. (past)
The hypnotist *has put* Olivia to sleep. (past participle)

Group 2 Some irregular verbs change form only once. Both the past form and the past participle are the same.

Present	Past	Past Participle
bring	brought	(have) brought
catch	caught	(have) caught
lead	led	(have) led
lend	lent	(have) lent
lose	lost	(have) lost
say	said	(have) said
sit	sat	(have) sat

Here are some sentences using irregular verbs from Group 2.

The tests *say* the suspect is lying. (present)
On that play, Oakland *lost* control of the ball. (past)
An octopus *was caught* in the fishing nets. (past participle)

Exercise A Choose the correct form of the verb.

1. The dog (leaded, led) the blind woman across the street.
2. I have (putted, put) my winter coat away.
3. Gene has (sayed, said) enough.
4. The bride's family (sat, sitted) in the front pew.
5. We have not (losed, lost) the game yet.
6. The water main had (bursted, burst).
7. No charges have been (brought, brung).
8. She (letted, let) down the hem of the skirt.
9. Ms. Natti (lent, lended) us her tape recorder.
10. The overdue fines will have (cost, costed) more than the book.

Exercise B Follow the directions for Exercise A.

1. Jack (caught, catched) the express bus.
2. Karen (sayed, said) nothing.
3. The warm air (bringed, brought) rain.
4. The boss (letted, let) Sam leave early.
5. A pair of footprints (leaded, led) to the window.

6. A few items (costed, cost) more in the 1950's.
7. Harry (lended, lent) me his dictionary.
8. Gwen jumped and (catched, caught) the ball.
9. We (sitted, sat) on the floor.
10. The driver had (lost, losted) her way in the fog.

Group 3 Verbs in this group add *-n* or *-en* to the past tense to form the past participle.

Present	Past	Past Participle
break	broke	(have) broken
choose	chose	(have) chosen
freeze	froze	(have) frozen
speak	spoke	(have) spoken
steal	stole	(have) stolen
wear	wore	(have) worn

These three sentences have Group 3 verbs:

Many construction workers *wear* hardhats. (present)
Berger *stole* third base. (past)
Cass's fishing line *has broken*. (past participle)

Exercise A Choose the correct form of the verb from the two forms given.

1. The burglar (stole, stolen) the television.
2. The ushers (wore, worn) bow ties.
3. Tara has (chose, chosen) to stay home.
4. The skater didn't realize he had (broke, broken) his ankle.
5. Someone had (stole, stolen) the equipment.
6. Jesse Owens (spoke, spoken) to the students.
7. Pete has (wore, worn) that shirt to the last three games.
8. The ice cream has not yet (froze, frozen).
9. The caseworker had never (spoke, spoken) with her before.
10. The dancer had (wore, worn) out another pair of shoes.

Exercise B Follow the directions for Exercise A.

1. Frank (froze, frozen) some of the spaghetti.
2. One of the trappers (chose, chosen) to continue west.
3. The windows were (froze, frozen) shut.
4. The springs have (wore, worn) out.
5. Elliot (spoke, spoken) without looking up.
6. Someone had (stole, stolen) their savings.
7. The splinter had (broke, broken) as she was prying it out.
8. I have (spoke, spoken) my last words on the subject.
9. The stranger (stole, stolen) quietly away.
10. The smaller army should have (chose, chosen) to retreat.

Group 4 In this group, the verbs change their final vowels. The vowel changes from *i* in the present tense, to *a* in the past tense, and *u* in the past participle.

Present	Past	Past Participle
begin	began	(have) begun
drink	drank	(have) drunk
ring	rang	(have) rung
sing	sang	(have) sung

Here are examples of irregular verbs from Group 4.

> I *drink* coffee with breakfast. (present)
> Bette Midler *sang* her new hit. (past)
> The Passover service *has begun*. (past participle)

Exercise A Choose the correct verb form.

1. I (drank, drunk) fresh orange juice in Florida.
2. Marvin Gaye (sang, sung) an old song.
3. "I have just (began, begun) to fight."
4. The meter reader (rang, rung) the doorbell.
5. Gary (began, begun) to think about his future.
6. Ms. Ramirez has (swam, swum) in Salt Lake.
7. Summer has finally (began, begun).

8. The telephone has not (rang, rung) once all day.
9. The group has (sang, sung) in that club before.
10. Natalie (swam, swum) across the pool underwater.

Exercise B   Follow the directions for Exercise A.

1. Ernestine has (began, begun) basic training.
2. Who (sang, sung) "Coward of the County"?
3. The patient (began, begun) coughing.
4. The woods (rang, rung) with birds' songs.
5. Maria has (rang, rung) up another victory.
6. The dog (drank, drunk) the rain water.
7. A shark (swam, swum) close to the boat.
8. This medicine can be (drank, drunk) in juice.
9. The basketball game had (began, begun) at eight o'clock.
10. We have not (swam, swum) in the Potomac for years.

Group 5 Irregular verbs in this group form the past participle from the present tense. The past participle looks more like the present tense than the past tense.

Present	Past	Past Participle
come	came	(have) come
do	did	(have) done
eat	ate	(have) eaten
fall	fell	(have) fallen
give	gave	(have) given
go	went	(have) gone
grow	grew	(have) grown
know	knew	(have) known
ride	rode	(have) ridden
run	ran	(have) run
see	saw	(have) seen
take	took	(have) taken
throw	threw	(have) thrown
write	wrote	(have) written

These examples use Group 5 verbs:

The Coopers *run* a laundry. (present)

Darnell *grew* a full beard. (past)

The coach *has taken* Robin out of the game. (past participle)

Exercise A   Choose the correct verb form from the two given.

1. We (ran, run) for shelter.
2. Wendy (rode, ridden) part of the way.
3. The rescue party had almost (gave, given) up hope.
4. Ten inches of snow had (fell, fallen) overnight.
5. Have you ever (ate, eaten) homemade ravioli?
6. He had (grew, grown) tired of waiting.
7. Jay (wrote, written) the message on the telephone book.
8. We (ate, eaten) lunch standing up.
9. Eileen has (rode, ridden) the world's largest roller coaster.
10. Claire (knew, known) she was right.

Exercise B   Follow the directions for Exercise A.

1. The news had not (came, come) as a surprise.
2. The temperature had (fell, fallen) quickly.
3. Jody (threw, thrown) salt on the icy sidewalk.
4. I have already (took, taken) that course.
5. Chrissy (saw, seen) that Jason was upset.
6. Dion (did, done) his homework before work.
7. The truck had (went, gone).
8. The typists (gone, went) back to work.
9. The carpenter had (wrote, written) down the measurements.
10. The horse had never (ran, run) on a muddy track before.

Part 6 Active and Passive Verbs

You have seen how the tenses of verbs indicate time. There is another way that verbs help you say exactly what you mean.

Let's look at an example. Suppose there is a fire, and you know who controlled it. You can say:

> Forest rangers controlled the fire.

However, you might not know who controlled the fire. Then you would probably say:

> The fire was controlled.

The subject of the first sentence tells who performed the action. When a subject performs the action of the verb, the verb is said to be active.

In contrast, the subject of the second sentence tells what received the action. When the subject is the receiver or the result of the action, the verb is said to be passive. The word *passive* means "acted upon."

Forming the Passive

The passive form of a verb is made with the past participle. A form of *be* is the helping verb.

Active	Passive
Dr. Chang *put* Lee's arm in a cast.	Lee's arm *was put* in a cast by Dr. Chang.
Mike's boss *has promoted* him to assistant manager.	Mike *has been promoted* to assistant manager by his boss.
Terry and Margie *have saved* all receipts.	All receipts *have been saved* by Terry and Margie.

Notice what happens to the direct objects in the sentences in the *Active* column above. Those direct objects become the subjects of the sentences in the *Passive* column. Only verbs that have objects (transitive verbs) can be changed from active to passive.

A verb is active when its subject performs the action stated by the verb.

A verb is passive when its subject names the receiver or result of the action stated by the verb.

Exercise A   Write the verb in each sentence. After each, write *Active* or *Passive* to tell what kind it is.

1. Scuba divers use a form of sign language.
2. The referee started the count.
3. Gina made a storage shed under the porch.
4. The petition was signed by seventy people.
5. The privates saluted the officer.
6. War was declared by Congress.
7. Jamal added pepper sauce to the stew.
8. A silver trophy was presented to Tracey.
9. The decision was upheld by a higher court.
10. Take the flag down at sunset.

Exercise B   Change the verbs in the following sentences from passive to active. Rewrite the sentences.

1. The horn was played by Brian.
2. The explorers were led by Father Marquette.
3. The school's new name was chosen by the students.
4. The stock car was driven by Neal.
5. Some posters will be done by Anita.
6. The fat was trimmed off by the butcher.
7. All shop projects must be approved by Mr. Morales.
8. A tree was planted by the block club.
9. The telephone had been taken off the hook by someone.
10. Electrical power had been cut off by the storm.

REVIEW Using Verbs

Recognizing Verbs   Write the verb in each sentence.

1. Horror movies are artistic sometimes.
2. Mary will be the driver.
3. Simon is afraid of heights.
4. A computer prepares the bills.
5. Have you ever wired a lamp?
6. Dan sent her some roses for her birthday.
7. The miner could barely stand in the tunnel.
8. Willie may have already left for school.
9. Something must be bothering Maureen.
10. Val has been watching the clock all day.
11. Did Caroline buy a car?
12. Where have you worked before?
13. How does Hector find time for guitar lessons?
14. Her arm had been badly injured.
15. The license plates have been removed.

Irregular Verbs   Write the correct verb form from the two given.

16. Al has (wrote, written) new lyrics.
17. The hurricane (did, done) a lot of damage.
18. Herman might have (ran, run) into some problems.
19. Linda (sitted, sat) on the radiator.
20. The slush had (froze, frozen) on the sidewalks.
21. The reporter (catched, caught) the politician at a bad time.
22. Mice had (ate, eaten) through the wrapper.
23. Maybe Hank (spoke, spoken) too soon.
24. His sister has (gave, given) him good advice.
25. The car's upkeep has (costed, cost) Ann a lot.

Using Modifiers

Imagine trying to tell about your home or your job by using only nouns, pronouns, and verbs. Nouns and pronouns name. Verbs show action or state-of-being.

> We live in an apartment.   I am a typist.

You can see, however, that these words are not enough to express much information. You need to use other words that describe these names and actions.

> We have *always* lived in *this small, cozy* apartment.
> *Fortunately*, I am a *full-time* typist with a *flexible* schedule.

The differences in these two sets of examples result from the use of modifiers. Modifiers are words that modify, or change, other words.

Besides describing, modifiers can also help you explain and express feeling.

> I accept your invitation.
> I *gratefully* accept your *thoughtful* invitation.

If you didn't use modifiers, your writing would seem empty and dull. By using modifiers, you can express precise ideas. In this section you will learn to recognize and use the two kinds of modifiers.

Part 1   Using Adjectives

One kind of modifier is an **adjective**.

An adjective is a word that modifies a noun or pronoun.

Adjectives can tell three different kinds of things about nouns or pronouns.

Which one or ones?

this studio, *that* streetlight, *those* machines, *these* cars

What kind?

loud music, *soft* pillow, *sweet* drink, *cheerful* nurse

How many or how much?

four plants, *enough* food, *tremendous* joy, *few* fans

Proper Adjectives

One special kind of adjective is formed from a proper noun. It is a **proper adjective**.

Proper adjectives refer to specific persons, places, or things. They are always capitalized. These are some examples:

Swiss cheese	the Jewish religion
a Republican governor	French pastry

Predicate Adjectives

A second kind of adjective is the predicate adjective.
Most adjectives come before the words they modify.

Sweet, soft tunes filled the studio.
(*Sweet* and *soft* modify *tunes*.)

The predicate adjective, though, comes after the noun or pronoun it modifies. A **predicate adjective** follows a linking verb and modifies the subject of the sentence.

Your T-shirt is *unusual*.
(*Unusual* modifies the subject, *T-shirt*.)

Everything looks *strange*.
(*Strange* modifies the subject, *everything*.)

Unusual and *strange* are predicate adjectives. They follow linking verbs, *is* and *looked*. Each one modifies the subject of the sentence.

Articles

Three special adjectives, *a*, *an*, and *the*, are called **articles.**
The is called the **definite article**. It refers to a specific person, place, or thing.

The penalty went to the Vikings. (a particular penalty)

A and *an* are called **indefinite articles**.

Please find *a* chair. (any chair)
Pam wants *an* ice cube. (any ice cube)

Notice that *a* is used before a consonant sound (*a cart, a field, a smile*). *An* is used before a vowel sound (*an oval, an area, an edge*). The sound, not the spelling, is important. We say *a hurry* but *an honest bid*, for instance.

Diagraming Adjectives

In a sentence diagram, an adjective appears below the word it modifies. It is placed on a slanted line.

All new members have special cards.

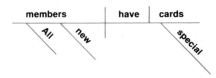

Predicate adjectives are diagramed in a different way. Like predicate nouns and pronouns, they are placed on the main line. Between the verb and the predicate adjective is a slanted line.

This melody sounds familiar.

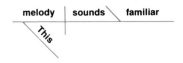

A compound predicate adjective is on a split line.

The chicken is tender and crispy.

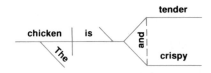

Exercise A Write each adjective. After each adjective, write the word it modifies. Ignore articles.

1. The new towel left green lint on everything.
2. The large goldfish was chasing the small one.
3. Fresh corn, ripe tomatoes, and shiny cucumbers filled the basket.
4. Jeff rubbed some ointment on the sprain.
5. Jaguars are British cars.
6. A former professional actress is coaching us.

7. Most people think of cornbread as a Southern food.
8. Is there an American style of cooking?
9. There are many definitions of modern art.
10. He had wide cheekbones and a square chin.

Exercise B   Write the predicate adjectives in these sentences.

1. Almond shells are soft.
2. White canaries are rare.
3. Marsha seems forgetful today.
4. His excuse sounded sincere to me.
5. That pronunciation of *New Orleans* sounds French.
6. Most of the refugees were hungry and sick.
7. Are you nervous?
8. Does the engine sound good to you?
9. The first half of the game was slow and dull.
10. Quite suddenly the sky became golden.

Part 2 Adjectives in Comparisons

Frequently, you learn about new things through comparisons. You compare something new with what you already know. You might describe a car as "*smaller* than most compacts." Or you might refer to the new mayor as *more powerful* than the former mayor. Adjectives help you to make such comparisons.

The Comparative

Adjectives have special forms for expressing comparisons. If you are comparing one person or thing with another, use the **comparative** form of an adjective. Here are some examples.

> This van is *smaller* than that one.
> Which is the *better* job?
> Recently, fuel has become much *more expensive*.

The comparative is made in two ways:

1. Add -er to short adjectives like *tall* and *sweet*:

heavy + er = heavier   wise + er = wiser
hot + er = hotter   tight + er = tighter

Notice that the spelling of some adjectives changes in the comparative form.

2. Use *more* for longer adjectives like *comfortable*:

more reasonable   more sensible

The comparative of most adjectives ending in *-ful* or *-ous* is formed with *more*.

more graceful   more ridiculous

The Superlative

If you are comparing a person or thing with all others in its class, use the **superlative** form of the adjective. Also, use the superlative for comparing a person or thing with two or more others. Here are some examples:

Samantha is the *most confident* person I know.
The cheetah is the *fastest* animal of all.
Of the three desserts, this pie is *highest* in calories.

Superlative forms of adjectives are made by adding either *-est* or by using *most*. Adjectives that add *-er* for the comparative add *-est* for the superlative. Adjectives that use *more* for the comparative use *most* for the superlative.

Adjective	Comparative	Superlative
wide	wider	widest
new	newer	newest
bitter	more bitter	most bitter
hopeful	more hopeful	most hopeful
realistic	more realistic	most realistic

Keep these three points in mind when you use comparison:

1. **To compare two people or things, use the comparative. To compare more than two, use the superlative.**

> The defense is *stronger* than the offense.
> Naomi told the *funniest* joke I've ever heard.

2. **Use the word *other* when you compare something with everything else of its kind.**

> Wrong: Adams is harsher than any judge.
>   (This sentence says that Adams is not a judge.)
> Right: Adams is harsher than any *other* judge.
> Wrong: This commercial is more clever than any one on TV.
> Right: This commercial is more clever than any *other* one on TV.

3. **Do not use *-er* with *more,* or *-est* with *most*.**

> Wrong: This is the most dullest game of the season.
> Right: This is the *dullest* game of the season.

Irregular Comparisons

Certain comparatives and superlatives are formed in unusual ways.

Adjective	Comparative	Superlative
good	better	best
well	better	best
bad	worse	worst
little	less or lesser	least
much	more	most
many	more	most
far	farther	farthest

Exercise A   If a sentence is correct, write *Correct*. If it is incorrect, write it correctly.

1. Althea is the more ambitious of the three students.

2. I bought the most warmest boots in the store.
3. Norma plays a gooder game than any other guard.
4. He can jump farrer than much taller contestants.
5. Her argument is more reasonabler than yours.
6. This winter is worse than last winter was.
7. That was the baddest disaster in aviation history.
8. Cliff made more home runs than any person on the team.
9. Dan seems more efficienter than any other orderly.
10. Ms. Sydris is the better educated of the two candidates.

Exercise B   Follow the directions for Exercise A.

1. Solar energy costs littler than most other kinds.
2. That plaid is more cheerfuller than the other.
3. Your cold seems worser today.
4. Ted was more accurater than any other typist.
5. Bottled water is much more expensiver than tap water.
6. Certainly copperheads are more dangerouser than black snakes.
7. That job offers more benefits but a smaller salary than the other.
8. The toboggan run is the bestest in New England.
9. The Bengal tiger had eight cubs, the most largest number ever born in captivity.
10. Chess is harder for me than any other game.

Part 3   Using Adverbs

Another kind of modifier is the adverb. With adverbs, you can express yourself clearly and vividly. Adverbs tell *how, when, where,* or *to what extent* about something.

Adverbs are words that modify verbs, adjectives, and other adverbs.

Using Adverbs with Verbs

Adverbs often modify verbs. Then they tell *how*, *when*, *where*, or *to what extent* something happened.

Adverbs tell *how* about verbs:

Sharon *confidently* faced the audience.

Al teetered *dangerously* on the rooftop.

Adverbs can tell *when* about verbs:

Dolores *finally* collapsed at the finish line.

Many employees have been fired *lately*.

Adverbs also tell *where* about verbs:

A rock concert will be held *here* next week.

Two birds flew *inside*.

Finally, adverbs can tell *to what extent*:

The blaze *almost* destroyed the nursing home.

Jose could *barely* speak.

Study the following list of adverbs:

How?	When?	Where?	To What Extent?
gloomily	soon	there	barely
terribly	then	behind	not
heroically	afterward	around	partly
slowly	recently	close	nearly

Using Adverbs with Adjectives and Other Adverbs

In addition to modifying verbs, adverbs also modify adjectives and other adverbs. Look at these sentences:

Business is *quite* brisk on weekends.

(*Quite* tells to what extent. It is an adverb modifying the adjective *brisk*.)

The trainer treated the animals *very* harshly.

(*Very* tells to what extent. It is an adverb modifying the adverb *harshly*.)

Certain adverbs often modify adjectives or other adverbs. Here are some examples.

too	rather	truly
extremely	so	more
fairly	most	just
nearly	really	somewhat

All these adverbs tell *to what extent* something is true.

Forming Adverbs

One way to form adverbs is to add *-ly* to adjectives.

serious + ly = seriously   usual + ly = usually
public + ly = publicly   direct + ly = directly

This addition of *-ly* sometimes results in a spelling change for the adjective.

simple + ly = simply   greedy + ly = greedily
full + ly = fully

A few adverbs are not formed from adjectives. Some examples are *just*, *too*, *so*, and *quite*.

That blues singer is *quite* good.
Matt put *too* much sauce on his sundae.

Some adverbs are also used as adjectives. Two examples of such words are *fast* and *low*.

The pit crews for the racecars moved *fast*.

(*Fast* is an adverb, modifying the verb *moved*.)

Mullins made a *fast* break for the end zone.
(*Fast* is an adjective, modifying the noun *break*.)

During her spin, the skater crouched *low* on the ice.
(*Low* is an adverb, modifying the verb *crouched*.)

Sara cleared the *low* hurdles easily.
(*Low* is an adjective, modifying the noun *hurdle*.)

Diagraming Adverbs

Like an adjective, an adverb is placed on a slanted line. That line is attached to the word the adverb modifies. This diagram shows an adverb that modifies a verb.

The health department routinely inspects restaurants.

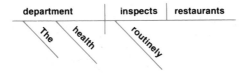

When adverbs modify adjectives or other adverbs, they are diagramed in this way:

Quite often Don wears very flashy clothes.

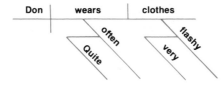

Exercise A Write the adverbs in these sentences. After each adverb write the word it modifies.

1. She speaks clearly now.
2. Donna climbed down carefully.
3. Suddenly the muffler fell off.
4. He works rather slowly.

5. The bus arrived very late.
6. The weather seems unusually cold today.
7. Hal smiled gently at his brother.
8. Finally the clerk looked up.
9. Strangers can be very kind sometimes.
10. The pressure rose too quickly.

Exercise B   Follow the directions for Exercise A.

1. The engine started rather slowly this morning.
2. These bills have not been paid yet.
3. The soldiers cheered happily.
4. Rarely has she insisted so firmly.
5. Sheldon always moves into the lead early.
6. Somewhere an alarm was whining shrilly.
7. Later Dwayne skated less cautiously.
8. Janet soon became more serious.
9. I do not know a less tactful person than Pat.
10. Recently the city balanced its budget.

Part 4   Adverbs in Comparisons

Adverbs help you to compare actions. You might say, for instance, "I wake up early, but Abby wakes up *earlier*." Or you might say, "Of all the horses, this one runs *fastest*." With comparisons like these, you can express ideas clearly. Adverbs, like adjectives, have special forms for making comparisons.

The Comparative

For comparing one action with another, use the **comparative** form of an adverb. This is an example:

This car rides *more smoothly* than that one.

Form the comparative in one of these two ways:
1. By adding *-er* to short adverbs like *hard* and *soon*.

WBBM has been broadcasting *longer* than WLAK.

2. By using *more* with most adverbs ending in *-ly*.

> Gil does business *more honestly* than other builders.

The Superlative

The **superlative** form of an adverb compares one action with two or more others. Here are some examples:

> Of the three contenders, that boxer hits *most powerfully*.
> The last dart came *closest* to the bull's-eye.

The superlative is formed either by adding *-est* or *most*. Adverbs that add *-er* for the comparative add *-est* for the superlative. Adverbs that use *more* for the comparative use *most* for the superlative.

Adverb	Comparative	Superlative
early	earlier	earliest
high	higher	highest
carefully	more carefully	most carefully

Remember these points about adverbs in comparisons:

1. To compare two actions, use the comparative. To compare more than two actions, use the superlative.

> Computers solve problems *more quickly* than people do.
> Of all the snacks, the Fritos disappeared *most quickly*.

2. Use the word *other* when you compare with every other action of the same kind.

> Wrong: "Mean Max" plays more roughly than any football player.
> Right: "Mean Max" plays more roughly than any *other* football player.

3. Do not use *-er* with *more*, or *-est* with *most*.

> Wrong: With a sledge hammer, you could hit more harder.
> Right: With a sledge hammer, you could hit harder.

Irregular Comparisons

From the comparative to the superlative form, some adverbs change completely. Here are a few examples:

Adverb	Comparative	Superlative
well	better	best
much	more	most
little	less	least
far	farther	farthest

The old Camero runs *well*.
The new Firebird runs *better*.
The Celica runs *best* on the open road.

Exercise A Write the comparative and superlative forms.

1. late
2. wildly
3. often
4. frequently
5. near
6. gladly
7. sharply
8. bravely
9. briefly
10. low

Exercise B If a sentence is correct, write *Correct*. If there is an error in the comparison of adverbs, write the sentence correctly.

1. The red Frisbee soared more farther than the green one.
2. Sal will play her part less awkwardly after a few rehearsals.
3. Computerized laser beams cut fabric efficientlier than machines do.
4. Handle the thermometer more carefullier.
5. A hammer works more simply than almost any tool.
6. Jackson draws the most skillfully of the two cartoonists.
7. Of the three drummers, Lynn plays more imaginatively.
8. That turntable works the bestest of the four.
9. Few machines run more smoothlier than this one.
10. Maybe the crew will work more better after lunch.

Part 5   Adjective or Adverb?

When you read these sentences, which one sounds right?

>The outlaws fought *desperate*.
>The outlaws fought *desperately*.

You are correct if you said the second sentence. To modify the verb *fought*, an adverb (*desperately*), not an adjective (*desperate*), is needed.

At times you may be confused about whether to use an adjective or an adverb. To decide, ask yourself:

1. What kind of word does the modifier tell about?

   If your answer is an action verb, adjective, or adverb, use the adverb.

   If your answer is a noun or pronoun, use the adjective.

2. What does the modifier say about the word it goes with?

   If it tells *how, when, where,* or *to what extent,* use the adverb.

   If it tells *which one, what kind,* or *how many,* use the adjective.

An adjective tells	An adverb tells
*Which one *What kind *How many	*How *When *Where *To what extent
About a noun or pronoun	About a verb, adjective, or adverb

Exercise A   List each adjective and adverb, together with the word each modifies. Do not list articles.

1. One acrobat leapt effortlessly into the air.

2. She shoveled the soft snow easily.
3. Finally the long, dreary play ended.
4. Suddenly the red light went on.
5. Clumsy bulldozers lumbered past.
6. Many guests had dressed formally.
7. That bread is more nutritious than these rolls.
8. Several pushy starlings drove the hungry sparrow away.
9. Tonight my best friend will get here.
10. The immediate future seems somewhat unpredictable.

Exercise B Choose the correct modifier from the two in parentheses. Tell whether it is an adjective or an adverb.

1. The fans went (wild, wildly) when the score became tied.
2. The patient seems (alert, alertly).
3. Mel stirred the gravy (careful, carefully).
4. His reply was (tactful, tactfully).
5. I am (dreadful, dreadfully) sorry.
6. Regina acted (real, really) glad to see us.
7. The day had begun (peaceful, peacefully).
8. Matt can be (awful, awfully) sensitive.
9. The omelet tasted (awful, awfully).
10. Katie finished the work (quick, quickly).

Adverb or Predicate Adjective?

As you have learned, a predicate adjective is used with a linking verb, and it modifies the subject. Besides forms of *be*, other linking verbs are *become, seem, appear, look, sound, feel, taste, smell,* and *grow*.

The rescue *looked* easy.

That rumor *sounds* unbelievable.

Jamie *feels* sick.

The verbs used above, *looked*, *sounds*, and *feels*, can also be action verbs. So can *grow*, *appear*, *smell*, and *taste*. As action verbs, these verbs are used with adverbs instead of predicate adjectives. Adverbs tell *how*, *when*, *where*, or *to what extent* about action verbs.

These sentences use the same words both as linking verbs and as action verbs:

Linking Verbs with Adjectives	Action Verbs with Adverbs
The team *appeared* confident.	The submarine *appeared* suddenly.
The night *grew* cold.	My plants *grew* fast.
The granola *tasted* sweet.	Donna *tasted* the taco cautiously.

To determine whether to use an adverb or an adjective in a certain sentence, ask these questions:

1. Can you substitute *is* or *was* for the verb? If so, the modifier is probably an adjective.

2. Does the modifier tell *how*, *when*, *where*, or *to what extent*? If so, the modifier is probably an adverb.

Exercise Choose the right modifier for the following.

1. Water dripped (slow, slowly) from the ceiling.
2. Harriet looked (suspicious, suspiciously) at us.
3. Harriet looked (suspicious, suspiciously) to us.
4. Dracula laughed (soft, softly).
5. The rug felt (soft, softly) and thick.
6. Weeds can grow very (quick, quickly).
7. The defendant grew (nervous, nervously) during the delay.
8. Tina felt (careful, carefully) around the floor for her needle.
9. Rita appears careful and (competent, competently).
10. Patches of fog (sudden, suddenly) appeared.

Part 6   Troublesome Modifiers

The modifiers that follow are often confused or used incorrectly.

Them and Those

Those can be used correctly as an adjective.

Did the FBI trace *those* fingerprints?

Them is never an adjective. It cannot substitute for *those*.

Wrong: Put putty in them cracks.
Right: Put putty in *those* cracks.
Right: Put putty in *them*.

Here and There

You may hear incorrect phrases like "this here room" or "that there part." "This here" and "that there" repeat ideas unnecessarily. The meaning of *this* includes the idea of *here*. The meaning of *that* includes the idea of *there*. Avoid "this here" and "that there."

Kind and Sort

Kind and *sort* are singular. *Kinds* and *sorts* are plural. No matter what words follow, use *this* or *that* with *kind* and *sort*. Use *these* and *those* with *kinds* and *sorts*.

This kind of truck has four axles. (singular)
Those sorts of batteries don't last long. (plural)

Good and Well

Good and *well* have similar meanings, but the words are not the same. You cannot always substitute one word for the other.

Look at the differences in these sentences:

This is a *good* magazine. (The adjective *good* modifies the noun *magazine*.)

Jesse types *well*. (The adverb *well* modifies the verb *types*.)

Good is always an adjective. It describes people, places, and things. It never tells about actions.

Well can be either an adjective or an adverb. In the sentence above, *well* is used as an adverb modifying an action verb. *Well* can also be used after a linking verb to mean "in good health."

Since Monday, my brother hasn't been *well*.
(*Well* is a predicate adjective modifying *brother*.)

That tape deck works *well*.
(*Well* is an adverb modifying the action verb *works*.)

To tell about an action, use *well*.

The Double Negative

Two negative words used together when only one is necessary is called a double negative. Avoid using double negatives.

Wrong: Lopez didn't make no free throws.
Right: Lopez did*n't* make *any* free throws.

Wrong: Shawn never throws nothing away.
Right: Shawn *never* throws *anything* away.

Wrong: I don't like none of those pictures.
Right: I do*n't* like *any* of those pictures.

Not is a negative word. Its shortened form (*n't*) is part of contractions like *hasn't* and *didn't*. Do not use other negative words after such contractions.

Common negative words include *no, none, not, nothing,* and *never.* Instead of such words, use *any, anything,* or *ever* after a negative contraction.

Gail has*n't ever* outscored that center.
The summit meeting did*n't* resolve *anything*.
Some storekeepers wo*n't* accept *any* credit.

Other negative words are *scarcely*, *barely*, and *hardly*. Avoid using them with negative contractions.

Wrong: I couldn't barely stay awake for the late show.
Right: I could *barely* stay awake for the late show.

Wrong: The new laws aren't scarcely enforced.
Right: The new laws are *scarcely* enforced.

Exercise A   Choose the correct word from the two given.

1. The movie was one of (them, those) documentaries.
2. (This, This here) perfume is made from gardenias.
3. (Them, Those) vitamins cost more than food.
4. (This, These) kind of paperback does not fall apart.
5. You may use (that, that there) phone.
6. The candidate felt (good, well) about her chances.
7. Cheese and mustard taste (good, well) together.
8. Diane checked the engine (good, well).
9. The job was going (good, well).
10. Turkey reheats (good, well).

Exercise B   Correct the double negatives in the following sentences. If a sentence contains no double negative, write *Correct*.

1. The band didn't know no old songs.
2. Please don't serve me none of that pie.
3. The supervisor hasn't said nothing about overtime.
4. I hadn't barely touched the accelerator.
5. Nobody hasn't seen Aaron lately.
6. That drill press didn't never work properly.
7. The tornado siren hadn't scarcely started wailing.
8. I didn't hardly recognize anybody at first.
9. The pawnbroker gives nothing to nobody.
10. Carol wouldn't ever tell anybody a lie.

REVIEW Using Modifiers

Recognizing Adjectives Write each adjective in these sentences. Tell which word it modifies. Do not include articles.

1. Natural fabrics require more care than artificial ones.
2. She made the necklace from bright wooden beads.
3. I listened to the Spanish station.
4. Several local stores sell Chinese vegetables.
5. Those three old men sit on that bench every day.
6. Have you seen a small calico cat, by any chance?
7. He almost tripped on the torn linoleum.
8. Perry always wears a black beret.
9. The new tenants work odd hours.
10. Gentle voices and calm hands soothed the hysterical patient.

Predicate Adjectives Write the predicate adjective.

11. Hal is often very witty.
12. Lately Ron has been less talkative.
13. Solar eclipses are not at all mysterious.
14. New ideas are always welcome here.
15. Real vanilla suddenly became very expensive.

Adjectives in Comparison Choose the correct adjective.

16. This summer is (more hot, hotter) than last summer was.
17. Of my four interviews, the one at Sears went (better, best).
18. Hong Kong flu is (worse, worst) than a cold.
19. Clyde is the (most valuable, valuablest) player.
20. A picture can be (more powerful, powerfuller) than a speech.

Recognizing Adverbs   Write the adverbs and the words they modify.

> Example: Put the package down.
>   *down* modifies *put*

21. Mattie is not an aide.
22. The power often goes out.
23. Two of the guests left very early.
24. Can anybody drive too cautiously?
25. Somewhere nearby there is a Burger Chef's.
26. Big white snowflakes floated lazily down.
27. Sometimes he behaves strangely.
28. No situation comedy is ever too dull for him.
29. Nat never saw them again.
30. The day was unusually warm for April.

Choosing the Right Modifier   Write the correct modifier.

31. Move (closer, more close) to the front of the room.
32. The rebels fought (more fiercely, fiercelier) than the invaders.
33. Harry sings even (worse, worst) than Fred.
34. That was the (baddest, worsest, worst) blizzard in our history.
35. Of my two aunts, Pam writes to me (more often, most often).
36. Everybody was playing (good, well) by the end of the game.
37. The coffee tasted (good, well).
38. Eileen read the contract (careful, carefully).
39. He didn't look (attractive, attractively) in (any, no) style.
40. (This, These) kind of cartridge works (good, well).

Using Prepositions and Conjunctions

Short sentences like these can sometimes express what you mean.

> Tim called.
> The spy escaped.

Frequently, though, you will want to provide more information. Modifiers are useful for that purpose.

> Tim called early.
> The foreign spy escaped.

There are other ways to add information. Maybe you want to say when Tim called. Maybe you want to add that the spy was never seen again. You will need different kinds of words to connect these ideas to your sentences.

> Tim called early *in* the morning.
> The foreign spy escaped *and* was never seen again.

Relationships dealing with people, actions, and things are expressed by words that connect other words. In this section you will learn about the two kinds of connecting words: **prepositions** and **conjunctions**.

Part 1 What Are Prepositions?

To join words or word groups, **connectives** are used. One important kind of connective is the **preposition**. Prepositions show relationships. Notice the different relationships in the following sentences:

> The road runs *over the mountain*.
> The road runs *through the mountain*.
> The road runs *around the mountain*.

The prepositions *over*, *through*, and *around* show relationship between *mountain* and the verb *runs*. *Mountain* is the object of the preposition in all of the above sentences. Like all prepositions, *over*, *through*, and *around* connect their objects to another part of the sentence.

However, prepositions do not show relationships all by themselves. Each preposition begins a *phrase*, a group of words without a subject or verb. As a whole, the **prepositional phrase** makes the relationship clear. The prepositional phrases in the above sentences are *over the mountain*, *through the mountain*, and *around the mountain*. The following sentences, too, have prepositional phrases:

> The crowds were entertained *by a band*.
> Nick poured two cups *of coffee*.
> The driver hopped *into the rig*.

A preposition is a word used with a noun or pronoun, called its *object*, to show the relationship between the noun or pronoun and some other word in the sentence.

A prepositional phrase consists of a preposition, its object, and any modifiers of the object.

372

Words in the list below are often used as prepositions. Quite a few, like *toward*, *below*, *near*, and *at*, help to show location. Others like *during*, *since*, and *before*, show a relationship of time. Some show other types of relationships. Study these prepositions and consider the relationship each one suggests.

Words Often Used as Prepositions

about	behind	during	off	to
above	below	except	on	toward
across	beneath	for	onto	under
after	beside	from	out	until
against	between	in	outside	up
along	beyond	inside	over	upon
among	but (*except*)	into	past	with
around	by	like	since	within
at	concerning	near	through	without
before	down	of	throughout	

Exercise A   Find the prepositional phrases in these sentences.

1. Several squad cars raced to the scene.
2. I propped a chair against the door.
3. Something was under the rug.
4. Geneva already looks like a success.
5. The neighbors had a meeting concerning the vandalism.
6. The smell of garlic spread throughout the house.
7. After the movie we looked for a restaurant.
8. Ryan is, without a doubt, the best choice for captain.
9. Under attack from the press, the city manager resigned.
10. A group of volunteers organized the telethon.

Exercise B   Follow the directions for Exercise A.

1. I felt nothing but sympathy for them.
2. Keith drives a truck for Meyer's Bakery.

3. During the trial, cameras were barred from the court.
4. On the way to the station, we had a flat tire.
5. The quarterback walked toward the bench without a word.
6. The tar stuck to the soles of my shoes.
7. On Monday, Meg goes to her first job interview.
8. Over the bleachers and into the street soared the ball.
9. By the way, Jeff is outside the door.
10. Nothing like that had ever happened in the city.

Preposition or Adverb?

Many words used as prepositions may also be used as adverbs. How can you tell when a word is an adverb and when it is a preposition?

A preposition is never used alone. It is always followed by a noun or pronoun as part of a phrase. Therefore, if the word is in a phrase, it is probably a preposition. However, if the word has no object, it is probably an adverb.

> Camilla's little sister always tags *along*. (adverb)
> The circus performer walked *along the ledge*. (preposition)
>
> A group of reporters waited *outside*. (adverb)
> A limousine stopped *outside my door*. (preposition)

Exercise A Write *Adverb* or *Preposition* for each sentence to indicate how the italicized word is used.

1. The burglar climbed *up* this pole.
2. Put the bleach *up* out of reach.
3. The puck slipped *past* the goalie into the net.
4. Rick shook the beach bag *out*.
5. The ball was clearly *outside* the line.
6. The ball was *out*.
7. Keep the dog *outside*.
8. Who left the book *outside* in the rain?
9. Watch *out* for the potholes.
10. Angela pressed a button *inside* the drawer.

1. Chris was *in* a happy mood.
2. On Friday the dentist will not be *in*.
3. Push the tile back *into* place.
4. The match was *over*, and she had won.
5. Guards patrol *along* the border.
6. Lena sent a card at Christmas but hasn't written *since*.
7. His foot went right *through* the floor.
8. Goldie was *through* with the job.
9. A tow truck drove *by*, but it didn't stop.
10. Can you back *up*?

Part 2 Prepositional Phrases as Modifiers

Modifiers are frequently single words. Groups of words, however, may also be modifiers. Prepositional phrases modify various sentence parts. These phrases modify words the same way that adjectives or adverbs do.

An adjective phrase is a prepositional phrase that modifies a noun or pronoun.

Hollywood is the home *of many stars*.
    (*Of many stars* is an adjective phrase, modifying the noun *home*. It tells *what kind* of home.)

The coach is the woman *on the sidelines*.
    (*On the sidelines* is an adjective phrase, modifying the noun *woman*. It tells *which one*.)

Many *of the parachutists* do free falls.
    (*Of the parachutists* is an adjective phrase, modifying the pronoun *many*. It tells *what kind*.)

The above sentences show that adjective phrases tell *which one* or *what kind* just as adjectives do.

Adverbs tell *how, when, where,* and *to what extent* about verbs. Adverb phrases modify verbs in the same way.

Adverb phrases are prepositional phrases that modify verbs.

The Olympics were held *at Lake Placid*.
> (*At Lake Placid* is an adverb phrase that tells *where*. It modifies the verb *were held*.)

During the winter the factory closes.
> (*During the winter* is an adverb phrase that tells *when*. It modifies the verb *closes*.)

The figure skater moved *with graceful polish*.
> (*With graceful polish* is an adverb phrase. It tells *how* about the verb *moved*.)

At times, one prepositional phrase may follow another. The second phrase is often an adjective phrase that modifies the object in the first phrase.

Kenneth sat on a stack of newspapers.
> (*On a stack* is an adverb phrase. It tells *where* about the verb *sat*. *Of newspapers* is an adjective phrase modifying the noun *stack*.)

Half of the people in America watch the Super Bowl.
> (The adjective phrase *of the people* tells *what kind* about the noun *half*. *In America* is an adjective phrase describing the noun *people*.)

Diagraming Prepositional Phrases

To diagram a prepositional phrase, place it under the word it modifies.

Wild horses run free in the canyon.

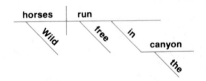

A preposition with two or more nouns or pronouns as objects in the prepositional phrase is diagramed this way:

At the zoo, we sketched pictures of the lions and the leopards.

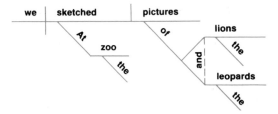

Exercise A Copy these sentences. Circle each prepositional phrase. Draw an arrow from the phrase to the word it modifies. Tell whether the phrase is an adjective or an adverb phrase.

1. Walt scored fourteen points in twenty minutes.
2. The carpenter slipped off the ladder.
3. The Mardi Gras parade goes along Canal Street.
4. Ms. Reyes solved the problem about our claim.
5. The tape pulled a patch of paint from the wall.
6. Many of the viewers responded to the poll.
7. The information in the ad was incorrect.
8. In summer we eat dinner on the porch.
9. The bank served coffee to the customers in line.
10. The paper with no title belongs to me.

Exercise B Follow the directions for Exercise A.

1. During the bus ride I talked with my seat mate.
2. The dime slipped between the slats of the boardwalk.
3. Gold and silver jewelry rose sharply in price.
4. Two of the candidates withdrew after the first primary.
5. Few of the landlords live on the premises.
6. The watchdog slept under the counter.
7. People in street shoes are not allowed in the gym.
8. At the party Ed danced only with Dawn.
9. The country of Burma isolates itself from the West.
10. Nobody but Sue could think of a plan like that.

Part 3   What Are Conjunctions?

A second kind of word that shows relationships is the conjunction. A conjunction is a word that connects words or groups of words.

Notice how conjunctions are used in the following sentences:

> The transmission *or* the brakes need repair.
>> (connects nouns)
>
> The FDA tests drugs *and* cosmetics.
>> (connects nouns)
>
> The clown winked *and* smiled at us.
>> (connects verbs)
>
> Proudly *and* happily, Sue looked at her family.
>> (connects adverbs)
>
> We bike in summer *and* during the fall.
>> (connects prepositional phrases)

Conjunctions, like prepositions, show a relationship between the words they connect. However, in contrast to prepositions, conjunctions link similar kinds of words. These might be two nouns or two phrases, for example. Another difference is that conjunctions do not have objects.

Coordinating Conjunctions

A **coordinating conjunction** joins single words or groups of words of the same kind. The most common coordinating conjunctions are *and*, *but*, and *or*.

Words joined by coordinating conjunctions are called compound constructions. Examples of compound constructions include compound subjects, compound direct objects, and compound verbs.

> William *and* Lena work on an assembly line.
>> (*And* links *William* and *Lena*, making them a compound subject of the verb *work*.)

The glasses fell *and* shattered.
   (*And* connects *fell* and *shattered*, forming a compound verb.)

Dana lost weight *but* gained it back.
   (*But* connects the two predicates.)

San Francisco is hilly *and* scenic.
   (*And* connects two predicate adjectives.)

The couple argued quietly *but* openly.
   (*But* connects two adverbs.)

A hurricane hit Cuba, Florida, *and* the East Coast.
   (*And* connects the three parts of the compound direct object.)

Congress gave the FBI *and* CIA new powers.
   (*And* connects the compound indirect object.)

Carolyn greets everyone with a joke *or* a kind word.
   (*Or* connects compound objects of a preposition.)

Correlative Conjunctions

Conjunctions that are used in pairs are called **correlative conjunctions**. These are some correlative conjunctions:

both . . . and	not only . . . but (also)
either . . . or	whether . . . or
neither . . . nor	

Ella sings *both* blues *and* jazz.
Good discipline is *not only* firm *but also* fair.
Each card player must *either* bid *or* pass.
Neither money *nor* power insures happiness.
We discussed *whether* to leave *or* to stay.

Exercise A   Find the conjunctions in the following sentences. Tell what words or word groups are connected by the conjunctions.

1. Ms. Doyle bought and installed a new sink.
2. Snow and colder weather are predicted.
3. The photograph was too old and fuzzy to use.

4. Jason spoke shyly but clearly to the recruiter.
5. Either a check or a credit card will do.
6. I asked whether Nick or Betsy had called.
7. Both the soup and the crackers are homemade.
8. That gossip is not only untrue but also unkind.
9. He neither knew nor cared.
10. Julie finally arrived but stayed only a few minutes.

Exercise B Write the kind of compound construction in each sentence. Write the construction with its conjunction.

1. Karen teaches both judo and karate.
2. The headlights and the radio are working.
3. Is the holiday "President's Day" or "Washington's Birthday"?
4. Either Ms. Glass or Mr. Santo interviews applicants.
5. The boots are neither warm nor waterproof.
6. He has raced not only at Daytona but also at Indianapolis.
7. There are naval bases at both San Diego and Waukegan.
8. Did Amy or Mandy win?
9. He is underweight but healthy.
10. She pivoted and tossed the ball.

REVIEW Using Prepositions and Conjunctions

Recognizing Prepositional Phrases Write the prepositional phrase or phrases in each sentence.

1. Everyone but Jerry rode the ferris wheel.
2. The old path was slippery with moss.
3. Needles from the tree showed up for months after Christmas.
4. Remove the stuffing from the turkey immediately.
5. The lake looked like glass under the fierce sun.
6. Fred sat and dozed all night in the bus station.
7. Without a worry in the world, she set off for California.
8. Isaac drove out beyond the city limits.
9. Most of the pitchers and catchers have started spring training.
10. For six months he dieted and exercised.

Prepositional Phrases as Modifiers Write the prepositional phrase in each sentence. Label each phrase *Adjective* or *Adverb* to tell how it is used.

11. The alley was littered with garbage after the thaw.
12. I have a message for you from Yvonne.
13. She fastened the belt of her raincoat.
14. During the game Willie became ill.
15. The alarm went off at seven o'clock.
16. We pushed through the defense without much difficulty.
17. Efren will be stationed at Fort Bragg for two more months.
18. The car with the hood ornament belongs to me.
19. The drug store on the corner is open until nine.
20. The woman by the window is from Chile.

Conjunctions For each sentence, write the compound construction with its conjunction.

21. Her eyeshadow was a blend of green and blue.
22. The sea snake is not only fast but also deadly.
23. The rainbow faded but reappeared.
24. That number reaches both the police and the fire department.
25. You can use either oil or butter.
26. He neither fouled nor scored during the game.
27. Wayne scrubbed not only the burners but also the oven.
28. We will send a basket of flowers or fruit.
29. Mosquitoes and sandflies made the beach unpleasant.
30. Joyce will take the shuttle bus or a taxi.

Review of Parts of Speech

Part 1   The Parts of Speech

You have studied nouns, pronouns, verbs, adjectives, adverbs, prepositions, and conjunctions. All of these classes of words are called **parts of speech**. A word may be a particular part of speech because of the way it is used in a sentence.

Altogether, there are eight parts of speech. In addition to the seven groups listed above, there is another part of speech. It is called the interjection.

What Is an Interjection?

An interjection is a word or group of words used to express strong feeling.

An interjection may be either a phrase or a single word that shows strong feeling. Those feelings might be either fear, horror, happiness, sorrow, or surprise, for example. Interjections are followed by exclamation points.

Look at the following interjections:

Ouch! That hurts.
Aha! I've found the solution.
Oh, no! We lost the ball.

You have now studied all eight parts of speech:

The Parts of Speech			
nouns	**verbs**	**adverbs**	**conjunctions**
pronouns	**adjectives**	**prepositions**	**interjections**

Exercise A   Write what part of speech each italicized word is.

1. The *noise* came from upstairs.
2. Mack certainly *needs* a vacation.
3. *Terrific!* There's an empty seat.
4. The conductor *checked* the doors.
5. Donna stretched the canvas *herself*.
6. The television is still not working *well*.
7. The truck was stuck *under* a viaduct.
8. Lamar keeps a first-aid kit *and* a lantern in the car.
9. You made a *wrong* move.
10. *Several* of the apartments are vacant.

Exercise B   Follow the directions for Exercise A.

1. *Uh, oh!* This ice cream bar is melting.
2. The drain is backing up *again*.
3. The country of *Thailand* was once called *Siam*.
4. Priscilla bought a *Japanese* motorcycle.
5. *You* are carrying the pizza box upside down.
6. Who *wishes* upon stars?
7. Simon looks *good* in that hat.

8. I have *never* been to a parade.
9. He always stretches his legs out *into* the aisle.
10. I will replace *or* pay for the damaged album.

Part 2 Using Words as Different Parts of Speech

One word can often be used as more than one part of speech. For example, the same word might be a verb in one sentence and a noun in another.

There is only one way to tell what part of speech any word is. You must know how that word is used in a sentence.

These sentences show examples of one word used as two different parts of speech:

The director *cast* Redford in the starring role. (*Cast* is used as a verb.)

Amid applause, the *cast* bowed. (*Cast* is used as a noun, the subject of the verb *bowed*.)

Susan and Lars *work* as zookeepers. (*Work* is used as a verb.)

Soon the *work* week may shrink to four days. (*Work* is used as an adjective, modifying *week*.)

The old woman travels *alone*. (*Alone* is used as an adverb, modifying the verb *travels*.)

For days, Bert was *alone* in the cave. (*Alone* is used as a predicate adjective.)

Park in the lot, please. (*Park* is used as a verb.)

A horse-drawn carriage circled the *park*. (*Park* is used as a noun, the direct object of the verb, *circled*.)

Every day we eat lunch on the *park* bench. (*Park* is used as an adjective, modifying the noun, *bench*.)

Greg turned *around* and went home. (*Around* is used as an adverb, modifying the verb *turned*.)

Put salt *around* the edge of the glass. (*Around* is used as a preposition.)

Great! I was hoping for this. (*Great* is used as an interjection.)
Einstein was a *great* scientist. (*Great* is used as an adjective, modifying the noun *scientist*.)

Exercise A   Write what part of speech each italicized word is.

1. We pay several kinds of *taxes*.
2. Sweden *taxes* its citizens heavily.
3. *Skid* marks can be used as evidence.
4. Light bikes *skid* easily.
5. *No!* Don't throw the instructions away.
6. *No* information was available.
7. Janet lunged toward the *finish* line.
8. *Finish* your story.
9. Pat applied a light *finish* to the wood.
10. I did not have the exact *change*.

Exercise B   Follow the directions for Exercise A.

1. Many people *shop* on Saturdays.
2. The Beckers own a shoe-repair *shop*.
3. From his window he watches the world go *past*.
4. As we rode along, I watched the scenery slip *past* us.
5. The *past* week has been very busy.
6. Randy lives in the *past*.
7. Maria checked the car for *rust* spots.
8. This metal *rusts* easily.
9. *That* joke was not funny.
10. Did she really say *that*?

REVIEW Review of Parts of Speech

Identifying Parts of Speech Read each sentence. Then copy the italicized word. Write what part of speech the word is in that sentence.

1. *Certainly*! Help yourself.
2. Morrison is *my* favorite novelist.
3. *That* color is called magenta.
4. The *morning* stars glittered above the treetops.
5. Mothballs hung among the *wool* clothes.
6. Gerry *bags* groceries on weekends.
7. *Leave* your boots in the hall.
8. *Overnight*, the leaves turned gold.
9. Oil *spills* kill sea creatures.
10. Gene's clock has no *alarm*.
11. The laundromat is a *very* sociable place.
12. Dreams are *different* from daydreams.
13. Several countries have red, white, *and* blue flags.
14. Penny arrived *early* for practice.
15. Suddenly, the shade flew *up*.
16. A deep wrinkle appeared *between* her eyes.
17. N*either* of these sweaters is in style.
18. Do *not* throw water on a grease fire.
19. I had never seen anything *like* it.
20. *This* is a good time for a break.
21. Can you fix *this* electronic game?
22. Delicious *smells* drifted from the bakery.
23. The bacon *smells* good.
24. This is Nelson's *last* season.
25. Some styles *last* for a long time.

Using Verbals

In previous sections you have learned about the eight parts of speech:

nouns	verbs	adverbs	conjunctions
pronouns	adjectives	prepositions	interjections

In addition to the parts of speech, our language also contains three other kinds of words. They are **gerunds, participles**, and **infinitives.** All three look like verbs. Therefore, they are called **verbals**. A verbal is a word that is formed from a verb but is never used as a verb. In this section you will become familiar with the three kinds of verbals.

Part 1 Using Gerunds

A gerund is a verb form that is used as a noun. Gerunds end in *-ing*. They may be used in all the ways that nouns are used. Like a noun, a gerund may be used as a subject.

> *Smoking* is hazardous to your health.
> (*Smoking* is a gerund, the subject of the verb *is*.)

Like a noun, a gerund may be used as a direct object.

Some states allow *gambling*.
(*Gambling* is a gerund, the object of the verb *allow*.)

Like a noun, a gerund may be used as an object of a preposition.

Noah lost twenty pounds by *exercising*.
(*Exercising* is a gerund, the object of the preposition *by*.)

Gerund Phrases

In many sentences, the gerund is not used alone. Often a gerund has a modifier or an object or both. Together, they form a **gerund phrase**. The whole gerund phrase is used like a noun.

Because a gerund is formed from a verb, it can have an object.

Winning Olympic medals was Heiden's goal.
(*Winning* is a gerund; *medals* is the object of *winning*. The phrase *winning Olympic medals* is the subject of the verb *was*.)

Because a gerund is formed from a verb, it can be modified by adverbs.

The troops began *turning back*.
(*Turning* is a gerund; *back* is an adverb modifying *turning*. The phrase *turning back* is the object of the verb *began*.)

Because a gerund is used as a noun, it can be modified by adjectives.

That comedian has *good timing*.
(*Timing* is a gerund; *good* is an adjective modifying *timing*. The phrase *good timing* is the direct object of the verb *has*.)

Gerunds can also be modified by prepositional phrases.

Telescopes are used for *looking at the stars*.
(*Looking* is a gerund; *at the stars* is a prepositional phrase modifying *looking*. The entire gerund phrase is the object of the preposition *for*.)

All of the above examples show that gerunds are used as nouns, even though they look like verbs. *Smoking, gambling, exercising, winning, turning, timing,* and *looking* all resemble verbs. However, because they are used as nouns, they are gerunds. Modifiers and objects that are used with them form gerund phrases.

Diagraming Gerunds

To diagram a gerund or gerund phrase used as a subject or direct object, place it on a line above the main line. The line for the gerund is drawn as a step. The gerund's modifiers are placed on slanted lines below it. Its object appears on the horizontal line following the gerund.

Starting a business is very risky.

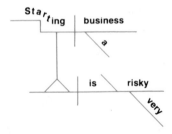

Marshall heard soft singing in the hallway.

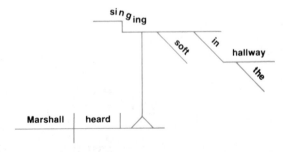

When a gerund or gerund phrase is used as the object of a preposition, it is diagramed below the main line. The preposition belongs on a slanted line going down from the word it modifies.

Once again, the gerund appears on a line drawn as a step.

The detective began by searching the room.

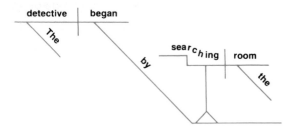

Exercise A Find the gerunds or gerund phrases in these sentences.

1. Shopping can be hard work.
2. Braking on ice is difficult.
3. Monty tried gluing the cup back together.
4. Training lions is actually not possible.
5. She makes a good living.
6. A misunderstanding caused the argument.
7. Begin by budgeting your time.
8. Scheduling the events was tricky.
9. I used that towel for drying the dog.
10. Who enjoys defrosting a refrigerator?

Exercise B Follow the directions for Exercise A.

1. Skipping lunch won't hurt Lee.
2. The politician began by discussing the economy.
3. He can't tell a joke without giggling.
4. The chef began stuffing the turkey.
5. Rhonda stopped dancing around the room.
6. Parking in the alley is prohibited.
7. He does push-ups without bending his knees.
8. She has a bad habit of interrupting.
9. The IRS encourages filing tax forms early.
10. Your mistake was thinning the paint.

Part 2   Using Participles

A participle is a verb form that is used as an adjective.

You know about the **past participle** as one of the principal parts of a verb. Usually, it is formed by adding *-d* or *-ed* to the present tense, as in *scrape—scraped* or *trust—trusted*. The past participles of irregular verbs are formed differently and must be learned separately: *ride—ridden*, *bring—brought*.

Besides the past participle, there is another kind of participle. It is called the **present participle**. Present participles are always formed by adding *-ing* to the present tense: *scrape—scraping, trust—trusting, ride—riding, bring—bringing*.

The following list shows more participles:

Verb	Past Participle	Present Participle
attack	attacked	attacking
fry	fried	frying
lose	lost	losing
give	given	giving

As verbals, participles are always used as adjectives. Participles modify nouns and pronouns.

> *Laughing*, Rita wiped the pie from her face.
>   (*Laughing* is a present participle modifying the noun *Rita*.)
> *Panting*, he ran into the emergency room.
>   (*Panting* is a present participle modifying the pronoun *he*.)
> Only *registered* voters were surveyed.
>   (*Registered* is a past participle modifying the noun *voters*.)
> Tom made a *refreshing* dessert with pineapple juice.
>   (*Refreshing* is a present participle modifying the noun *dessert*.)

Participial Phrases

A participle is not always used alone. Often a participle has a modifier or an object or both. Together, they form a **participial phrase**. The entire participial phrase is used as an adjective.

Because a participle is formed from a verb, it may have an object.

The man *ringing our doorbell* looks angry.

> (*Ringing our doorbell* is a participial phrase modifying *man*. *Doorbell* is the object of the participle *ringing*.)

Because a participle is formed from a verb, it may be modified by adverbs.

> We walked along *brightly lighted* streets.
> (*Brightly* is an adverb modifying the participle *lighted*.)

A participle may also be modified by prepositional phrases.

> *Made by hand*, these rugs are works of art.
> (*Made by hand* is a prepositional phrase modifying *rugs*. *By hand* is a prepositional phrase modifying the participle *made*.)

All of the preceding examples show that participles are used as adjectives, even though they look like verbs. While *laughing*, *panting*, *registered*, *refreshing*, *ringing*, *lighted*, and *made* all look like verbs, they are not used as verbs. Since they are used as adjectives, they are called participles. Modifiers and objects used with them form participial phrases.

Diagraming Participles

To diagram a participle, place it below the noun or pronoun it modifies. Place the participle on an angled line. Place modifiers of the participle on lines slanted down from it. An object appears after the participle on a horizontal line.

Waving a flag, the man signalled oncoming traffic.

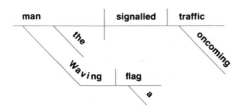

Exercise A Write the participles or participial phrases in these sentences. Show which word the participle or phrase modifies.

1. Remembering the main switch, she raced to the basement.
2. Complaining loudly, the customer demanded a refund.
3. The gusting wind ripped the loose shingles off.
4. Loosening his tie, James breathed deeply.
5. A boiled egg has fewer calories than a hamburger.
6. The coach restored the team's badly shattered morale.
7. The crowd on the platform looked anxiously at the train roaring past.
8. We watched the laughing children.
9. The yearbook brought back nearly forgotten memories.
10. He wore a wrinkled shirt and a baggy suit.

Exercise B Follow the directions for Exercise A.

1. Quickly pulling on her gloves, the surgeon rushed into the room.
2. Marcie told us an amazing story.
3. The captain read the list of soldiers missing in action.
4. The smoldering chair suddenly burst into flames.
5. The hair stylist groaned at Bess's tangled hair.
6. He piled whipped cream onto the sundae.
7. Grant wrote the terms of surrender with ink borrowed from Lee's aide.
8. Luckily, there was only one broken ornament.
9. His loved ones gathered around the hospital bed.
10. Using a calculator, he balanced his checkbook.

Gerund or Participle?

Gerunds and participles, the two kinds of verbals you have studied, may look exactly the same. Both gerunds and present participles are formed by adding -*ing* to verbs. If they look alike, how can you tell them apart?

To tell whether a word is a gerund or a present participle, look at how it is used. If it is used as a modifier, it is a participle. If it is used as a noun, it is a gerund.

Compare these two sentences:

Returning to school will prepare me for a better job.

(The gerund phrase *returning to school* is the subject of the verb *will prepare*.)

Returning to work, Gail noticed new faces.

(The participial phrase *returning to work* modifies the noun *Gail*.)

Exercise For each sentence, write the gerund or participle and say which each is. Be prepared to explain your answer.

1. Complaining will not help.
2. Steaming the wrinkles might work.
3. Pam is the player dribbling the ball.
4. Pinching his finger in the drawer, he yelped.
5. What is a tuning fork?
6. Fixing the hem with a safety pin is an emergency repair.
7. The man leaning against the post is Mr. Bobek.
8. Taping the pieces, Rob made a mistake.
9. Just watching the waves from the shore makes her seasick.
10. During the movie Steve had a bad coughing fit.

Part 3 Using Infinitives

Finally, the third kind of verbal is the **infinitive. An infinitive is a verbal form that usually begins with the word to.** *To* is called the **sign of the infinitive**. Here are some infinitives:

to tell	to wish	to draw	to open
to buy	to see	to plan	to take

Note: As you have learned, the word *to* can be a preposition. *To* is a preposition when it is followed by its object, a noun, or a pronoun. When *to* is followed by a verb, though, it is the sign of the infinitive. Look at these examples:

Prepositional Phrases	Infinitives
The boys went to the game.	The situation started to improve.
Everything is back to normal.	Our plane stopped to refuel.

Infinitive Phrases

Infinitives, just like gerunds and participles, are not always used alone. Many infinitives are used with modifiers and objects. An infinitive, together with its modifiers and objects, forms an **infinitive phrase**.

Because an infinitive comes from a verb, it is like a verb in certain ways. Like a verb, an infinitive may have an object.

> *To make new friends*, Jenny joined some clubs.
>> (*Friends* is the direct object of the infinitive *to make*.)
> The manager has agreed *to give us longer breaks*.
>> (*Us* is the indirect object and *breaks* is the direct object of the infinitive *to give*.)

Because an infinitive is formed from a verb, it may be modified by adverbs.

> I plan *to repay the loan immediately*.
>> (*Immediately* is an adverb modifying the infinitive *to repay*.)
> Yolanda promised *to come back soon*.
>> (*Back* and *soon* are adverbs modifying the infinitive *to come*.)

An infinitive may also be modified by prepositional phrases.

> Astronauts are trained *to live in outer space*.
>> (*In outer space* is a prepositional phrase modifying the infinitive *to live*.)
> This vacuum cleaner is guaranteed *to work for five years*.
>> (*For five years* is a prepositional phrase modifying the infinitive *to work*.)

Uses of the Infinitive Phrase

Unlike gerunds and participles, infinitives can be used as more than one part of speech. Infinitives and infinitive phrases can function as the following: nouns, adjectives, or adverbs.

Infinitives and infinitive phrases can be used in ways that nouns are used. Specifically, they may be subjects or direct objects, as well as predicate nouns.

Subject:	*To sign a petition* is a citizen's right.
	(*To sign a petition* is the subject.)
Direct Object:	Janet wanted *to refinish the bookcase*.
	(*To refinish the bookcase* is the direct object.)

Infinitives and infinitive phrases can also be used as adjectives or adverbs. If an infinitive or infinitive phrase modifies a noun or pronoun, it is functioning as an adjective. If it modifies a verb, adjective, or adverb, it is functioning as an adverb.

Adjective:	In case of fire, this is the switch *to pull*.
	(*To pull* modifies the noun *switch*.)
Adjective:	Do you have anyone *to counsel you*?
	(*To counsel you* modifies the pronoun *anyone*.)
Adverb:	Bonnie was hired *to process insurance claims*.
	(*To process insurance claims* modifies the verb *was hired*.)
Adverb:	The field was too muddy *to play on*.
	(*To play on* modifies the adjective *muddy*.)
Adverb:	Ron didn't run enough *to get into shape*.
	(*To get into shape* modifies the adverb *enough*.)

All of these examples show that while infinitives look like verbs, they are not used as verbs. Instead, infinitives and their phrases are used as nouns, adjectives, and adverbs.

Split Infinitives

At times you may see a modifier between the word *to* and the verb of an infinitive. A modifier in that place is said to split the infinitive. In general, a split infinitive sounds awkward and should be avoided.

Awkward:	Kate plans to *carefully* study.
Better:	Kate plans to study *carefully*.

Diagraming Infinitives

To diagram an infinitive or infinitive phrase used as a noun, place it on a bridge above the main line. *To*, the sign of the infinitive, is shown on an angled line. The infinitive belongs on a horizontal line. Modifiers appear on lines slanted down from the infinitive. An object is shown on a horizontal line following the infinitive.

The actor tried to remember his lines.

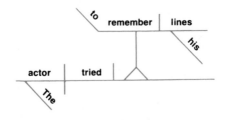

To diagram an infinitive or infinitive phrase used as a modifier, place it under the word it modifies. Modifiers and objects of the infinitive appear as explained above.

Ms. Minsky is the person to see about repairs.

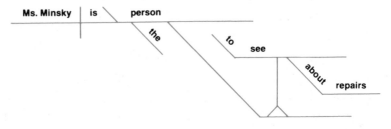

Exercise A Write each infinitive or infinitive phrase.

1. To give up snacks was their goal.
2. Grace attempted to find a foothold.
3. I used a carton to prop the table up.
4. How was he supposed to know that?
5. Glenn likes to walk in the rain.
6. Visitors are not allowed to feed the animals.
7. Rochelle did not mean to bump into you.
8. To get to the library is my project for today.
9. The patient was encouraged to walk to the lounge.
10. To win by default is unsatisfying.

Exercise B Follow the directions for Exercise A.

1. To travel there by bus would take two days.
2. To get to the interview on time, I must leave at 6:00 A.M.
3. Gina is too thin to worry about calories.
4. Did anyone bother to time the race?
5. Were you asked to pay for a transfer?
6. Jess has no time to waste.
7. Did you remember to ask for a receipt?
8. Use ammonia and water to clean the ring.
9. Don't even try to put that fire out yourself.
10. Juanita promised to send the negative to us.

Part 4 A Review of Verbals

Verbals, as you have learned, are verb forms. However, they are never used as verbs. They are used as other parts of speech.

The three kinds of verbals are gerunds, participles, and infinitives. All three may be used alone or in phrases. These phrases are called gerund phrases, participial phrases, and infinitive phrases. In phrases, all three kinds of verbals may have objects or modifiers or both.

Gerunds are the verb forms used as nouns. Gerunds, which end in -*ing*, may be used in all the ways nouns are used.

> Steve enjoys *shopping*. (direct object)
> *Shopping for bargains* sometimes pays off. (subject)
> Adam goes to Franco's Market for *his weekly grocery shopping*. (object of preposition)
> By *shopping wisely*, we save money. (object of preposition)

Participles are verb forms used as adjectives. Participles modify nouns and pronouns just as adjectives do. Present participles end in -*ing*. Past participles of regular verbs end in -*d* or -*ed*.

> *Writing carefully*, Greg signed the contract.
> Pam sat at a special *writing* table.
> *Writing on a blackboard*, the coach reviewed strategy.
> We watch the reporter *writing his story*.

Infinitives are verb forms that start with the word *to*. Infinitives may be used as three different parts of speech. They may be nouns, adjectives, or adverbs.

> *To take over the government* was the rebels' goal. (noun, subject)
> The photographer wants *to take pictures at the party*. (noun, object.)
> Peterson Avenue is the best route *to take*. (adjective)
> Marcy left *to take Jeremy home*. (adverb)
> The battery is easy *to take out*. (adverb)

Exercise A   Find the verbal in each sentence. Write the verbal or verbal phrase. Tell whether the verbal is a gerund, a participle, or an infinitive.

1. Anita wants to wear a costume to the party.
2. I carried the buttered popcorn back to our seats.
3. Dominick asked to speak with the manager.
4. Within five minutes he had mended the badly torn shirt.
5. Carol began by explaining her experiment.
6. Joking happily, Tony left for work.
7. The soldiers passed the time by joking together.
8. The starched collar felt too stiff to Vince.
9. Would you wear a silk shirt with faded jeans?
10. Carefully observing the current, she steered the boat.

Exercise B   Follow the directions for Exercise A.

1. The lawyer questioned the badly shaken witness.
2. The prosecuting attorney objected to the questions.
3. Waking up Gregory is no easy job.
4. Waking up quickly, she ran to the window.
5. With a puzzled look, Jeremy examined the engine.
6. The bank will send the cancelled checks to you.
7. Tiptoeing is normal for him.
8. Looking for an exit can waste valuable time.
9. I had hoped to drive you to the airport.
10. Do you want to rent a locker?

REVIEW Using Verbals

Recognizing Gerunds Write each gerund or gerund phrase.

1. The reporters were accused of spying.
2. The constant traveling tired the flight attendant.
3. Hosing the car down will wash the mud off.
4. I hate beginning the day without breakfast.
5. Don't buy anything there without bargaining first.

Recognizing Participles Write each participle or participial phrase.

6. The housing market is bad right now.
7. Crops ruined by the flood included corn and beans.
8. Did you buy insulated wire?
9. Tammy has several very annoying habits.
10. Exhausted after the day's work, Lyle sat down to relax.

Recognizing Infinitives Write each infinitive or infinitive phrase.

11. Chip wanted to ask you but was too shy.
12. Leave yourself time to check your answers.
13. Ms. Martinez managed to locate the apartment.
14. Jacob will have to budget more carefully.
15. We had hoped to see more of the city today.

Recognizing Verbals Write each verbal or verbal phrase. Label it *Gerund, Participle*, or *Infinitive*.

16. We often regret words spoken in anger.
17. Adjusting to the climate was difficult.
18. Carrying the goldfish bowl, he tripped and fell.
19. Sandy needs to find a steady job.
20. Pete offered to walk with them to the store.

Making Subjects and Verbs Agree

Two people who accept the same idea are said to agree. Words, too, can agree. The subject and verb in a sentence agree when they are alike in certain ways. In this section you will find out how to make subjects and verbs agree.

Part 1 Making Subjects and Verbs Agree in Number

The **number** of a word refers to whether the word is singular or plural. A word is **singular** when it refers to one thing. A word is **plural** when it refers to more than one thing. When a subject and verb are the same in number, they agree.

A verb must agree in number with its subject. A singular subject belongs with a singular verb. A plural subject belongs with a plural verb.

Singular	Plural
He *guesses*.	They *guess*.
She *arrives*.	They *arrive*.
Food *spoils*.	Eggs *spoil*.
The balloon *rises*.	The balloons *rise*.

As you can tell from the examples, most singular verbs end in -*s*. The plural verbs do not end in -*s*.

Usually, subject and verb agreement seems natural. You may have trouble, though, if you are not sure which word is the subject of the sentence. Remember that to find the subject, first find the verb. Then ask *who?* or *what?* before the verb.

> These posts in the ground support the fence.
>> *Verb*: support
>> *What supports?* posts
>> The subject is *posts*.

The subject of the verb is never in a prepositional phrase. A prepositional phrase often appears between the subject and the verb of a sentence. Ignore phrases when you are trying to make subjects and verbs agree.

> *Water* from the streams *runs* into the river.
> *One* of the factories *has* a job opening.
> The *people* on our block *were* helpful.

Phrases beginning with words like *with*, *together with*, *including*, *as well as*, and *in addition to* are also not part of a subject.

> The *glue*, as well as the paper, *is stuck* to my hand.
> My *jacket*, together with my vest, *is* at the cleaners'.
> *Cereal* with milk *makes* a good breakfast.

Exercise A   Choose the verb that agrees with the subject.

1. The peaches in the bowl (is, are) ripe.
2. Those men in the picture (looks, look) familiar.
3. The woman in the big sunglasses (is, are) the coach.
4. The waters of the Nile (overflows, overflow) annually.
5. The director of the projects (has, have) resigned.

6. The opponents in the election (is, are) friends.

7. The visit from his friends (has, have) cheered him up.

8. Some beetles, as well as the chameleon, (changes, change) colors.

9. The workers, together with the boss, (demands, demand) a safety check.

10. All of the musicians, including Celia, (gets, get) paid promptly.

Exercise B   Follow the directions for Exercise A.

1. Her denial of the rumors (was, were) published in the newspaper.

2. The dancer in red suspenders (is, are) out of step.

3. Boxes on this conveyor (requires, require) special handling.

4. A car with no plates (is, are) usually stopped.

5. The mind as well as the muscles (needs, need) exercise.

6. Complaints about city services (goes, go) to the mayor.

7. The handles on that suitcase (is, are) loose.

8. Hank's nerves of steel (seems, seem) to be melting.

9. The vision in both her eyes (seems, seem) to be better.

10. Mae's sketches, together with her photos, (shows, show) talent.

Part 2   Compound Subjects

A compound subject joined by *and* is plural. Therefore, it requires a plural verb.

> Flannel *shirts* and wool *socks* **keep** me warm.
> *Loggins* and *Messina* **have performed** here before.

If the parts of a compound subject are joined by *or* or *nor*, the verb should agree with the subject nearer to the verb.

> Neither Adam nor his *cousins were* at the reunion.
> The bank or the grocery *store cashes* my paychecks.

Choose the verb that agrees with the subject.

1. The cuffs and the collar (is, are) too tight.
2. Batfish and viperfish really (exists, exist).
3. Those stripes and this plaid (looks, look) wrong together.
4. Kay and Ben (attends, attend) night classes.
5. Doughnuts and coffee (was, were) served.
6. Warmth and light (was, were) provided by the fire.
7. Neither the salad nor the dessert (is, are) included.
8. Neither pears nor apples (requires, require) peeling.
9. Either the computer or the programmers (is, are) at fault.
10. Either the needle or the tubes (needs, need) to be replaced.

Exercise B   Follow the directions for Exercise A.

1. The trains and the buses (is, are) running late.
2. Her coordination and speed (improves, improve) daily.
3. Pancakes and syrup (is, are) both high in calories.
4. Neither pancakes nor waffles (is, are) high in protein.
5. Either Claire or her sisters (feeds, feed) the stock.
6. Either her sisters or Claire (feeds, feed) the stock.
7. Both Claire and her sisters (feeds, feed) the stock.
8. Neither the paper nor the string (is, are) secure.
9. Either rats or squirrels (has, have) chewed this rope.
10. The fare and the cost of a transfer (has, have) increased.

Part 3   Indefinite Pronouns

To make a verb agree with an indefinite pronoun used as its subject, you must know if the pronoun is singular or plural. As you have learned, some indefinite pronouns are singular while others are plural. Still others may be either singular or plural.

The following indefinite pronouns are **singular**:

another	each	anything	one	neither
anybody	either	everything	somebody	nobody
anyone	everybody	everyone	someone	no one

Everyone needs leisure time.
Somebody in this room *is* the winner.
Each of the girls *is* in a carpool.

The following indefinite pronouns are **plural**:

both   few   many   several

Many of my friends *work* overtime.
Both of the elevators *are broken*.

The following indefinite pronouns are **singular** when they refer to one thing. They are **plural** when they refer to several things.

all   any   most   none   some

All of this paper *is* for decorations.
All of the reporters *have* deadlines.
Most of this money *is* counterfeit.
Most of the Senators *travel* to foreign countries.
Some of my work *is* difficult.
Some of the vineyards *are* open to visitors.

Exercise A   Choose the verb that agrees with the subject.

1. Nobody even (suspects, suspect) the surprise.
2. Something in the oven (smells, smell) good.
3. Another of those big jets (has, have) crashed.
4. Everybody in the building (wants, want) to move.
5. Few of the vents (is, are) open.
6. None of the cheese (is, are) moldy.
7. Most of the players (is, are) under contract.
8. All of the fat (was, were) trimmed off.
9. All of the bikers (wears, wear) helmets.
10. Most of the students (works, work).

Exercise B   Follow the directions for Exercise A.

1. Few of the musicians still (takes, take) lessons.
2. Neither of the solutions (seems, seem) correct.
3. Everything in the islands (has, have) changed.

4. Nothing from the stores (fits, fit) him well.
5. Either of the ties (goes, go) with the suit.
6. Both of the ties (goes, go) with the suit.
7. Most of the park (is, are) closed after dark.
8. Some of the instructions (makes, make) no sense.
9. Some of the wood (looks, look) rotten.
10. Each of these games (needs, need) batteries.

Part 4 Other Problems of Agreement

Doesn't and Don't

The verb *doesn't* is always singular. *Doesn't* is used with the subjects *she*, *he*, and *it*. *Don't* is used with all other personal pronouns.

It *doesn't* seem right.   We *don't* argue.
She *doesn't* care.   I *don't* drive.
He *doesn't* live here.   They *don't* understand.

Sentences Beginning with *There*

In sentences beginning with *there*, *here*, or *where*, the subject comes after the verb. Look ahead to find the subject of the sentence. Use the verb that agrees with that subject.

There *are* some *letters* here for you.
Here *is* a *piece* of sugarless gum.
Where *are* the application *forms*?

Exercise A Choose the verb that agrees with the subject.

1. The coach (doesn't, don't) look pleased.
2. Where (is, are) the rubber bands?
3. The stapler (doesn't, don't) have any staples in it.

4. There (was, were) two errors on the bill.
5. Shauna (doesn't, don't) ever seem hungry.
6. This glue (doesn't, don't) stick to vinyl.
7. (Doesn't, Don't) the subway stop at Clark Street?
8. (Doesn't, Don't) the lights look lovely?
9. (Isn't, Aren't) there any parking places?
10. Here (is, are) my keys.

Exercise B   Follow the directions for Exercise A.

1. (Doesn't, Don't) everybody like some kind of music?
2. (Where's, Where're) my yellow sandals?
3. (There's, There're) some ice cubes in the freezer.
4. The situation (doesn't, don't) look good.
5. Those movers certainly (doesn't, don't) move fast.
6. Where (is, are) the loudspeakers?
7. (Here's, Here're) a good spot.
8. Here (is, are) the latest scores.
9. (Doesn't, Don't) graham crackers contain wheat?
10. There (is, are) no cures for some diseases.

REVIEW Making Subjects and Verbs Agree

Making Subjects and Verbs Agree   Number your paper from 1 to 20. Write the verb that agrees with the subject.

1. Only the dents in the fender (is, are) rusty.
2. The coat with leather buttons (belongs, belong) to me.
3. Other clerks in addition to Phil (is, are) bonded.
4. Floods in India (kills, kill) many people.
5. Smoke as well as flames (means, mean) danger.
6. That truck and the van (gets, get) poor gas mileage.
7. (Is, Are) two slices of bacon enough?
8. Allergies and asthma sometimes (disappears, disappear).
9. The cause of the explosions (has, have) been found.
10. Several of the windows (do, does) not open.
11. One of the space heaters (is, are) very old.
12. Most of the painting (has, have) been done.
13. Few of the tellers (works, work) on Saturday.
14. Some of the milk (has, have) spoiled.
15. All of the students (takes, take) math.
16. Neither the lobby nor the stairs (is, are) well lit.
17. Either the downspouts or the gutter (is, are) clogged.
18. There (is, are) hot peppers in that sauce.
19. Where (is, are) the brakes?
20. Annette probably (doesn't, don't) remember me.

Using Compound and Complex Sentences

In preceding sections, you have studied sentence parts and how they work together. Now you are ready to examine four different kinds of sentences. In this section, you will learn about simple sentences, compound sentences, complex sentences, and compound-complex sentences.

Part 1 A Review of the Sentence

Any sentence has two basic parts. These basic parts are the subject and the predicate.

Subject	Predicate
The bus	left.
The last bus from the city	left at midnight.

The **subject** of a sentence names the person or thing about which something is said. The **predicate** tells something about the subject.

The **simple predicate** is the verb. The **simple subject** is the subject of the verb. Within the subject of the sentence are the simple subject and its modifiers. Within the predicate, are the verb, objects, and predicate words, and their modifiers.

Compound Parts in a Sentence

Any of the parts within a sentence may be **compound**. In other words, each one may have more than one part.

Compound subject:	Cats, dogs, and other stray animals are taken to the city pound.
Compound verb:	Sheila turned and walked away.
Compound predicate:	Pat glazed the clay pot and then baked it in the kiln.
Compound object:	The 76ers' lineup includes Erving, Collins, and Jones.
Compound object of the preposition:	Fashion models in magazines and newspapers look perfect.
Compound predicate word:	That injury is neither severe nor painful.

The Simple Sentence

While the preceding sentences have compound parts, each still expresses only one main idea. Such sentences, like all of those you have been studying, are called **simple sentences**.

A simple sentence is a sentence with only one subject and one predicate. However, the subject, the predicate, and any of their parts may be compound.

You are now prepared to tell simple sentences from other types of sentences.

Exercise A Copy each of the following simple sentences. Then draw a line between the subject and the predicate.

1. Editorials and news stories have different purposes.
2. Humans and other primates walk upright.

3. Marshall and Ed set out for the stadium.
4. Bert sorted and filed the letters.
5. The waitress looked up and hurried over.
6. Political cartoons can be funny or serious.
7. Sue loaded the wheelbarrow and pushed it away.
8. The clinic opens at seven and closes at five.
9. The manager hired typists, machinists, and keypunch operators.
10. The saguaro cactus can grow fifty feet high and weigh six tons.

Exercise B Write the compound subjects, verbs, and objects you find in these simple sentences.

1. He won the Cy Young Award and a big contract.
2. Dancers and athletes must practice daily.
3. Dave tasted and then carefully seasoned the chili.
4. Frank danced and sang in the variety show.
5. That reporter investigates consumer fraud and other swindles.
6. Arsonists destroy both life and property.
7. Are the stores and banks closed today?
8. Both heating costs and cooling costs have gone up.
9. The spy hid the notes under the rugs and in books.
10. Mel, Ann, and Nat got a permit and went into business.

Part 2   The Compound Sentence

When two simple sentences express related ideas, they are sometimes joined to form one sentence. The sentence that results has more than one subject, each with its own predicate. It is called a **compound sentence**.

A compound sentence consists of two or more simple sentences joined together. The parts of the compound sentence may be joined by a coordinating conjunction (*and, or, but*) or by a semicolon(;). Look at the following examples.

Many horror films are truly scary, **but** others are simply silly.

The quintuplets were born last month, **and** they are still in the hospital.

Does Todd work at the bakery, **or** does he work for the city?

Some comic strips are syndicated; they are purchased by various newspapers across the country.

Why are compound sentences used? Why don't writers use only simple sentences? This passage will help you to see why.

Barry works for the city. He drives a snowplow. Most of the time he has regular hours. During snowstorms, Barry is on call.

Repeating simple sentences one after another becomes dull and tiresome. Notice how much better the same paragraph sounds with compound sentences.

Barry works for the city, and he drives a snowplow. Most of the time he has regular hours, but during snowstorms, Barry is on call.

Diagraming Compound Sentences

Once you know how to diagram simple sentences, you can diagram compound ones. A diagram simply shows that a compound sentence is two or more simple sentences joined together. The simple sentences are diagramed one below the other. Then the two sentences are connected with a dotted line. The coordinating conjunction sits on a "step" in the dotted line.

Lennie dashed for the bus, but he missed it.

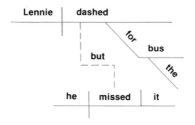

Exercise A   Label three columns *Subject/Verb, Conjunction* and *Subject/Verb*. For each sentence, fill in the columns.

Example: Ray types and takes shorthand, but he wants outdoor work.

Subject/Verb	Conjunction	Subject/Verb
Ray/types, takes	but	he/wants

1. Maine has lovely beaches, but the water is cold.

2. Wild elephants eat a variety of foods, but elephants in zoos eat hay, apples, and carrots.

3. The plan seemed silly, but it worked.

4. The bus is very late, or maybe we missed it.

5. Emma opened a checking account, and she deposited her check.

6. Lydia makes the calls, and Jan visits the customers.

7. Nobody seemed interested, and I canceled the reservations.

8. Shall we give her a party, or would she prefer a gift?

9. Did Dee and Ken find jobs yet, or are they still looking?

10. Rummage sales and thrift shops offer bargains, but they have few selections.

Exercise B Follow the directions for Exercise A.

1. The wrecked cars are shredded, and the pieces are melted down.

2. Hank baked some oatmeal cookies, and he served them to his friends.

3. You can tell the truth, or you can take the consequences.

4. The lipstick and polish match, but they are too light.

5. Ms. Wright wants to buy the house, but she cannot get a mortgage.

6. The weather was cold and damp, but the fans did not mind.

7. Not every player had signed a contract; some were still negotiating.

8. The car went into a skid, but Kelly pulled it out.

9. Are you allergic to something, or do you have a cold?

10. Nan has no checking account, but she does have cash.

Compound Sentence or Compound Predicate?

Can you tell the difference between a compound sentence and a simple sentence that has a compound predicate? Both have two verbs. Furthermore, a coordinating conjunction is used within both compound predicates and compound sentences.

> Keane *was ahead in the polls* but *lost the election*.
> (This compound predicate is joined by *but*.)
> *Keane was* ahead in the polls, but *he lost* the election.
> (This is a compound sentence joined by *but*.)

There is one clearcut way to tell if a sentence is compound or if it has a compound predicate. If each verb has its own subject, then the sentence is compound. If the verbs share the same subject, then only the predicate is compound.

> s.   v.   v.
> *Smugglers buried* gold under the sea and *recovered* it later.
> (This simple sentence has a compound predicate. Both verbs, *buried* and *recovered*, have the same subject, *smugglers*.)

> s.   v.   s.   v.
> *Smugglers buried* gold under the seas, and *divers recovered* it later.
> (This is a compound sentence. The verb *buried* has its own subject, *smugglers*. The verb *recovered* has its own subject, *divers*.)

> s.   v.   v.
> *Rachel walked* into the day-care center and *smiled* warmly.
> (The conjunction *and* joins the compound predicate of this simple sentence. Both verbs, *walked* and *smiled*, have the same subject, *Rachel*.)

> s.   v.   s.   v.
> *Rachel walked* into the day-care center, and the *children smiled* warmly.
> (This compound sentence is actually two simple sentences joined by the conjunction *and*.)

Exercise A Decide whether the following sentences are compound sentences or simple sentences with compound predicates. Write *Compound Sentence* or *Compound Predicate* on your paper.

1. He turned off the gas and padlocked the valve.
2. She does not look like her father, but she acts like him.
3. Norm yells, and Lisa mumbles.
4. Will you stay on the job, or will you quit?
5. The magician performed amazing tricks and entertained us all evening.
6. Jeff raises parakeets and sells them from his home.
7. Laurie discovered the error but did not correct it.
8. Did you see or hear anything suspicious?
9. Have you eaten, or can I make you a snack?
10. Curiosity is admirable, but nosiness isn't.

Exercise B Follow the directions for Exercise A.

1. The tools were old, and they needed repair.
2. The doctors went on strike, but they treated emergencies.
3. Antibiotics cure many diseases but do not help colds.
4. I have an idea, but I don't know for sure.
5. The hospital ran out of funds and had to close.
6. Nobody but Gwen could think of such a scheme and carry it out.
7. He must have been delayed, or maybe he has forgotten.
8. The linoleum was worn and torn but shone with wax.
9. Did Kay make the basket, or did Linda make it?
10. The National Guard was put on alert but was not called.

Punctuating Compound Sentences

One of two punctuation marks is used in a compound sentence. Either a **comma** before a coordinating conjunction or a **semicolon** is needed to separate the two parts of a compound sentence. A punctuation mark shows the division between the two parts. It also shows where to pause in reading the sentence.

When a comma is used in a compound sentence, it belong before the coordinating conjunction. Notice how the comma is used in these compound sentences:

      s.   v.   s.   v.

First Cary nailed the wallboard in place, **and** then Laura taped it.

      s.   v.   s.   v.

Some people hide their feelings, **but** others display them openly.

Instead of a comma and a conjunction, a semicolon may be used in a compound sentence.

      s.   v.   s.   v.

Samantha is superstitious; she avoids black cats.

      s.   v.   s.   v.   v.

Melissa met Phil on a bus; they were married two years later.

Often a semicolon is used with a **conjunctive adverb**. Conjunctive adverbs are adverbs like *however, nevertheless, therefore, otherwise, furthermore,* and *consequently*. They help to join the two parts of a compound sentence. In addition, they show the relationship between the parts.

      s.   v.   v.   s.   v.

Roberto does not swim; *consequently*, he stays away from boats.

      s.   v.   s.   v.

Sherman was ahead in the polls; *however*, she lost the election.

As you can see, a conjunctive adverb is placed after a semicolon, and it is followed by a comma.

Either a comma or a semicolon separates the parts of a compound sentence. However, no punctuation is used between the parts of a compound predicate. Look at these simple sentences with compound predicates.

      s.   v.   v.

A witness went to the police and told his story.

      s.   v.   v.

Linda gets less pay now but enjoys her work more.

Finally, no commas are necessary in very short compound sentences.

The Rangers won and everyone cheered.

Exercise A Commas and semicolons have been omitted between the parts of the following compound sentences. For each sentence, write the two words between which punctuation belongs. Put in the comma or semicolon. If a sentence needs no punctuation, write *correct*.

1. Jackie Wilson hasn't sung for years but many remember him.
2. Tyrone lost a quarter in the machine and wrote to the manufacturer.
3. Fabian and Rick Nelson were once famous singers but are now forgotten.
4. We wrote to our Congresswoman she answered promptly.
5. The apartment is on the corner and gets lots of light.
6. Eileen is good at her work moreover, she enjoys it.
7. The new filling fell out and Dawn complained to the dentist.
8. I get no sick leave otherwise, I would have stayed home.
9. Did Cora fill out the census form or did you?
10. Neal belongs to a union however, he crossed the picket line.

Exercise B Follow the directions for Exercise A.

1. Jenny found the water meter and copied down the reading.
2. Clayton has an answering machine therefore, he misses no calls.
3. The snake was coiled it was about to strike.
4. Mac is happy with his job and his parents are proud of his success.
5. Squeeze toothpaste from the bottom the tube will last longer.

6. Many great civilizations have fallen and others have taken their places.

7. Terry jumped from the plane and her parachute opened.

8. The bag tore groceries spilled everywhere.

9. Rose and Don helped us but would take no pay.

10. Should I straighten the picture or does it look all right?

Part 3   The Complex Sentence

You have learned about simple sentences and compound sentences. Another kind of sentence, the **complex sentence**, can also help you to express your ideas. In order to understand the structure of a complex sentence, you must first know what a **clause** is.

A clause is a group of words containing a verb and its subject.

According to this definition, a simple sentence is a clause. It has a verb and a subject.

s.   v.
James retired from baseball.

s.   v.
The trip ended too soon.

However, the structure of sentences will be easier to understand if you think of a clause as a *part of a sentence*. Think of a clause as *a group of words within a sentence*.

Compound sentences contain clauses. Compound sentences have two or more groups of words, each having a subject and verb. Look at these examples:

s.   v.   s.   v.
We applied too much paste, and the wallpaper slid off the wall.

s.   v.   s.   v.
The twins look alike, but their personalities are very different.

Clause or Phrase?

Keep in mind that clauses differ from phrases. Both clauses and phrases are sentence parts. However, a clause has a subject and a verb. A phrase does not.

Phrases: since Friday
before my appointment

s.   v.
Clauses: since the campaign began

s. v.
before I went to the dentist

Subordinate Clauses

The clauses of a compound sentence are actually two separate sentences. Each one can stand on its own. Each is a **main clause**. A main clause, also called an **independent clause**, is a clause that can stand alone as a sentence.

Subordinate clauses, or **dependent clauses**, are clauses that cannot stand alone. A subordinate clause is not a complete sentence. Study these examples:

s.   v.
Because the dam burst

s.   v.
When the strike was over

Both of the subordinate clauses above contain subjects and verbs. However, neither of them expresses a complete thought. Neither of them can stand alone. Both leave you wondering *then what?*

A word that begins a subordinate clause has an important function. Without *because* and *when*, the clauses above would be sentences. Words like *because* and *when* are called **subordinating conjunctions**. They *subordinate*, or make *dependent*, the words they introduce. Most, but not all, subordinate clauses begin with subordinating conjunctions.

420

These words are often used as subordinating conjunctions:

Words Often Used as Subordinating Conjunctions

after	because	so that	when
although	before	than	whenever
as	if	though	where
as if	in order that	till	wherever
as long as	provided	unless	while
as though	since	until	

Note: Most of the words above can be used in different ways. They are subordinating conjunctions only when they begin clauses.

Morever, subordinate clauses do not always begin with subordinating conjunctions. Clauses may begin with words like these:

that	who, whom, whose	which	why
what, whatever	whoever, whomever	how	

Exercise Using *if*, *because*, *when*, *after*, and *since*, make subordinate clauses out of these sentences.

1. The lamp was unplugged.
2. Paul dislikes seafood.
3. A wire is loose.
4. Kit stole third base.
5. The steps have been repaired.
6. I have no more change.
7. Lightning struck the shed.
8. Delia used live bait.
9. The orchard is open to the public.
10. The heavy rains caused mudslides.

Definition of the Complex Sentence

Now that you know the difference between main clauses and subordinate clauses, you can understand the complex sentence.

A complex sentence is a sentence that contains one main clause and one or more subordinate clauses.

Main Clause	Subordinate Clause
The tape recorder will start	when you press this button.
The President wouldn't decide	until he consulted his advisers.
Frankenstein is a character	that Mary Shelley created.

Exercise A Copy each subordinate clause in these complex sentences. Underline the subject once and the verb twice.

1. Mike knows that we trust him.
2. Margie asked where the pliers were.
3. This is the last time that we will play in this gym.
4. Did you see the Grand Canyon while you were there?
5. Does Carson realize that he needs a ticket?
6. Although his nickname is Lucky, he isn't.
7. For as long as I can remember, we have shopped at that grocery store.
8. It looks as though the secret is out.
9. Sam works on the car whenever he has a chance.
10. Whenever Carl eats anything, he records the calories.

Exercise B Follow the directions for Exercise A.

1. Ask Allison if she remembers the tune.
2. Weeds grow wherever there are gardens.
3. Gene always talks as if he has a sore throat.
4. Whenever Rae is in town, we have a family reunion.
5. Donna painted the gutters black so that they would retain heat.
6. Don't sign anything before you have read it.

7. General Sherman said that terror was a weapon.
8. Erin wondered why the dogs were barking.
9. If she cannot sell the van, she will refinance it.
10. One wood tick can be deadly unless it is removed from the victim.

Part 4   Adverb Clauses

By definition, a complex sentence contains a subordinate clause. The subordinate clause may be one of three kinds. One kind is the **adverb clause**. An adverb clause has the same function as an adverb.

An **adverb** modifies a verb, an adjective, or another adverb. It tells *how*, *when*, *where*, or *to what extent*.

Adverb: Doug fishes *here*.

An **adverb phrase** is a prepositional phrase used as an adverb.

Adverb phrase: Doug fishes *from this pier*.

An adverb clause is a subordinate clause used as an adverb.

Adverb clause: Doug fishes *whenever he can*.

Adverb clauses, like adverbs and adverb phrases, tell *how*, *when*, *where*, or *to what extent*. They modify verbs, adjectives, and adverbs. Don't forget that a clause, unlike a phrase, has a subject and a verb.

Diagraming Adverb Clauses

To diagram an adverb clause, place it on a separate horizontal line below the main line. With a dotted line, connect the adverb clause to the word it modifies in the main clause. Place the subordinating conjunction on the dotted line.

The town has grown since a factory opened here.

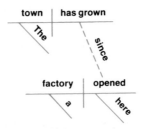

Exercise A   Copy the adverb clause from each sentence.

1. When a bus is crowded, Rita waits for the next one.

2. John stays inside whenever the smog is thick.

3. Though Jay seemed to listen, his mind was on his own problems.

4. Because rayon is a wood product, it is a natural fabric.

5. Cleo met nice people wherever she traveled.

6. Although slang is lively, it quickly becomes outdated.

7. Dr. Sanchez answers questions more carefully than the other doctors do.

8. Turn the television off if no one is watching it.

9. Nothing is a bargain unless you need it.

10. Even the judge was surprised when the defendant pleaded guilty.

Exercise B   Follow the directions for Exercise A.

1. Betsy takes her camera wherever she goes.

2. Although he definitely heard the reporter's question, he ignored her.

3. Treatment cannot be started until the lab report is in.

4. Since the building became vacant, it has been a trouble spot.

5. When the sun sets, the windows look goldplated.

6. Tim lost control of the car as he rounded the curve.

7. Lonnie must quit unless his hours are changed.

8. After Tasha passed the test, she celebrated.

9. As long as you are up, please let the dog in.

10. Because the funds were cut, the day-care center closed.

Part 5   Adjective Clauses

A second kind of subordinate clause is the **adjective clause**. An adjective clause has the same function as an adjective.

An **adjective** modifies either a noun or pronoun.

    Adjective: Leslie found *three silver* coins.

An **adjective phrase** is a prepositional phrase that modifies a noun or pronoun.

    Adjective phrase: Wendy needs a pair *of crutches*.

An adjective clause is a subordinate clause used as an adjective to modify a noun or pronoun.

    Adjective clause: The truck *that was towing my car* broke down.

Adjective clauses, like adjectives and adjective phrases, tell *what kind* or *which one*. They usually appear directly after the noun or pronoun they modify. Adjective clauses, unlike adjective phrases, have subjects and verbs.

There are several words that can introduce adjective clauses. *Where* and *when* are two of them.

    Damen is the street *where the accident occurred*.

    This is the time *when the tide goes out*.

Relative Pronouns

Besides *when* and *where*, the words *who*, *whom*, and *whose* are also used to begin adjective clauses. *Who, whom,* and *whose* are called **relative pronouns**. They relate a clause, called a **relative clause**, to a noun or pronoun in the sentence. Sometimes *that* and *which* are relative pronouns.

Here are the words used as relative pronouns:

       who   whom   whose   that   which

The relative pronoun in a complex sentence is special because it has these three functions:

1. It introduces an adjective clause.
2. It links the clause to a word in the main clause.
3. It serves a function within the clause. Its role may be subject, object, or predicate pronoun of the verb within the adjective clause. Otherwise, it may be the object of a preposition in the clause. The relative pronoun *whose* is used as an adjective.

> Lynn was one of the runners *who finished the marathon*.
>> (*Who* is the subject of *finished*.)
>
> The pen name *that Samuel Clemens used* was Mark Twain.
>> (*That* is the direct object of *used*.)
>
> We saw the galley, *which is the kitchen of a ship*.
>> (*Which* is the subject of *is*.)
>
> The people *with whom I work* bought me a birthday cake.
>> (*Whom* is the object of the preposition *with*.)
>
> People *whose taxes are late* may be fined.
>> (*Whose* modifies *taxes*, the subject of the clause.)

Sometimes you may be confused about whether *who* or *whom* is the correct relative pronoun. To decide, see how the pronoun is used within the clause. Remember to use *who* as the subject form and *whom* as the object form.

Diagraming Adjective Clauses

To diagram an adjective clause, place it on a separate line under the main line. A dotted line connects the relative pronoun to the word in the main clause that the adjective modifies.

> Do you know anyone who repairs motorcycles?

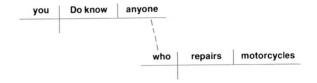

The clerk with whom Val spoke gave her incorrect information.

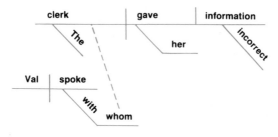

Exercise A Copy each adjective clause. Write the word it modifies.

1. The fish that has the worst reputation is the piranha.
2. She is the reporter who uncovered the scandal.
3. Many of the people to whom we sent questionnaires replied.
4. Sojourner Truth was one of the abolitionists who supported women's rights.
5. Smoke filled the only hallway that was open.
6. The room where Mary practices is soundproof.
7. Tell her about the time when the accelerator stuck.
8. Did you read the notice that was posted in the hall?
9. That was the last time that I saw Bernie.
10. Houdini was the magician who was known for escapes.

Exercise B Follow the directions for Exercise A.

1. Bowlers whose scores are high can enter the tournament.
2. Lee Street, which runs east, is the quickest route.
3. The town where he was born no longer exists.
4. The duffel bag in which she packed the clothes was torn.
5. The base to which she was assigned was in Hawaii.
6. Do you remember the day when you first entered school?
7. Martin Luther King, Jr. was someone who combined philosophy and action.
8. Horror movies were the kind that Ms. Zima liked least.
9. The wind was the only sound that we heard.
10. Workers who put in overtime got a bonus.

Part 6   Noun Clauses

The noun clause is the third kind of subordinate clause. **A noun clause is a clause used as a noun in a sentence.** A noun clause can be used any way that a noun can be used. It can be a subject, an object of the verb, a predicate word, or an object of a preposition. Unlike adverb and adjective clauses, noun clauses do not modify.

Uses of Noun Clauses

Subject: *What he expects* is perfection.
Direct object: Can you explain *how you solved the problem?*
Object of preposition: The mayor agreed with *whatever the neighborhood group said.*
(The clause is the object of the preposition *with.*)
Predicate noun: Joe's objection was *that the law was out of date.*

These examples show that many noun clauses begin with the words *that* and *what.* The words *whatever, who, whom, whoever,* and *whomever* can also introduce noun clauses. *Where, when, how,* and *why* are used, too.

Diagraming Noun Clauses

To diagram a noun clause, use a bridge extended from the point where the clause is used in the sentence. Place a word that introduces a clause on a line above the clause.

1. Noun clause used as subject

What propels this plane is a jet engine.

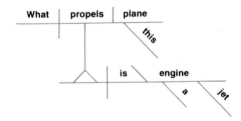

2. Noun clause used as object of the verb

Mark said that he lives on a houseboat.

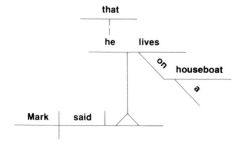

3. Noun clause used as object of a preposition

We talked about how we had become friends.

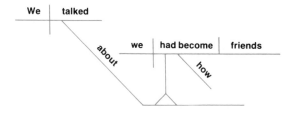

Exercise A Copy the noun clauses. Tell how each clause is used.

1. Christmas Eve is when the stores are most crowded.
2. Anita asked where the new highway would go.
3. I forgot what I should do next.
4. Travers said that he would be gone for a long time.
5. Why Bobbi said that worries me.
6. Set the dial at whatever number is recommended.
7. We will support whomever the committee chooses.
8. What Clark needs is more privacy.
9. Nobody knows how long the strike will continue.
10. Ms. Varner will hire whoever is best qualified.

Exercise B Follow the directions for Exercise A.

1. Do you know why the class was canceled?

2. Give these clothes to whoever wants them.

3. Lou complained that the referee had ignored the foul.

4. Newspapers speculated about how the mayor would react.

5. The scientists calculated that the satellite would land in the ocean.

6. The lawyer must support what she says with evidence.

7. Jim muttered that the decision was unfair.

8. Why bears hibernate is a bit of a puzzle.

9. Don't just sit and wonder why the roof leaks.

10. Whatever he does is helpful.

Part 7 A Review of Subordinate Clauses

You have learned about the three kinds of subordinate clauses. These are the adverb clause, the adjective clause, and the noun clause.

The only way to identify the kind of clause is to look at its use in the sentence. A clause used as a noun is a noun clause. A clause used as a modifier is an adverb or adjective clause, depending on the word modified.

Exercise A Write the subordinate clause in each sentence. If the clause is used as a noun clause, tell how it is used in the sentence. If the clause is used as an adjective or adverb clause, tell what it modifies.

1. I suspect that the trouble is in the engine.

2. Who would have believed that this could happen?

3. Ted asked because he is taking a poll.

4. Ted asked how old the bike was.

5. Keep going until you reach an intersection.

6. That was the book that made Baldwin's reputation.

7. Bev is the only member of the choir who sings solos.

8. How Gillespie discovered his unique sound is a good story.

9. Lena traveled alone when she was in Mexico.

10. Twilight is the time when some people feel lonely.

Exercise B Follow the directions for Exercise A.

1. That explains why the smoke detector went off.
2. Who asked who is in charge here?
3. Chuck exercises while he washes the dishes.
4. Sunday, which is the pastor's busiest day, passed quickly.
5. Dr. Weiss, who chaired the conference, teaches here.
6. The writer who is quoted most often is Shakespeare.
7. There is a shuttle helicopter that carries passengers from the city to the airports.
8. China is the country that has the largest population.
9. I put the message where Sara would be sure to see it.
10. After all, Terry works because she has to.

Part 8 Clauses as Sentence Fragments

Earlier, you learned about sentence fragments. The kind of fragments you studied did not have subjects and verbs.

> A successful business   Jogged along the road

There is another kind of fragment that does have a subject and verb. It is a subordinate clause. Because a clause does not express a complete thought, it is a sentence fragment. It is only part of a sentence. It is not meant to stand alone.

Look at how these word groups differ:

> Jennifer smiled   When Jennifer smiled

The first word group is a sentence. Because the second word group uses the subordinating conjunction *when*, it is a sentence fragment. Subordinate clauses should be used only within sentences.

A subordinate clause must not be written as a complete sentence. It must always be joined to a main clause.

Fragment: Because he lost his keys
Sentence: Because he lost his keys, Eric was locked out of his apartment.
Fragment: What the code meant
Sentence: The agent explained what the code meant.

Exercise A Number your paper from 1 to 10. Decide whether the groups of words below are sentences or fragments. Write *S* for *Sentence* and *F* for *Fragment*. Add words to make each fragment a complete sentence. Punctuate and capitalize where necessary.

1. Why is there no hot water
2. What a gyroscope is
3. When is Easter this year
4. Before a game Millie skips dinner
5. Before I saw that movie
6. The cook who made the tacos
7. June asked who had made the team
8. When the Ice Age was over
9. Because fish are sensitive to vibrations
10. Until the storm is over

Exercise B Follow the directions for Exercise A.

1. Remember when we saw the falling star
2. How do you get to school
3. The night when the water main burst
4. Sal left
5. Because Sal had already left
6. The panda which is not really a bear
7. Just before the game was over
8. What did Marla say to you
9. What the fight was about
10. Since breakfast I have had nothing to eat

Part 9 The Compound-Complex Sentence

You can already recognize simple, compound, and complex sentences. The fourth kind of sentence is the **compound-complex sentence.**

A compound-complex sentence consists of two or more main clauses and one or more subordinate clauses.

In other words, think of a compound-complex sentence as a compound sentence plus a subordinate clause. Within a compound-complex sentence, two sentences are joined. At least one of them has a subordinate clause, which may be an adjective, adverb, or noun clause. Between the main clauses is either a coordinating conjunction or a semicolon.

Here are some examples of compound-complex sentences:

Main Clause   Main Clause   Subordinate Clause

Carol felt dizzy, and we noticed that she looked pale.

Subordinate Clause   Main Clause   Main Clause

When a shark was sighted, the beach was closed, and everyone went home.

Exercise Identify the two main clauses and the subordinate clause in these compound-complex sentences.

1. She realized that Art was listening, and she lowered her voice.

2. I played in the band before I took a job, but now I don't have time.

3. Ike knew that the machine would not fit through the doorway, and he called his boss.

4. Watch where you're going, or you will slip.

5. Don't ask why you were invited; just accept.

6. Watch the machine, and you'll see how it works.

7. Usually the goalie is the player who is most important; this game was unusual.

8. Al wanted to enlist, but he was rejected because he has asthma.

9. Egypt hated its Persian conquerors; it was glad when Alexander the Great defeated them.

10. American Indians had cures that impressed European doctors; however, most of the cures are now lost.

Part 10   A Review of Sentences

There are four basic kinds of sentences.

A **simple sentence** contains one subject and one predicate. Parts of the simple sentence, however, may be compound. A simple sentence tells one idea.

> s.   v.   v.
> Lou was born in Ohio but grew up in Oregon.

A **compound sentence** is made up of two simple sentences. These simple sentences are connected by a comma and coordinating conjunction or by a semicolon. Sometimes a conjunctive adverb follows the semicolon. A compound sentence expresses two related ideas.

> s.   v.   s.   v.
> Lou was born in Ohio; however, he grew up in Oregon.

A **complex sentence** contains one main clause and one or more subordinate clauses. The subordinate clauses may be used as adverbs, adjectives, or nouns. A complex sentence expresses one main idea and one or more dependent ideas.

> s.   v.   s.   v.
> *Although Lou was born in Ohio*, he grew up in Oregon.

A **compound-complex sentence** contains two main clauses and one or more subordinate clauses. The subordinate clauses may be adverb, adjective, or noun clauses. A compound-complex sentence expresses two main ideas, as well as one dependent idea.

                s.   v.   s.   v.   s.

Although Lou was born in Ohio, he grew up in Oregon; now he

      v.

lives in New Mexico.

Exercise A For each sentence, write *Simple*, *Compound*, *Complex*, or *Compound-Complex* to show what kind it is.

1. Denny and his friends went to a movie.
2. Mike said that he would be late.
3. Are these keys yours, or do they belong to Troy?
4. Kathy wrote a letter to the editor, and the letter was published.
5. Did you buy the car because you liked its looks?
6. How pretty the room looks!
7. The salesclerk explained how the amplifier worked.
8. If you have any suggestions, write them down.
9. Carpet beetles eat rugs; however, the larvae can be easily killed.
10. Nobody but Jim stayed and helped after the party.

Exercise B Follow the directions for Exercise A.

1. The Watsons bought postcards, but they forgot to send them.
2. Tony put the pizza in the oven and set the timer.
3. Before you leave, look at these pictures.
4. Doesn't Ed realize that he is being immature, or doesn't he care?
5. A van pulled up, and the band piled in.
6. How many people live in that apartment building?
7. She stopped drilling when the patient raised his hand.
8. Lower the thermostat if you want to save energy.
9. The album that Christina bought was warped.
10. Until Ann moved, she walked or biked to work.

REVIEW Using Compound and Complex Sentences

Compound Sentences Copy each sentence. In each part, underline the subject once and the verb twice. Then add punctuation if it is needed.

1. Sid's aim was off consequently the ball veered.
2. The grapefruit looked ripe but it tasted sour.
3. Nora and Mae checked the basement but they found nothing.
4. Hal draws the blueprints and Kay or Chip gives the estimates.
5. Today is a holiday no mail is delivered.

Complex Sentences Write each subordinate clause.

6. Ms. Baptiste is the woman who runs the program.
7. Don't spread the frosting until the cake has cooled.
8. The passenger whose luggage was lost was reimbursed.
9. I didn't know that you worked at Head Start.
10. We could not tell where the noise was coming from.

A Review of Sentences For each sentence, write *Simple, Compound, Complex*, or *Compound-Complex*.

11. When computers are near radioactivity, their memories can fail.
12. Wood-burning stoves and fireplaces are becoming popular as fuel costs rise.
13. Lucy bought and repaired a chair for less than five dollars.
14. Lincoln announced that Lee had surrendered, and then he ordered the band to play "Dixie."
15. Posters brighten a room; moreover, they cost little.

The Right Word

In preceding sections you have examined the sentence and its parts. In this section you will examine some general ideas about the English language and some specific words that cause confusion.

Part 1 Standard and Nonstandard English

The language that is presented in this textbook would be appropriate at all times and in all places. It is **standard English**. Standard English is the language used by educated people. It is the language that is correct in any situation.

If you do not use standard English in certain situations, some people may think of you as less careful or less intelligent.

Language that is not considered correct or acceptable by all people in all situations is called **nonstandard English**.

Compare these examples of standard and nonstandard English:

Standard	Nonstandard
They were hurt badly.	They was hurt bad.
Lou and I have gone on that road before.	Me and Lou has went on that there road before.
There aren't any people anywhere.	There ain't no people anywheres.

Part 2 Formal and Informal English

Even if you always use standard English, you will use different levels of language at different times. For instance, you wouldn't use the same words in a letter requesting a job interview as you would on the phone to a friend. Some situations are simply more formal than others. Likewise, the appropriate language is either formal or informal. Compare these examples:

Formal: Formed by the skeletons of marine organisms, a coral reef acts as a barrier against powerful ocean waves. Within the lagoon enclosed by a reef, fish and plant life flourish.

Informal: Isn't this coral reef fantastic? I can see lots of colorful fish and plants under the water. With scuba equipment, we could see more.

In general, formal English is marked by a more precise and factual presentation of information. It is marked also by longer sentences with longer words and fewer contractions. Formal English is appropriate for writing some papers, articles, and books. On the other hand, informal English is appropriate for speaking and for more casual writing situations.

Part 3 Other Types of Language

There are other uses of language that you may encounter in everyday situations. **Slang**, for example, is unusual, continually changing language. "Rap," "Get your act together," and "Power trip" are examples of slang. Slang expressions are acceptable only in the most informal speaking situations. Such expressions are not acceptable in your writing.

Sometimes when you read, you may find language you do not understand because it is no longer used. Outdated language is called **archaic** or **obsolete**, and it is usually labeled so in a dictionary.

In addition, certain language related to sports, music, science, law, and the military often has special meanings. Consequently, a word may have different meanings under different circumstances. On board a ship, for example, the word *up* is used to mean "windward." However, on a baseball field *up* is used to mean "at bat."

All of these uses of language are appropriate at certain times. However, using certain language in the wrong situation is inappropriate and confusing. For example, neither using slang in a business report nor formal English in a shopping list is a suitable or sensible use of language. As you become more skillful with standard English, you will be better able to use language appropriate to a particular time and place.

Part 4 Words Often Confused

Certain words are often confused because they look alike or sound alike or because they have similar meanings. However, the words grouped in the following list are not alike. One word cannot substitute for another. Study this list of words often confused. Practice using the right word at the right time.

adapt means "to adjust."

adopt means "to take up and use as one's own."

> Can you *adapt* this engine for a smaller bike?
> The club recently *adopted* a new motto.

advice means "an opinion."
advise is "to suggest or give advice to."

> Anita needed help and asked for *advice*.
> The campaign manager *advised* the candidate.

des′ ert means "a dry, barren region."
de sert′ means "to leave or abandon."
des sert′ (note the difference in spelling) is a sweet food served at the end of a meal.

> There is an oasis in the *desert*.
> Did the man *desert* his family?
> We will have coffee with *dessert*.

hear means "to listen to or to receive sound by the ear."
here refers to this place.

> Did you *hear* the newscaster's comments?
> New townhouses will be built *here*.

its is a possessive, meaning belonging to *it*.
it's is a contraction for *it is* or *it has*.

> The show is in *its* third season.
> *It's* curtain time!

lead (lēd) means "to guide or head." Its past tense is *led*.
lead (led) is a soft metal.

> Please *lead* us home.   Ryan *led* us the wrong way.
> Strips of *lead* hold the pieces of stained glass together.

loose means either "not tight" or "free and untied."
lose means "to be unable to find or keep." It is also the opposite of *win*.

> Since I lost weight, my clothes are *loose*.
> Did you *lose* your job?
> Usually I *lose* at games.

principal means "leading, chief, or highest in importance."
principle refers to a basic truth, rule, or law.

The *principal* water supply comes from underground.
One *principle* of a democracy is rule by the people.

stationary means "not moving, fixed."
stationery refers to materials for writing, especially paper and envelopes.

That *stationary* ship is a floating museum.
Nicole's *stationery* has her initials on it.

their shows possession by *them*.
there means "in that place."
they're is the contraction for *they are*.

Their plates were loaded with food.
The doughnut shop is *there* on the corner.
They're listening to their new albums.

to means "toward or as far as."
too means "also or extremely."

This rickety old staircase leads *to* the attic.
Dwayne plays the trumpet and the trombone *too*.

weather refers to the condition of the atmosphere, including its heat or cold, wetness or dryness.
whether indicates a choice between two things.

The *weather* was unusually calm.
Stacy couldn't decide *whether* to go out or to stay home.

who's is the contraction for *who is* or *who has*.
whose is the possessive form of *who*.

Who's the drummer for Pink Floyd?
Whose bike did you borrow?

your shows possession by *you*.
you're is the contraction for *you are* or *you were*.

I'd recognize *your* voice anywhere.
You're leaving now, aren't you?

Exercise   Choose the right word from the words given.

1. Camels are used for crossing the (desert, dessert).
2. The play was (adapted, adopted) slightly for TV.
3. (Their, There, They're) is the snow shovel.
4. Do you know (who's, whose) in command?
5. We'll be taking inventory next week (to, too).
6. (Your, You're) name is in the newspaper!
7. David gave me some good (advice, advise).
8. Those gymnasts never (loose, lose) their balance.
9. For (desert, dessert) the choices are sherbet or torte.
10. Many foster parents (adapt, adopt) homeless children.
11. The dancers rehearsed (their, there, they're) numbers.
12. (Weather, Whether) is affected by air pressure.
13. The sheriff (adviced, advised) us to avoid Route 66.
14. Shale is a (principal, principle) source of oil.
15. When you mumble, I can't (hear, here) you.

Part 5   Troublesome Verbs

The following pairs of verbs are often confused. Examine the differences between them.

Bring and *Take*

Bring refers to movement toward the person speaking. Example: Trucks *bring* goods here to the loading dock.

Take refers to motion away from the speaker. Example: Did you *take* the chipped plate back to the store?

Here are the principal parts of these verbs:

bring, brought, brought

Present: *Bring* home some bread, please.
Past: The doctor *brought* an assistant with her.
Past Participle: You *have brought* me good luck.

take, took, taken

Present: *Take* some coffee out to the workers.
Past: Carruthers *took* the ball out of bounds.
Past Participle: Somebody *has taken* my jacket.

Learn and Teach

Learn means "to gain knowledge or skill." Example: Did you *learn* what the code means?

Teach means "to help someone learn." Example: Will you *teach* me how to lift weights?

Here are the principal parts of these verbs:

learn, learned, learned

Present: *Learn* your lines before Monday.
Past: Beth *learned* how to place kick.
Past Participle: We *have learned* a lot about tropical fish.

teach, taught, taught

Present: Julia Child *teaches* viewers about cooking.
Past: The foreman *taught* us to use the drill press.
Past Participle: Derek *has taught* his dog simple commands.

Let and Leave

Let means "to allow or permit." Example: *Let* us in.

Leave means "to go away from" or "to allow something to remain." Example: *Leave* the boxes here.

Here are the principal parts of these verbs:

let, let, let

Present: The rangers *let* people into the park.
Past: Jane *let* the dog in.
Past Participle: The supervisor *has let* us work overtime.

leave, left, left

Present: *Leave* the door open, please.
Past: Barrett *left* his business card on the table.
Past Participle: The photographer *has left* without her camera.

Lie and Lay

Lie means "to rest in a flat position" or "to be in a certain place." Example: Lie on your back.

Lay means "to place." Example: Lay your cards down.

These are the principal parts of these verbs:

lie, lay, lain

Present:	Lie down on the examining table.
Past:	The keys lay on the seat.
Past Participle:	All day Brian has lain under a palm tree.

lay, laid, laid

Present:	Lay the logs on the fire.
Past:	The plumber laid out his tools on the floor.
Past Participle:	The workers have laid the tile.

May and Can

The helping verb may refers to permission. May also indicates that something is possible. Might is another form.

> May I continue?   Nancy might forget.

The helping verb can refers to ability. Can means being able, physically or mentally, to do something. Another form is could.

> How far can you run?   Nobody could see.

May and might and can and could have no principal parts.

Rise and Raise

Rise means "to go upward." Example: Warm air rises.

Raise means "to lift or make something go up." Example: Raise your left hand.

Here are the principal parts of these verbs:

rise, rose, risen

Present: Gliders *rise* with the wind.

Past: The symphony members *rose* and bowed.

Past Participle: Because of heavy rains, the river waters *have risen*.

raise, raised, raised

Present: Every year the owner *raises* our rent.

Past: The mechanic *raised* the car on a lift.

Past Participle: The judge *has raised* the fine.

Sit and *Set*

Sit means "to occupy a seat." Example: *Sit* next to me.
Set means "to put." Example: *Set* the tee here.
These are their principal parts:

sit, sat, sat

Present: *Sit* in the penalty box for a while.

Past: Lauren and I *sat* in the balcony.

Past Participle: All season Roberts *has sat* on the bench.

set, set, set

Present: *Set* your packages on the table.

Past: Ann *set* the message next to the phone.

Past Participle: They *have set* their luggage on the conveyor belt.

Exercise   Choose the right verb from those given.

1. The driver (let, left) me operate the forklift.
2. Exhausted, Meredith (lay, laid) on the couch all day.
3. (Bring, Take) those keys over here, please.
4. The instructor (learned, taught) us how to spot faulty wiring.
5. Don't (sit, set) that paint brush on my jacket.
6. (May, Can) I please borrow your saw?
7. The nurse (rose, raised) Diana's hospital bed.

8. (Let, Leave) the dough (rise, raise) for two hours.
9. A pile of bills (lay, laid) on the desk.
10. The passengers (sat, set) in small lifeboats.
11. Kim has (brought, taken) us some egg rolls.
12. The mail carrier (let, left) our package outside in the rain.
13. We must (bring, take) these cans out to the recycling center.
14. Lee (rose, raised) the hood of the car.
15. (Lie, Lay) the packing slip on top of the crate.

Part 6   Usage Problems

The following words are often used incorrectly. To avoid problems, study these examples of standard usage.

accept means "to agree to something or to receive something willingly."

except means "to leave out." *Except* also means "not including."

> The Raiders *accepted* the fifteen-yard penalty.
> No one is *excepted* from the terms of the contract.
> We have all the ingredients *except* corn syrup.

all right is the correct spelling. *Alright* is nonstandard and should be avoided.

> *All right*, I'll stop by later.   Do I look *all right*?

among refers to more than two people or things.
between refers to only two people or things.

> There was a fake stone *among* the jewels.
> We split the Hershey bar *between* the two of us.

amount refers to a certain quantity that cannot be counted. It is used with singular nouns.

number refers to items that can be counted. It is used with plural nouns.

Frieda poured a small *amount* of milk into a cup.
A large *number* of travelers visit the Grand Canyon.

bad is an adjective. Besides modifying nouns and pronouns, *bad* also is used with linking verbs like *feel*.
badly is an adverb. It is used only with action verbs.

> Ramon feels *bad* about the mix-up.
> Chris had a *bad* day yesterday.
> Gustafson pitches *badly*.

beside means "at the side of." It points out location.
besides means "in addition to."

> We sat *beside* the wood-burning stove.
> *Besides* tacos, I also like tamales and enchiladas.

borrow means "to receive something on loan." Don't confuse it with *lend*, meaning "to give out temporarily."

> Nonstandard: Will you borrow me your fishing pole?
> Standard: Will you *lend* me your fishing pole?
> Standard: May I *borrow* your fishing pole?

fewer refers to numbers or things that can be counted.
less refers to a certain amount or quantity.

> There are *fewer* people here today.
> This recipe calls for *less* flour.

Exercise Look for sentences with nonstandard usage. Rewrite those sentences, using the right words. If a sentence is correct, write *Correct* after that number.

1. All right, I'll use less onions.
2. We shared the supplies between the four of us.
3. Eliza works fewer hours on weekends.
4. When he makes a mistake, Ken feels badly.
5. Besides papers, the newsstand also sells magazines.
6. Only a small amount of tickets are unsold.
7. Everyone accept Judith went home early.

8. The personnel department accepts applications.

9. Lisa's parents will borrow her some furniture for her apartment.

10. The patient seems alright today.

11. There is a picnic table besides the stream.

12. Both quarterbacks played bad in last night's game.

13. A large amount of old buildings have been renovated.

14. Many people are trying to use less fuel.

15. Between the four of us, we should be able to think of a solution.

had of and **off of** are nonstandard. In both cases, *of* is unnecessary and should be omitted.

Nonstandard:	If you had of helped, I'd be done by now.
Standard:	If you *had* helped, I'd be done by now.
Nonstandard:	The clasp came off of Gena's necklace.
Standard:	The clasp came *off* Gena's necklace.

himself and **themselves** are standard usage. *Hisself, theirselves,* and *themself* are nonstandard.

Nonstandard:	The mayor hisself led the parade.
Standard:	The mayor *himself* led the parade.
Nonstandard:	The campers found theirselves in a dark cave.
Standard:	The campers found *themselves* in a dark cave.

in means "inside something."
into tells of motion from the outside to the inside of something.

Nonstandard:	The tightrope walker fell in the net.
Standard:	The tightrope walker fell *into* the net.
Nonstandard:	Drop your ballot in this box.
Standard:	Drop your ballot *into* this box.

kind of and **sort of** are not acceptable as modifiers. To be correct, use *rather, fairly, slightly,* or *somewhat* instead.

| Nonstandard: | Danny is sort of shy. |
| Standard: | Danny is *rather* shy. |

Nonstandard:	I have been kind of lonely lately.
Standard:	I have been *somewhat* lonely lately.

like is a preposition. Using *like* as a conjunction before a clause is not fully accepted. Especially in writing, *as* or *as if* is better.

Nonstandard:	Jay looks like he's pleased.
Standard:	Jay looks *as if* he's pleased.
Nonstandard:	Just like I thought, the tank was empty.
Standard:	Just *as* I thought, the tank was empty.

of is used incorrectly in phrases like *would of, must of,* or *couldn't of.* The proper word to use is the verb *have* or its contractions: *would have, must have, couldn't have, might have, shouldn't have.*

Nonstandard:	Alex shouldn't of run away.
Standard:	Alex shouldn't *have* run away.

percent is correct only when it follows a number.
percentage is used when there is no number.

The supermarket's profit is 3 *percent*.
A large *percentage* of the votes went to O'Neal.

says is present tense. It is not standard usage to indicate past action. Use *said* instead. *Goes* is also mistakenly used for *said*. Avoid this incorrect usage.

Nonstandard:	Jan saw Les and says, "Where have you been?"
Standard:	Jan saw Les and *said*, "Where have you been?"
Nonstandard:	Then he goes, "I've been waiting for you."
Standard:	Then he *said*, "I've been waiting for you."

that, which, and **who** are all relative pronouns. *That* may refer to people, animals, or things. However, *which* is used only for animals and things. *Who* refers only to people.

The bookcase *that* Tom built is in the hallway.
Yvonne is one friend *that* can be trusted.
Yom Kippur, *which* is a Jewish holiday, is a time of prayer.
The athletes, *who* came to these games have trained for years.

Exercise Look for sentences with nonstandard usage. Rewrite those sentences, using the right words. If a sentence is correct, write *Correct* after that number.

1. The strangers made theirselves comfortable.

2. Karen looks like she's having a good time.

3. Viewers could hear the coach, which was wearing a microphone.

4. The salesperson gets a percentage of each sale.

5. If Mike had of been in a better mood, he wouldn't of been so quiet.

6. Dick came up to me, and he says, "I'm sorry."

7. Randy tossed an important letter in the wastebasket.

8. Betty thought, as I did, that the house was sort of shaky.

9. That is the woman which drives the lead car.

10. A stunt man dove in a tiny pool.

11. Ted stood by hisself in the corner.

12. One glass fell off of the table.

13. Did you sand the wood just as I told you?

14. "You should of seen the scary part," Mandy said.

15. Late at night the trucker became kind of tired.

REVIEW The Right Word

Using Words Correctly Choose the correct word from the words given in parentheses.

1. (Your, You're) taking a course in wilderness survival, aren't you?

2. Do you know (who's, whose) books these are?

3. (Its, It's) hard to study (here, hear).

4. The realtor's (advice, advise) was to sell the property.

5. The spy changed his name and (adapted, adopted) a new identity.

6. Michelle's brother (lead, led) the search party.

7. The bakery sells fancy (deserts, desserts).

8. (Bring, Take) your tickets to me at the box office.

9. The Suziki method (learns, teaches) young children to play the violin.

10. Brandon (let, left) a big muskie get away.

11. "The Amazing Reynaldo" (lay, laid) on a bed of nails.

12. (May, Can) I finish the pie, please?

13. The elevator (rose, raised) to the top floor.

14. We'll (sit, set) outside and listen to the music.

15. People (sat, set) their tickets on the counter.

16. (All right, Alright), I'll make several copies.

17. I'll divide this small (amount, number) of Pepsi (among, between) the three of us.

18. Michael (goes, said), "I could (of, have) told you that."

19. Adam replaced the muffler (hisself, himself).

20. The singers (who, which) made this record are (kind of, fairly) well known.

Capitalization

The use of capital letters makes your writing easier to read. Capital letters call attention to certain special words, as well as to words that begin sentences.

There are specific rules for capitalizing words. This section will present these rules. If you have questions about capitalization, refer to this section.

Proper Nouns and Adjectives

Capitalize proper nouns and proper adjectives.

Common nouns are the names of whole groups of people, places, or things. **Proper nouns** are the names of particular persons, places, or things. **Proper adjectives** are adjectives formed from proper nouns.

Common Noun	Proper Noun	Proper Adjective
state	**T**exas	**T**exan
mountains	**A**lps	**A**lpine
country	**S**pain	**S**panish

The following rules will help you to determine if a noun is a proper noun.

Names and Titles

Capitalize people's names. Also capitalize the initials or abbreviations that stand for names.

> **A. E. H**ousman   **A**lfred **E**dward **H**ousman
> **J**ohn **W. C**oltrane   **J**ohn **W**illiam **C**oltrane

Capitalize the titles used with people's names. Also capitalize the initials or abbreviations that stand for those titles. Always capitalize *Ms.*, *Miss*, *Mrs.*, and *Mr.*

> **R**ev. Adam Moses   **P**rofessor Helmer
> **M**r. Eugene O'Malley   **D**r. Lucille Ortez
> **G**en. J. G. Fine   **M**ayor Young

Do not capitalize a title that is used without a name. It is a common noun.

> Sarah Kimpel was made a vice-president of her company.

Capitalize titles of very high importance, even when they are used without names.

> the **P**resident of the **U**nited **S**tates
> the **S**ecretary of **S**tate
> the **Q**ueen of **E**ngland
> the **P**ope
> the **S**ecretary-**G**eneral of the **UN**

Family Relationships

Capitalize such family words as *mother, father, grandma*, and *uncle* when they are used as names. If the noun is preceded by a possessive word or by *a* or *the*, it is not capitalized.

> We planned an anniversary party for Mom and Dad.
> My mother left Japan when she was ten.
> Last year Grandma started ice-skating.
> The aunt I have never met is Aunt Bobbie.

The Pronoun *I*

Capitalize the pronoun *I*.

I meant what I said.   Yes, I'll go.

The Supreme Being and Sacred Writings

Capitalize all words referring to God, to the Holy Family, and to religious scriptures.

the **A**lmighty	the **S**on of **G**od	the **B**ible
the **L**ord	the **O**ld **T**estament	the **T**almud
the **B**lessed **V**irgin	the **H**oly **G**ospel	**A**llah

Capitalize personal pronouns referring to God.

They prayed to the Lord and gave **H**im thanks.

Exercise A Copy these sentences. Change small letters to capital letters wherever necessary.

1. My brother and i like danish pastries.
2. When was indira gandhi the prime minister of india?
3. According to mom, pizza is not an italian food.
4. The children recited bible verses for rev. parks.
5. Mayor martinez has a large mexican-american constituency.
6. The british author g. k. chesterton wrote about a priest, father brown, in his detective stories.
7. The manager is ms. suzy kraske.
8. Sometimes president johnson was called l.b.j.
9. Did senator baker sponsor the bill?
10. Has sgt. jones reported to the captain yet?

Exercise B Follow the directions for Exercise A.

1. Do lt. graves and her husband live on the base?

2. None of the doctors but dr. cane make house calls.
3. When my grandmother is sick, dad takes care of her.
4. Was president herbert hoover related to j. edgar hoover?
5. Many russian troops are stationed near the chinese border.
6. Recently uncle bob reread the new testament.
7. None of my other aunts are like aunt dorothy.
8. My sister lynn and i volunteered to help at the telethon.
9. She lit a candle to st. jude, who prays for impossible cases.
10. The new dean of the college is dr. rachel shapiro.

Geographical Names

In a geographical name, capitalize the first letter of each word except articles and prepositions.

The article *the* used before a place name is not part of the name. Therefore it is not capitalized.

Continents:	South America, Australia, Asia, Africa
Bodies of Water:	the Red River, Lake Superior, the Pacific Ocean, the Bering Sea, Chesapeake Bay, Salt Creek
Land Forms:	the Mohave Desert, Channel Islands, Cape Horn, Mt. Rainier, Grand Canyon, the Great Plains, Shenandoah Valley
Political Units:	Michigan, Houston, Scotland, Republic of Korea, Province of Alberta, Sixth Congressional District, the Middle East
Public Areas:	Washington Memorial, Rocky Mountain National Park, Peabody Museum, Disneyland, Indiana Dunes
Roads and Highways:	Peachtree Avenue, Route 6, Interstate 101, Indiana Tollway, Central Street, Governor's Highway

Directions and Sections

Capitalize names of sections of the country.

The **E**ast is more urban than the **W**est.
Hillary wants to move to the **S**outhwest.

Capitalize proper adjectives that come from names of sections of the country.

Southern fried chicken   a **N**orthern state
a **M**idwestern farmhouse   a **W**est **C**oast resort

Do not capitalize directions of the compass.

Brookfield is west of Chicago.
Go east to the second stoplight.

Do not capitalize adjectives that come from words showing direction.

The White Mountains are in northern Vermont.
The tornado is moving in a southerly direction.

Exercise A   Find the words in these sentences that should be capitalized. Write the words using the necessary capital letters.

1. I live in the fourth congressional district.
2. The new england settlers made the most of their natural resources.
3. Go east on main street to reach the lake.
4. Is north america larger than south america?
5. The dead sea is an inland sea.
6. Is greenland an island?
7. Much of our shellfish comes from chesapeake bay.
8. Leaves turn later in the south than in the north.
9. Dale grew up in dayton, ohio, and has a midwestern accent.
10. We drove south through the great smoky mountains.

Exercise B Follow the directions for Exercise A.

1. Does interstate 74 run through champaign county?
2. The statue of liberty is located on liberty island.
3. He is buried in arlington national cemetery.
4. Is nevada rich in minerals?
5. Sid's cousin lives in east moline, a city in illinois.
6. The indian ocean is west of australia.
7. The northeast is heavily industrialized.
8. Many counties in colorado have indian or spanish names.
9. The longest river in africa is the nile river.
10. The beaches on the east coast are very popular.

Names of Organizations and Institutions

Capitalize the names of organizations and institutions, including political parties, governmental bodies or agencies, schools, colleges, churches, hospitals, clubs, businesses, and abbreviations of these names.

Democratic Party	Glenbrook Hospital
Federal Aviation Administration	Chicago Motor Club
Wright Junior College	Pacific Stereo
Trinity Lutheran Church	FBI

Do not capitalize words like *hospital*, *school*, and *company* when they are not used as parts of names.

Four companies made bids for the contract to build a new school.

Names of Events, Documents, and Periods of Time

Capitalize the names of historical events, documents, and periods of time.

Battle of Bunker Hill	Bill of Rights	the Crusades
World War II	the Elizabethan Age	Magna Carta

Months, Days, and Holidays

Capitalize names of months, days, and holidays, but not the names of seasons.

November	Memorial Day	spring
Monday	Fourth of July	winter

Races, Languages, Nationalities, and Religions

Capitalize the names of races, languages, nationalities, and religions. Also capitalize any adjectives that come from these names.

Japanese	Italian	Moslem	Latin
English	Indian	Judaism	Catholic

School Subjects

Do not capitalize the names of school subjects, except specific course titles followed by a number.

math	World History 300
art	Consumer Problems I

Remember that the names of languages are always capitalized.

Spanish	English	German	Russian

Ships, Trains, Airplanes, and Automobiles

Capitalize the names of ships, trains, airplanes, and automobiles.

U.S.S. *Lexington*	*San Francisco Zephyr*	*Pontiac Firebird*

B.C., A.D.

Capitalize the abbreviations *B.C.* and *A.D.*

Augustus ruled Rome from 27 **B.C.** to **A.D.** 14.

Exercise A   Write the words that should be capitalized. Use the necessary capital letters.

1. She teaches biology at oakland community college.
2. The day-care center is in mt. olivet baptist church.
3. Shawn built a model of the *liberator*, a world war II bomber.
4. The crusades were wars against the moslems.
5. The *orient express* was a unique train.
6. In june i begin my summer job at the hospital.
7. Michael reese hospital offers its employees english and other college courses.
8. Our business I test is on the monday after thanksgiving.
9. The jewish holiday of hanukkah lasts eight days.
10. Ina translates chinese speeches at the united nations.

Exercise B   Follow the directions for Exercise A.

1. Dee has a degree in math and works for the irs.
2. The egyptians developed the first lunar calendar in about 4241 b.c.
3. Mr. elam teaches art at delgado junior college.
4. Lee got a mortgage guaranteed by the fha from the first national bank.
5. The a.m.a. is not a union.
6. Thornton worked for blue cross until last winter.
7. The fiat she drives is a company car.
8. My u.s. history teacher told us to memorize the bill of rights.
9. On saturday the pirates will play the cubs.
10. The world survived without aspirin until a.d. 1893.

First Words

Sentences and Poetry

Capitalize the first word of every sentence and the first word of most lines of poetry.

> The plane passed the sound barrier. People in the area heard the boom.

> The woods are lovely, dark, and deep,
> But I have promises to keep . . .
> —from "The Road Not Taken," by Robert Frost

Sometimes in modern poetry, the lines of a poem do not begin with capital letters.

Quotations

Capitalize the first word of a direct quotation.

A **direct quotation** tells the exact words of a speaker or writer.

> William Shakespeare wrote, "The course of true love never did run smooth."

A **divided quotation** is a direct quotation broken into two parts by words such as *she said* or *he remarked*. The first word of the second part is not capitalized unless it starts a new sentence.

> "It is true," said Carrie, "that we can never please everyone."
> "It is true," said Carrie. "We can never please everyone."

Letter Parts

Capitalize the first word in the greeting of a letter. Also capitalize the name of the person addressed, or words like *Sir* and *Madam* that stand for names.

> Dear Ms. Oppenheim: Dear Sir or Madam:

460

In the complimentary close, capitalize only the first word.

Sincerely yours,   Very fondly,

Outlines

Capitalize the first word of each item in an outline. Also capitalize the letters before each line.

    I. Film comedians
      A. Silent film comedians
        1. Individuals
        2. Groups
      B. Comedians of the 1930's

Titles

Capitalize the first word and all important words in the titles of chapters, magazine articles, short stories, essays, poems, television programs, radio programs, and songs or short pieces of music.

Chapter title:	Chapter 6, "The Astronauts"
Magazine article:	"Behind the Scenes with the Who"
Short story:	"Too Early Spring"
Essay:	"A World at Peace"
Poem:	"My Last Duchess"
Television program:	"The Tonight Show"
Song:	"Happy Days Are Here Again"

Capitalize the first word and all important words in titles of books, newspapers, magazines, plays, movies, works of art, and long musical compositions.

Book title:	*Gnomes*
Newspaper:	*Boston Globe*
Magazine:	*Consumer Reports*
Play:	*No Place To Be Somebody*
Movie:	*Breaking Away*
Work of art:	*Winged Victory*
Long musical composition:	*Barber of Seville*

Exercise A Write the words that should be capitalized. Use capital letters correctly.

1. i listen to "radio mystery theatre."

2. "did Sal get a role in *romeo and juliet?*" asked Liz.

3. the American national anthem is "the star-spangled banner."

4. "did you have the winning number?" asked Rae.

5. "why," asked Nina, "don't you think before you speak?"

6. "stop!" called Jake. "that's my suitcase."

7. carrie's story "a prairie summer" appeared in *seventeen*.

8. dear mr. nolan:

   your subscription to *ms.* is about to expire. we have enclosed a renewal form so that you will not miss an issue.

                    sincerely yours,

9. have you ever seen the movie *animal crackers?*

10. we discussed "notes of a native daughter" from *slouching towards bethlehem*.

Exercise B Follow the directions for Exercise A.

1. "when i was young," said Joe, " 'sesame street' didn't exist."

2. marta said that she didn't know the words to "silent night."

3. II. native american art
      A. practical arts
         1. wampum
         2. ceremonial bowls

4. the painting *government bureau* looks frightening.

5. the *sun-times* is a Chicago newspaper.

6. read Chapter 4, "defensive driving," in *let's drive right*.

7. i enjoyed the article "nicknames and social status" in *psychology today*.

8. "did anybody," asked Lori, "take my copy of *time* magazine?"

9. matt recited the entire poem, "the skeleton in armor."

10. "would you like to hear Beethoven's *ninth symphony?*" asked Ann. "there's an extra ticket."

REVIEW Capitalization

Using Capital Letters Correctly Copy each of these sentences. Change small letters to capital letters wherever necessary.

1. dr. moore is a surgeon at st. francis hospital.
2. is loyola university a catholic school?
3. one great apache chief was chief cochise.
4. the southern pecan pie at emory's diner is good.
5. we found lithuanian easter eggs in a shop near central park.
6. the jewish prophet isaiah lived in the eighth century b.c.
7. the story of adam and eve is in genesis.
8. drive north through canada to reach alaska.
9. the state of hawaii is composed of islands.
10. does modern dance I satisfy the physical education requirement?
11. read "the laughing man" in *nine stories* by j. d. salinger.
12. was the white house burned down in the war of 1812?
13. our english class discussed the story "the black madonna."
14. was senator long formerly a member of the republican party?
15. chevrolets are manufactured by general motors.
16. *the dollmaker* by harriet arnow is about appalachia and detroit during world war II.
17. mary baker eddy founded the christian science religion.
18. "last sunday," said pat, "the minister requested contributions for southeast asian refugees."
19. the mormons settled salt lake city.
20. the first woman philosopher in recorded history was hypatia, who died in a.d. 415.

Punctuation

Road signs guide you when you drive. Similarly, punctuation marks guide you when you read. Punctuation marks show readers where to stop or slow down or change direction.

When you write, your punctuation signals your reader. It shows groups of words that belong together. It indicates how sentences should be read. Generally, punctuation helps your reader to understand your meaning.

End Marks

End marks are the punctuation marks that indicate the end of a sentence. The **period**, the **question mark**, and the **exclamation point** are the three kinds of end marks.

The Period

Use a period at the end of a declarative sentence.

A **declarative sentence** is a sentence that makes a statement. You use declarative sentences when you tell something.

The rate of inflation is rising.

Use a period at the end of most imperative sentences.

An **imperative sentence** is a sentence that orders or requests someone to do something.

Step to the rear of the elevator, please.

Imperative sentences sometimes express strong excitement or emotion. For those sentences, exclamation points, rather than periods, are used.

Watch out!   Don't move!

Use a period at the end of an indirect question.

An **indirect question** tells that someone asked a question. However, it does not give the exact words of the question.

The flight attendant asked if everyone was comfortable.

A **direct question** shows the exact words of the person asking the question. A direct question ends with a question mark. Notice how a direct question differs:

The flight attendant asked, "Is everyone comfortable?"

Use a period at the end of an abbreviation or an initial. An **abbreviation** is a shortened form of a word. An **initial** is a first letter that stands for a word.

Col. B. Johnson, Jr.   10 ft., 2 in.   2:00 P.M.

Some abbreviations do not use periods. If you aren't sure whether or not to use a period with an abbreviation, check the abbreviation in your dictionary.

FM (*Frequency Modulation*)
NATO (*North Atlantic Treaty Organization*)
FBI (*Federal Bureau of Investigation*)

Use a period after each number or letter for an item in an outline or a list.

(An Outline)	(A List)
I. Records	1. names
A. Olympic	2. addresses
1. Winter Sports	3. phone numbers

Use a period between dollars and cents and before a decimal.

$42.50 $1.59   2.06   .667

The Question Mark

Use a question mark at the end of an interrogative sentence.

An **interrogative sentence** is a sentence that asks a question.

What are your strong points?

The Exclamation Point

Use an exclamation point at the end of an exclamatory sentence.

An **exclamatory sentence** expresses excitement or other strong emotion.

That's a mess!   How great you look!

Use an exclamation point after an interjection.

An **interjection** is one or more words that show strong feeling. Sometimes the interjection is a sound.

Hurray!   What luck!   Oh my gosh!   Pow!

Exercise A Copy the following sentences, adding the necessary punctuation.

1. Well Look who's here
2. Doesn't he call the baby Sammy
3. The government agency that looks after working conditions is OSHA
4. Bill Mauldin became famous for his army cartoons
5. Does Dr Nunez have an office in this building

6. Bill asked the conductor if she could change a twenty for the $125 fare

7. Rev J A Weaver is the chaplain at the hospital

8. Open the door for Col Kale, please

9. That FM station doesn't come on until 6:00 AM

10. Is Tracey an RN or an LPN

Exercise B Follow the directions for Exercise A.

1. Which states are part of the USSR

2. The turkey weighs 8 lbs, 11 oz and costs $795

3. I Allergies
   A Reactions
      1 Sneezing

4. J Edgar Hoover was the first director of the FBI

5. Is her address still 805 S Elm Street

6. Ow That hurts

7. Sixty percent of the students answered the questionnaire

8. Ann asked if we were from St Paul

9. Does the FBI investigate airplane crashes

10. Carl asked whether Mt Fuji was in Japan

The Comma

A comma is used to separate words that do not go together. When you are speaking, you can pause for breaks in thought. When you are writing, however, you need commas for breaks. In this way, commas help you to communicate clearly.

Commas in a Series

Use a comma after every item in a series except the last one.

A series is three or more items of the same kind. You may use a series of words, phrases, or clauses.

Words: Flowers, candy, and other gifts crowded the hospital room.

Phrases: Vanessa hurried through the door, up the stairs, and into the president's office.

Clauses: The fire chief explained how the fire started, how it spread, and how much damage it caused.

Use commas after *first, second, third*, and so on, when these adverbs introduce a series.

The speaker told us how to succeed: first, believe in yourself; second, set goals; and third, work hard.

When there are two or more adjectives before a noun, use commas between them.

Tall, sleek, modern skyscrapers line Fifth Avenue.

Exercise A   Copy these sentences. Add commas where necessary.

1. Old newspapers full ashtrays and dirty cups littered the room.
2. Dr. Wade Dr. Yoshi and Dr. Bird were being paged.
3. Decals posters and notices covered the window.
4. Paul hesitated shrugged and agreed.
5. The tool is a clamp a wrench and a wire cutter all in one.
6. I wrote to the mayor the governor and the President.
7. Her thin lively face is almost never still.
8. He worked cheerfully carefully and quickly.
9. Cleo gathered the firewood started the campfire and set up the tent.
10. First shampoo your hair; second apply the conditioner; third massage it into your hair; fourth rinse thoroughly.

Exercise B   Follow the directions for Exercise A.

1. First listen; second question; third form your opinion.

2. The tall shy man carried an umbrella a briefcase and a hat.

3. The pain of a heart attack can be felt in the chest arms and lower jaws.

4. The attendant wiped the dust grime and dead bugs from the windshield.

5. Roger has an evening class on Mondays Tuesdays and Fridays.

6. The workers packed crates in the hot dusty plant.

7. Mary looked through her notebook around her desk and then in her locker.

8. Check the lining the seams and the quality of the material.

9. Small pale lights shone dimly through the thick wet snow.

10. Aspirin fluids and rest can help colds and the flu.

Commas with Introductory Words

Use a comma to separate an introductory word, a long phrase, or a clause from the rest of the sentence.

Yes, I have plenty of time. (introductory word)

After the last round of the match, Cosell interviewed both boxers. (prepositional phrases)

Frowning slightly, Blake reached for a chess piece. (participial phrase)

When you leave, lock the door. (adverb clause)

As you can see, commas are used after introductory words such as *yes* and *no*. They are also used after prepositional phrases, participial phrases, and adverb clauses that begin sentences.

Sometimes the comma may be left out. When there would be little pause in speaking, no comma is needed.

At night we made a fire.

Commas with Interrupters

Use commas to set off one or more words that interrupt the flow of thought in a sentence.

A doctor, therefore, needs malpractice insurance.

The players were, I believe, unusually rough.

Linda Ronstadt, for example, requires no back-up singers.

These words are additional examples of interrupters. Set them off with commas.

I believe	I suppose	however
by the way	in addition	furthermore
in fact	moreover	nevertheless

Exercise A Copy these sentences. Add commas correctly.

1. When I opened the window I knocked over the plant.
2. No there's still time.
3. Ira however hasn't registered to vote.
4. Holding the baby in one arm he clutched the groceries with the other.
5. After her first week on the job Marilyn began to feel confident.
6. As most of us grow older we become less sensitive to pain.
7. Moreover not all oil-producing countries belong to OPEC.
8. The United States for instance does not belong.
9. Ms. Barber I think is the expert.
10. Honey on the other hand does provide nutrition.

Exercise B Follow the directions for Exercise A.

1. Laura has an original style to say the least.
2. Although she dances Tina can't skate at all.
3. Therefore Curt declined the scout's invitation.
4. Briskly nodding to her nosy neighbor Celia strode by.

5. Your brother for instance is always very helpful.
6. Your Honda I am sorry to say is beyond repair.
7. In conclusion we must request a refund.
8. Furthermore tranquilizers can be deadly.
9. If you try again however you might succeed.
10. Watching television in Herb's opinion is a waste of time.

Commas with Nouns of Direct Address

Use commas to set off nouns of direct address.

When you speak or write to someone, you often use the person's name. The name of someone directly spoken to is a **noun of direct address**.

> Julie, listen to this song.
>
> The nearest gas station, Mark, is two miles away.
>
> Please, folks, stay in your seats.
>
> Are you ready yet, team?

As in the last example, nouns of direct address may sometimes be common nouns.

Commas with Appositives

Use commas to set off most appositives.

An **appositive** is one or more words that explain or identify another word. The appositive directly follows the word it explains.

> Most Chinese food is stir-fried in a wok, a rounded metal pan.
>
> The head nurse, Barbara Allen, instructs the aides.
>
> Langston Hughes, a poet and playwright from Missouri, wrote *Shakespeare in Harlem*.

As in the final example, an appositive may contain a prepositional phrase.

A noun used as an appositive is called a **noun in apposition**. If the noun in apposition is a single name, it is not usually set off by commas.

My friend Brian plays the drums.

Commas with Quotations

Use commas to set off the explanatory words of a direct quotation.

Explanatory words are statements like *she said*, *Martin asked*, or *JoAnne noted*. Such words are not part of the quotation.

Explanatory words often come before the quotation. Use a comma after these explanatory words.

Debbie said, "I don't agree with that candidate."

Now look at this quotation:

"I don't agree with that candidate," Debbie said.

The explanatory words come after the quotation in the sentence above. Notice that the comma at the end of the quotation belongs inside the quotation marks.

At times, a quotation is divided into two parts. The explanatory words then separate the two parts. This is a *divided quotation*:

"I don't agree," Debbie said, "with that candidate."

In a divided quotation, use a comma within the quotation marks after the first part of the sentence. Use another comma after the explanatory words.

Remember that indirect quotations do not show the speaker's exact words. No commas are used.

Debbie said that she doesn't agree with that candidate.

Commas in Compound Sentences

Use a comma before the conjunction between the two main clauses of a compound sentence.

The taxi stopped, and five people hopped out.

When the main clauses are very short and are joined by *and*, the comma is not necessary.

I blinked and she disappeared.

Very short main clauses are sometimes joined by *but* or *or*. Since the words *but* and *or* mark a change in the flow of thought, a comma is used.

Lisa fell, but she wasn't hurt.

Remember that compound sentences differ from sentences with compound subjects or predicates. There is no comma before the *and* that joins a compound subject or predicate.

The test pilot flew a new jet and landed it safely.

Exercise A Copy these sentences. Add commas where they are needed.

1. The car an old Chevy seemed to be abandoned.
2. "Run ten laps" said the coach.
3. "Tom" said Maureen "here is my sister Nell."
4. India already an enormous country has a rapidly growing population.
5. Charles works and he works hard.
6. He laughed politely but he was not amused.
7. Millie have you seen Jerome?
8. Shovel the snow off the roof or it might collapse.
9. Jim Thorpe played in several sports but is best remembered for football.
10. Alice Walker a novelist and an editor appeared on "Today."

1. "Did Elizabeth find that book yet Mel or is she still looking?" asked Carol.

2. Joan Baez is a singer but she also champions social causes.

3. Your taxi is here Gloria.

4. By the way Neal Ms. Mills called and wants you to call back.

5. Harry I would like you to meet Ms. Chen my math teacher.

6. We stood still and listened but we didn't hear a sound.

7. Did she take your case or did she refer you elsewhere?

8. The Congo river in Africa curves widely and it empties into the Atlantic.

9. "Your jokes" muttered Gil "are not funny."

10. Have you seen my brother Joy?

Commas in Dates

In dates, use a comma between the day of the month and the year.

July 4, 1776   May 8, 1982

When a date is part of a sentence, a comma follows the year.

Ralph Nader was born on February 27, 1934, in Winsted, Connecticut.

Commas in Place Names

Use a comma between the name of a city or town and the name of its state or country.

Nashville, Tennessee   Caracas, Venezuela

Rome, Italy   Oakland, California

If a sentence contains an address, use a comma after each item.

> Send your entry to Eastman Kodak Company, 343 State Street, Rochester, New York 14650.

A comma is not used between the state and the ZIP code.

Commas in Letters

Use a comma after the salutation of a friendly letter. Use a comma after the closing of a friendly letter or a business letter.

> Dear Erica,   Very truly yours,

Commas with Nonrestrictive Clauses

Use commas to set off nonrestrictive clauses.

A **nonrestrictive clause** is a clause that simply adds an idea to a sentence. The meaning of the sentence would be complete without it. The clause is not needed for the sense of the sentence.

A **restrictive clause** is a clause that is essential to the meaning of a sentence. For the sentence to make sense, the clause is needed. When a restrictive clause is dropped from a sentence, the meaning changes.

Nonrestrictive clause:	The Black Hawks, *who lost today,* moved to third place.
	The Black Hawks moved to third place. (The clause can be dropped from the sentence.)
Restrictive clause:	The player *who made the winning goal* was Bob Santini.
	The player was Bob Santini. (The meaning changes when the clause is dropped.)

To decide whether a clause is nonrestrictive, read the sentence without it. If the meaning doesn't change, the clause is nonrestrictive. It needs commas before and after it.

Restrictive clauses are often used to identify or to point out the person or thing they modify. Without such identification, the meaning of a sentence would not be clear. Nonrestrictive clauses, on the other hand, do not add any essential information to the sentence.

Restrictive clause:	The comedian who wears a white suit is Steve Martin. (The clause tells which one.)
Nonrestrictive clause:	Steve Martin, who wears a white suit, makes crazy faces.
	Steve Martin makes crazy faces.
	(The clause is not needed.)
Restrictive clause:	Carol Marin is the anchorperson who reports the news at 5 P.M. (The clause tells which one.)
Nonrestrictive clause:	Carol Marin, who reports the news at 5 P.M., explained the ruling.
	Carol Marin explained the ruling.
	(The clause is not needed.)

Commas To Avoid Confusion

Use a comma whenever the reader might otherwise be confused. Although no rule may apply, some sentences might be misread without commas.

For example, without commas, the following sentences could be misunderstood:

> Whatever you sing you sing well.
> Outside the fairgrounds were crowded.

With commas, the sentences are clearer.

> Whatever you sing, you sing well.
> Outside, the fairgrounds were crowded.

Exercise A Copy the following sentences. Add commas where necessary. Some sentences are correct.

1. Inside freshly baked bread awaited us.
2. The family that lived next door has moved to Wichita Kansas.
3. The address of the Northwest Campus is 3400 Broadway Gary Indiana 46408.
4. The first Ferris wheel which held more than a thousand passengers was built for the World's Fair in Chicago in 1893.
5. The Ferris wheel was designed by G. W. Gale Ferris of Galesburg Illinois.
6. The only antibiotic that the patient has had is penicillin.
7. Dear Ramona
    The roses that you sent were lovely. Thank you very much.
                    Sincerely yours
8. Sissy Spacek whom I like played the lead.
9. The first workable light bulb was invented in Menlo Park New Jersey in October 1879.
10. We bought Alaska on March 30 1867 for $7,200,000.

Exercise B Follow the directions for Exercise A.

1. The people I like like me.
2. When Josh walks through the furniture shakes.
3. The card was postmarked May 3 1980 and arrived on May 4.
4. If Loretta walks over Jay drives her home.
5. Earl Campbell who plays in the NFL did the commercial.
6. The electrician who wired this made a mistake.
7. The number that you called has been disconnected.
8. Carla who likes to travel is in Iowa.
9. The Jan Grey who won the trophy is not I.
10. Her address which she remembered to put on the letter is 522 Meade Avenue Chicago Illinois 60639.

The Semicolon

Use a semicolon to join the parts of a compound sentence if no coordinating conjunction is used.

The city has a phone number for emergencies; it is 911.

If the parts of a compound sentence contain several commas, separate the clauses with a semicolon.

The British flag is red, white, and blue; and the Irish flag is red, white, and green.

When there are commas within parts of a series, use semicolons to separate the parts.

The members of the band are Ross Alonzo, drums; Marcy Donovan, guitar; Jeb O'Donnell, bass; and Katie Spencer, banjo.

Use a semicolon before a conjunctive adverb that joins the clauses of a compound sentence.

As you have learned, the parts of a compound sentence are often joined by words like *however, therefore, moreover, otherwise, so, then, yet, besides, consequently,* and *nevertheless.* Such words, called **conjunctive adverbs**, follow a semicolon.

Jonathan fell asleep on the subway; consequently, he missed his stop.

The Colon

Use a colon after the greeting of a business letter.

Dear Sir or Madam: Dear Mr. Williams:

Use a colon between numerals indicating hours and minutes.

10:27 A.M.   3:30 P.M.

Use a colon to introduce a list of items. The colon indicates a pause before the items that follow.

> Air pollution comes from the following sources: cars, trucks, buses, factories, and smokers.

If there would be no pause in speaking, a colon is not used before a list.

> The six largest American cities are New York, Los Angeles, Chicago, Philadelphia, Detroit, and Boston.

Exercise A Copy the word before and after each missing semicolon or colon. Add the correct punctuation mark.

1. The train stops at these stations Grand, Western, and Belmont.
2. The park was filled with people the first day of spring had arrived.
3. Ramsey was not fired furthermore, he was not asked to resign.
4. The class starts at 800, but Barb is there by 745.
5. Sunspots interfere with computers, radios, and civil defense sirens and these solar flares also affect the weather.
6. These cities host nuclear power plants Crystal River, Florida Batavia, Illinois and Three Mile Island, Pennsylvania.
7. Beth had worked overtime she arrived home tired, cross, and hungry.
8. These books influenced public opinion greatly *Uncle Tom's Cabin, Oliver Twist, The Jungle,* and *Silent Spring.*
9. Dear Madam
   Please cancel my subscription to your newspaper.
10. Sandra enjoys fixing cars she wants to be a mechanic.

Exercise B Follow the directions for Exercise A.

1. We have abundant coal resources however, coal smoke is a pollutant.
2. The bus leaves at 215 you're just in time.

3. Dear Ms. Jackson
   Thank you for your generous contribution.
4. Brenda had an interview at 9:00 therefore, she set the alarm for 7:00.
5. Her collection includes records by Sonny Rollins, Nina Simone, and Bud Powell I was impressed.
6. Gravy gets lumpy quickly therefore, stir it constantly.
7. Vote for me I'll get things done.
8. Notify these departments immediately security, payroll, and personnel.
9. Ms. Kull is a dangerous imposter notify security, payroll, and personnel at once.
10. He turned in the air and caught the ball then he raced across the goal line.

The Dash

Dashes Used with Interrupters

As you have learned, commas set off words or short phrases, like *I believe* and *moreover*, that interrupt a sentence. When a long explanation interrupts the thought, however, use a **dash**.

> The "youth vote"—eighteen-year-olds got the vote in 1971—is sought by many politicians.
> Mother Nature's Restaurant—it specializes in health foods—opened in the old warehouse.

The Dash Before a Summary

Use a dash after a series if a summary statement follows.

> Louis Armstrong, Buddy Bolden, Bessie Smith, and Duke Ellington—they helped to develop jazz music.
> Chocolate chip, rocky road, peach, and peppermint—those are my favorite ice cream flavors.

Exercise   Copy these sentences. Insert dashes as needed.

1. The Civil Service exam I plan to take it will be given next Tuesday.

2. Louis, Robinson, Ali he had seen them all.

3. A folding canteen, a wrist compass, a water purifier, all could be found at the surplus store.

4. The brilliant colors yellow, red, lime caught the sun.

5. A school bus luckily it was empty blocked the alley.

6. The recession a few had predicted it had arrived.

7. She keeps records of medical expenses, interest payments oh, everything that is tax deductible.

8. Scissors, tweezers, toothpick, blade they were all included in the Swiss army knife.

9. "Turn the other cheek" that's what Brenda is saying.

10. Romeo and Juliet, Hamlet, Macbeth these are some of Shakespeare's most famous characters.

The Hyphen

Use a hyphen if part of a word must be carried over from one line to the next. Hyphens separate words only between syllables.

> I recognized an old, yellowed photo-
>   graph of my grandfather.

Only words of two or more syllables can be broken by a hyphen. Never divide one-syllable words, like *shout* or *height*, at the end of a line. Use your dictionary to check syllables.

Never leave a single letter at the end of a line. This division of *isolate* for example, would be incorrect: *i-solate*. Do not begin a line with a single letter either. This division of *imaginary* would be incorrect: *imaginar-y*.

Use a hyphen in compound numbers from twenty-one to ninety-nine.

> thirty-one days   seventy-nine clips

Use a hyphen in fractions.

a three-fifths majority   one-half of the distance

Use a hyphen in certain compound nouns, such as *editor-in- chief, sister-in-law, spin-off,* and *great-uncle*.

The *stand-in* for the part is my *brother-in-law*.

Use a hyphen or hyphens between words that make up a compound adjective used before a noun.

Mohr Corporation has excellent *on-the-job* training.
but: Workers are trained on the job.

When a compound adjective is used after a noun, as in the second example, it is not usually hyphenated.

Check a dictionary to find out if a word needs a hyphen. Here are some examples of compound adjectives:

eight-year-old girl	out-of-date fashions
run-down neighborhood	do-it-yourself project

Exercise   Write the word or words that should be hyphenated. Add the necessary hyphens. Use a dictionary if you need to.

1. A sharp eyed cabbie noticed the smoke.
2. The medium rare steak was delicious.
3. My brother in law is twenty two.
4. A six year old child can usually pedal a bike.
5. The two wheeler is on sale for twenty five dollars.
6. Forty five minutes can pass quickly.
7. The Vice President visited the ex mayor.
8. The half awake janitor dragged herself upstairs.
9. The first two thirds of the outline is organized well.
10. The Commander in Chief had arrived.
11. The dark eyed man had a worn out appearance.
12. With a short term loan, we were able to buy a car.
13. Self service stations have some drawbacks.
14. The half baked cake looked less than appetizing.
15. My great aunt bought me a warm up jacket.

The Apostrophe

One common function of the **apostrophe** is to form the possessive of nouns. To place the apostrophe correctly, you should know if a noun is singular or plural.

To form the possessive of a singular noun, add an apostrophe and an s.

rider + 's = rider's   Gus + 's = Gus's
employee + 's = employee's   Barbara + 's = Barbara's

To form the possessive of a plural noun that does not end in s, add an apostrophe and an s.

children + 's = children's   workmen + 's = workmen's

To form the possessive of a plural noun that ends in s, add only an apostrophe.

reporters + ' = reporters'   years + ' = years'
Simpsons + ' = Simpsons'   visitors + ' = visitors'

To form the possessive of indefinite pronouns, use an apostrophe and an s.

nobody + 's = nobody's   anyone + 's = anyone's

Apostrophes are not used with personal pronouns to show possession.

hers   ours   yours   its   theirs
The stopwatch is *ours*.

Use an apostrophe in a contraction.

In contractions words are joined and letters are left out. An apostrophe replaces one or more letters that are left out.

they've = they have   couldn't = could not
I'm = I am   hadn't = had not
we'll = we will   won't = will not
it's = it is (or has)   you're = you are

Use an apostrophe to show the omission of numbers in a date.

the Class of '80 (the Class of 1980)
a '78 Toyota (a 1978 Toyota)

Use an apostrophe and *s* to form the plurals of letters, figures, and words used as words.

three *s*'s   two 6's   *good-bye*'s   GI's

Exercise   Write the words that need apostrophes. Insert apostrophes where they are needed.

1. The citys budget is already strained.
2. My dentists drill is operated by a pedal.
3. Jesss locker is next to hers.
4. The teachers union votes tonight.
5. Its brakes dont work well.
6. Thats Deloress book, not yours.
7. Youre the peoples choice.
8. Shes not crossing her *t*s or dotting her *i*s.
9. Theyre using Nicks car, not theirs.
10. Nobodys future looks brighter than ours.
11. The nine Justices decision was unanimous.
12. Was Supermans cape blue?
13. Mens suits are on the third floor, arent they?
14. Ive bought a 73 Mustang.
15. Tanyas *for sures* are getting on my nerves.

Quotation Marks

Use quotation marks at the beginning and at the end of a direct quotation.

Quotation marks tell your reader that a speaker's exact words are being given. Here is an example:

Dennis said, "I have a headache."

An indirect quotation does not tell the speaker's exact words. Quotation marks are not used.

Dennis said that he has a headache.

Before a quotation, there are often explanatory words. Immediately after the words, insert a comma. Then begin the quotation with quotation marks. A period at the end of a sentence belongs *inside* the quotation marks.

Melissa said, "It's time for the news."

The explanatory words sometimes end the sentence. Then the quoted statement that begins the sentence is followed by a comma. The comma always belongs inside the quotation marks.

"It's time for the news," Melissa said.

Punctuating Divided Quotations

A quotation is sometimes divided into two parts by explanatory words. In that case, quotation marks enclose each part of the quotation.

"Sweet, sticky foods," the dentist noted, "promote tooth decay."

If the divided quotation is a single sentence, the second part begins with a small letter. Notice the example above. However, the second part may begin a new sentence. Then the second part starts with a capital letter.

"The Knicks staged an upset," the sportscaster said. "They won in the last second of play."

In the middle of a divided quotation, the explanatory words are followed by either a period or a comma. If the first part completes a sentence, use a period. If the sentence continues after the explanatory words, use a comma.

"From a distance," Julie noted, "the area looks deserted."

"New Hampshire is a key state," said the campaign manager. "It has the first primary election."

Write each of the following sentences three ways as a direct quotation.

1. Yes, Ted, you can use my camera. (said Larry)
2. Maybe the Steelers will sign him up. (said Bonnie)
3. I know that pigeons don't migrate. (insisted Thomas)
4. After a few days, I adjusted to the noise. (Marie admitted)
5. I'm afraid that the pattern needs alteration. (Rob noted)

Using Punctuation with Quotation Marks

Place question marks and exclamation points inside the quotation marks only if they belong to the quotation itself.

Jane asked, "Are you on a diet?"

The man shrieked, "We need help!"

Place question marks and exclamation points outside the quotation marks if they do not belong to the quotation.

Did the doctor say, "Your X-rays are normal"?

How thrilled I was to hear her say, "You're hired"!

Remember that commas and periods, as you have seen, always appear within quotation marks.

Exercise A Copy the following sentences. Punctuate them correctly with quotation marks, end marks, and commas. (There are three indirect quotations that need only end punctuation.)

1. Which team is Mark Aguirre on asked Joy
2. Who said that she wanted to leave early
3. I like your coat Ron said Is it new
4. The mayor said Nobody leaves the room until we have reached an agreement
5. Nobody leaves the room the mayor said until we have reached an agreement
6. Look out screamed Dwight
7. Dawn said that she knew him

8. Marty asked where the pipes ran
9. How awful I felt when the boss said You're late
10. Did Ed really say I've forgotten her name

Exercise B Write each of the following sentences as a direct quotation. In some examples, put the quotation first. In others, put the quotation last. For variety, divide some quotations.

1. Get out of the way!
2. Toast has as many calories as bread.
3. Do you have any insurance?
4. Have you ever played this game before?
5. I don't work in this department.
6. Did the drug store go out of business?
7. Leave me alone!
8. I said that I was sorry.
9. How many people live in this house?
10. Are gnomes the same as elves?

Using Long Quotations

When you are quoting two or more sentences by the same speaker, you may wonder how to use quotation marks. Study this example:

> "I work with primary colors," the artist said. "I think red, yellow, and blue are bold, clear, and forceful. They emphasize the lines of my painting."

Using Quotation Marks for Dialogue

Conversation between two or more people is called **dialogue**. Begin a new paragraph each time the speaker changes.

> "What do you think you'll be doing ten years from now?" Darryl asked.
> "That's a tough question," Al said. "Maybe I'll have a family of my own. At least I hope I will."

Carla said, "In ten years I think I'll have a good job. I think I'll travel out West, too."

"What about you, Darryl?" Al asked. "What will you be doing ten years from now?"

"I'll probably be sitting around," Darryl remarked, "wondering what I'll be doing ten years later."

Exercise Rewrite the following conversation. Make correct paragraph divisions, and use the right punctuation.

What makes you go to a doctor? asked Mary. I tend to go said Judy only when I'm very sick. I don't like to spend the money, and I don't like to spend the time. Angie said I make an appointment after I've exhausted my home remedies. Well said Jim I am distrustful. I go to the doctor if I already know what I have and what the cure is, but at no other time. You all sound ridiculous! said Lee. Don't you realize how important your health is?

Punctuating Titles

Use quotation marks to enclose the titles of magazine articles, chapters, short stories, essays, poems, television and radio programs, songs, and short pieces of music.

Magazine article:	"The Best in Off-Road Vehicles"
Chapter title:	Chapter 3, "Africa Explored"
Short story:	"The Killers"
Essay:	"Nature"
Poem:	"Chicago"
Television program:	"Taxi"
Song:	"Too Much Heaven"

Underline the titles of books, newspapers, magazines, plays, movies, works of art, and long musical compositions.

In writing or typing, such titles are underlined like this: Newsweek.

However, in print, these titles appear in italics.

Book title:	*Ordinary People*
Newspaper:	*Chicago Tribune*
Magazine:	*Rolling Stone*
Play:	*Eubie*
Movie:	*Kramer vs. Kramer*
Work of art:	*The Last Supper*
Long musical composition:	*American in Paris*

Exercise A   Copy the following sentences. Add quotation marks around titles or underline titles where necessary.

1. Who played in the movie Coal Miner's Daughter?
2. Is Mary Cassett's Portrait of a Young Girl in this museum?
3. The Outlandish Knight is a ballad.
4. John Brown's Body has the same tune as The Battle Hymn of the Republic.
5. One business newspaper is the Wall Street Journal.
6. Are reruns of M.A.S.H. being shown on TV?
7. She's seen the movie Star Trek twice.
8. We discussed the article The Invisible Threat.
9. Please read Chapter 1, Let Justice Be Done.
10. Pollyanna is a novel about a girl who's always glad.

Exercise B   Follow the directions for Exercise A.

1. She has old issues of Scientific American.
2. The article appeared in The New England Journal of Medicine.
3. Blazing Saddles was a comic Western.
4. We saw the musical The Evolution of the Blues.
5. The painting Winter hangs in the classroom.
6. The choir sang Go Tell It on the Mountain.
7. We listened to Beethoven's Pastoral Symphony.
8. At the funeral, Will the Circle Be Unbroken? was sung.
9. The professor said that Peter Pan was the saddest book in literature.
10. The Drama Club presented The Miracle Worker.

REVIEW Punctuation

End Marks and Commas Rewrite the following sentences. Add the missing punctuation.

1. Is the USS *Nimitz* still the world's largest warship
2. What a miser he is
3. Reba asked us to wake her at 5:00 AM
4. Ouch That shot hurt a lot Dr Dempski
5. Luanne have you met Ms Clay my music teacher
6. Squatting on his heels he drew a circle in the sand
7. *Sula* a novel by Toni Morrison is not available here
8. The address of the hospital where Roy works is 606 Clermont Road Batavia Ohio 45103
9. Jake and Fred however eat too much sleep too much and exercise too little
10. The mood in the mayor's office was peaceful but outside the city was growing angry

Semicolons, Colons, Dashes, and Hyphens Add semicolons, colons, dashes, and hyphens as you rewrite these sentences.

11. The day it had been a long one was almost over.
12. Pet goldfish aren't much trouble they're not much fun, either.
13. If you think it's time to quit, check again it's only 415.
14. Bermuda, Jamaica, Mexico he had brochures from all those beautiful, far away places.
15. Dear Sir
    We have received your order for these items the vise, the cutting shears, and the heavy-duty flashlight.
    We will send the first two items immediately however, we regret that the third item is out of stock.

Apostrophes, Quotation Marks, and Underlining Write each sentence, putting in necessary apostrophes, quotation marks, and underlining.

16. Time magazine was first published in the early 1920s.

17. Lu asked Why do you make your 7s that way?

18. The song Nobody isnt a favorite of hers.

19. Didnt the teacher say Please read the story Overdrawn at the Memory Bank in the book The Persistence of Vision?

20. Chris said that she had never heard Canadas anthem O, Canada.

21. I know I said Don that everybodys dues but mine are in.

22. Its true! she said. Josss picture is in todays Daily News.

23. The womens exercise equipment isnt in this closet.

24. Both doctors offices have copies of the poem If on the wall.

25. Teenagers styles of dress were different in the 50s, said Al.

Spelling

One skill that will never lose its value is good spelling. It is a skill that is valuable in all writing, ranging from a school report, to letters, to a job or credit application. In many jobs, too, some writing is required. At all times good spelling is noticed and admired.

At first, learning to be a good speller may seem difficult. The spelling of many English words does not seem to make sense. Many words are not spelled the way they sound.

However, becoming a good speller is not hopeless. There are patterns of spelling that many English words follow. There are general rules that make spelling easier. In addition, there are methods for attacking spelling problems. Using such tools, you can avoid many problems and improve your spelling. This section will show you some solutions.

How To Improve Your Spelling

1. Recognize and conquer your specific spelling problems. Do you make certain spelling errors over and over? Look over writing that you have done in the past. Make a list of the words you have misspelled. Try to master those words.

2. Pronounce words carefully. Are you misspelling words because you aren't pronouncing them right? For example, if you are writing *temperture* for *temperature* or *athelete* for *athlete*, you are probably mispronouncing the word. Work on pronouncing words more precisely.

3. Try to memorize the letters in new words. Do you look closely at the spelling of new or difficult words? That habit can help you to remember how new words are spelled. Practice spelling a new word by writing it several times.

4. Always proofread your writing. Do you misspell words out of carelessness? You may catch such errors if you examine what you write. Read over your work slowly, word by word.

5. Check difficult words in a dictionary. When you're unsure of a spelling, do you reach for the dictionary? Get into the habit of letting the dictionary help you to spell well.

6. Learn the few important spelling rules explained in this section.

How To Spell a Particular Word Correctly

1. Look at the word and say it to yourself. Be sure to pronounce it correctly. Say it twice, looking at the syllables as you say them.

2. Look at the letters and say each one. Sound out the words from its spelling. Divide the word into syllables and pronounce each syllable.

3. Without looking at your book or list, write the word.

4. Check to see if you spelled the word correctly. If you spelled the word correctly, repeat this process.

5. If you made an error, note what it was. Then repeat steps 3 and 4 until you have spelled the word correctly three times.

Rules for Spelling

Adding Prefixes

When a prefix is added to a word, the spelling of the word remains the same.

dis- + appear = disappear
mis- + inform = misinform
re- + apply = reapply

im- + mobile = immobile
pre- + mature = premature
un + noticed = unnoticed

Suffixes and Silent e

When a suffix beginning with a vowel is added to a word ending in a silent e, the e is usually dropped.

hide + -ing = hiding
sense + -ible = sensible
believe + -able = believable

date + -ing = dating
cube + -ic = cubic
celebrate + -ion = celebration

When a suffix beginning with a consonant is added to a word ending in a silent e, the e is usually retained.

grate + -ful = grateful
safe + -ty = safety
move + -ment = movement

life + -less = lifeless
bare + -ly = barely
strange + -ness = strangeness

The following words are exceptions. Learn them.

ninth   wholly   truly   argument

Exercise A Find the misspelled words. Spell them correctly.

1. The driver's car was weaveing strangely.
2. Peaceful cows were grazeing nearby.
3. The argument was completly unecessary.
4. The game was not wholely boreing.
5. Tish was disatisfied with the amount in her savengs account.
6. He practiced brakeing on ice.

7. Rita distrusted them completely.
8. The unlikely story was received impolitly.
9. The couragous deed was scarcly noticed.
10. He reentered school on the nineth of September.

Exercise B Add the prefixes and suffixes as shown. Write the new word.

1. recite + -al
2. forsake + -ing
3. remarkable + -ly
4. strange + -ness
5. mis- + matched
6. mis- + state
7. dis- + abled
8. un- + needed
9. prepare + -ation
10. waste + -ful
11. re- + instate
12. re- + action
13. re- + enforce
14. like + -able
15. like + -ly
16. leisure + -ly
17. dis- + service
18. il- + legible
19. wave + -ing
20. smile + -ing

Suffixes and Final *y*

When a suffix is added to a word ending in *y* preceded by a consonant, the *y* is usually changed to *i*.

pity + -ful = pitiful
body + -ly = bodily
sorry + -est = sorriest
ready + -ness = readiness

marry + -age = marriage
twenty + -eth = twentieth
lazy + -er = lazier
mystery + -ous = mysterious

Note this exception. When *ing* is added, the *y* does not change.

carry + -ing = carrying
worry + -ing = worrying

fly + -ing = flying
copy + -ing = copying

When a suffix is added to a word ending in *y* preceded by a vowel, the *y* usually does not change.

stay + -ed = stayed
relay + -s = relays

convey + -or = conveyor
enjoy + able = enjoyable

Adding the Suffixes -*ness* and -*ly*

When the suffix -*ly* is added to a word ending in *l*, both *l*'s are kept. When -*ness* is added to a word ending in *n*, both *n*'s are kept.

loyal + -ly = loyally open + -ness = openness
potential + -ly = potentially uneven + -ness = unevenness

Doubling the Final Consonant

In words of one syllable that end in one consonant preceded by one vowel, double the final consonant before adding -*ing*, -*est*, -*ed*, or -*er*.

hop + -ing = hopping big + -est = biggest
sip + -ed = sipped nap + -ing = napping
plan + -er = planner win + -er = winner

In words of one syllable that end in one consonant preceded by two vowels, the final consonant is not doubled.

dear + -est = dearest need + -ing = needing
groan + -ed = groaned cool + -er = cooler

Exercise Add the suffixes as shown. Write the new word.

1. hazy + -er
2. happy + -ly
3. pretty + -est
4. twenty + -eth
5. foggy + -er
6. icy + -est
7. scurry + -ed
8. employ + -ment
9. joy + -ous
10. marry + -age
11. mystery + -ous
12. dreary + -est
13. fuzzy + -ness
14. replay + -ed
15. delay + -ing
16. worry + -er
17. worry + -ing
18. lazy + -ly
19. deploy + -ed
20. coy + -ness

Words with the "Seed" Sound

Only one English word ends in -sede: supersede. Three words end in -ceed: exceed, proceed, succeed. All other words ending with the sound of seed are spelled cede.

> concede   secede   recede   precede

Exercise A   Find the misspelled words. Spell them correctly.

1. Margaret baged the groceries carefuly.
2. The child was poping the balloons out of meaness.
3. Jo dresses casualy.
4. The wind is realy roaring.
5. My vision is not usualy blured.
6. Lester went runing to find the nearrest phone.
7. His keeness made him a winer.
8. Finaly the clerks finished taging the garments.
9. After starring in the movie, he was mobed by fans.
10. Unmercifuly the agent draged the information out of the spy.

Exercise B   Add the suffixes as shown. Write the new word.

1. frail + -ly
2. hop + -ed
3. nip + -ing
4. thin + -ness
5. pour + -ed
6. brazen + -ness
7. civil + -ly
8. bleak + -er
9. mop + -ing
10. hear + -ing
11. rip + -ed
12. soap + -ed
13. lawful + -ly
14. flip + -ing
15. zip + -er
16. read + -er
17. knit + -ed
18. mean + -ing
19. dot + -ed
20. stop + -er

Words with *ie* or *ei*

For words with *ie* or *ei* pronounced as long *e* (e), there is a general spelling rule. The correct spelling is *ie* except after a *c*.

I before *E*

field	grieve	piece	fierce	chief
niece	shield	believe	relieve	retrieve
reprieve	pierce	shriek	grief	pier

Except after *C*

ceiling	receipt	perceive	deceit
receive	deceive	conceive	conceit

These words are exceptions to the rule. Study them.

leisure	either	weird
neither	species	seize

Exercise   Find the misspelled words in these sentences. Spell them correctly.

1. The dog, a retreiver, was barking feircely.
2. He succeded in persuading Maryland not to seceed.
3. Mr. Blair beleived that he was the heir; he was deceived.
4. The plasterer conceeded that the cieling had been poorly done.
5. I was releived to find the reciept.
6. Neither of the cheifs wore a headdress.
7. Seizing the intruder by the hair, Ellie caught the theif.
8. Either his conciet or his beliefs will bring him greif.
9. This memo superceeds the one you recieved yesterday.
10. Lu percieved that she needed more liesure time.

REVIEW Spelling

Read each sentence carefully. Find the misspelled words. Write each word correctly.

1. My neice goes jogging dayly.
2. I notifyed the doctor that the patient was wheezeing.
3. She beleives that war is imoral.
4. The cheif was mortaly wounded.
5. His poor coordinateion worries me.
6. I beleive you are exceding the speed limit.
7. I carryed it here; I'm not carrying it back.
8. Milt was cuting a peice of cake.
9. The theif's denyals decieved no one.
10. The singers' voices sounded realy gloryous.
11. That misstake was completly unecessary.
12. The dial was spining crazyly.
13. Nick was gazeing hopefuly at the pie.
14. Their greedyness was causing arguements.
15. Marion was glanceing around uneasyly.
16. Niether of them is good at disguiseing her dissapproveal.
17. The tide is receeding awfuly fast.
18. Rhoda looked for the reciept for the cieling fixture.
19. Fryed onions are fattening; so is whiped cream.
20. Plainness of speech is usualy admirable.

The Correct Form for Writing

The people who read what you write notice the content. Your ideas are important. You may forget, however, that readers also notice the form of your papers. Your writing is judged not only by its content, but also by its form.

Good form is precise, neat, and consistent. Such form will impress any reader, and present your ideas in their best light. Some schools set their own rules for the correct form for written work. In this section you will learn about the kind of form that is accepted by many schools.

Guidelines for Clear Writing

Neatness

Neat, legible papers can be read easily. Neatness also suggests that the writer cares about what he or she is writing. You can give your papers a neat appearance in several ways.

Legible Writing

Usually, typewritten papers are more legible than handwritten ones. If you do not have a typewriter, make your handwritten papers clear and legible. Write in ink, preferably blue or black. To make your handwriting easy to read, be sure that letters are distinct. Some letters look similar, like *a*'s and *o*'s, unless they are formed carefully. Other letters that can be confused are *e*'s and *i*'s.

The First Draft and the Final Copy

You cannot expect the first draft of a paper to be in perfect form. You write a first draft from your pre-writing notes or an outline. Then you need to correct or revise the first draft. At that time, you may need to change words, sentences, or whole sections.

After revising, you can make your final copy. Carefully proofread this new copy. You may find words left out or other errors. To insert a word, write it above the line. Use a caret (∧) to show where the word belongs. To change a word, draw a line through it, and write the correct word above it. If any page has more than about three corrections, you should recopy the page.

Acceptable Form

Using the correct form for writing involves more than simply making a paper neat. For a paper to have correct form, its various parts should be positioned correctly. Headings, titles, margins, and spacing should be in the correct form.

The Heading

The heading identifies your paper. It is usually placed in the upper right-hand corner of the first page. Place your name on the first line. Write the name of your class on the second line. Write the date on the third line. If a paper has a title page, the heading belongs in the upper right-hand corner of that page.

Except for page one, each page should be numbered. Beginning with page two, place the page number in the upper right-hand corner. You may want to put your name under the page number in order to identify all pages.

Some teachers require a different form for labeling your paper. Follow any special instructions you are given.

The Title

The title of a paper should appear near the top of the first page. In general, place the title two lines down from the last line of the heading. Two lines below the title, begin the first line of your paper.

The correct form for a title includes proper capitalization. Capitalize only the first letter of the first word and of all important words. Do not underline your title or place it in quotation marks.

Sometimes a title page is used when a paper is more than three pages long. The title page becomes the first page.

Margins and Spacing

To make a paper attractive, use correct margins and spacing. Margins of one inch at the top, bottom, and left side of the paper are suitable.

The right-hand margin should be fairly even. However, do not break too many words with hyphens in order to keep the margin straight. A safe rule is to avoid hyphens in more than two lines in a row.

Double-spacing makes typed papers look neat. Indent five spaces to begin each paragraph. Skip two spaces after the punctuation mark at the end of a sentence.

Writing Numbers

The form for writing numbers should be consistent. Numbers under 100 are usually spelled out. Larger numbers are written in figures.

> When Mark was *sixteen*, he moved *three* times.
> Union dues are *fifty* dollars a year.
> Anyone with an income of $3,300 or more must file a tax return.

A number at the beginning of a sentence is always spelled out.

> *Five hundred* people were evacuated.
> *Nine million* automobiles were produced here last year.
> *Fifty-five* miles per hour is the speed limit.

Figures rather than words are used for the following: dates, street and room numbers, telephone numbers, temperatures, page numbers, decimals, and percentages.

> On July 13, 1977, a blackout hit New York.
> The branch office is at 21 East Huron Street.
> Jennifer is in room 72 at the hospital.
> Our phone number was changed to 869-4288.
> In Florida, winter temperatures are about 65 degrees.
> The letters to the editor are on page 15.
> The track is 2.8 miles long.
> The divorce rate increased 3 percent last year.

For expressions of large sums of money or large quantities, commas are used to separate the figures. However, commas are not used in dates, serial numbers, page numbers, addresses, or telephone numbers.

> Correct: The bills printed last year amounted to $58,714,890.
> Correct: That record sold 1,000,850 copies.
> Incorrect: In 1,953 Jonas Salk developed a polio vaccine.
> Correct: In 1953 Jonas Salk developed a polio vaccine.

Exercise Copy these sentences, correcting any errors in the writing of numbers.

1. $75 is the cost of the rear wheel kit.
2. About twenty percent of the students work more than 20 hours a week.
3. The temperature drops below 40 degrees at least one hundred and eighty-two days a year here.
4. In the year seventeen hundred and ninety, the United States had a population of 3929214.
5. The planet Saturn takes twenty-nine point forty-six years to revolve around the sun.
6. The Atkins family moved to 11,502 Kedzie Street 6 years ago.
7. On November fourteenth, 1889, Nellie Bly circled the globe in seventy-two days.
8. 200 kilograms equal 440 pounds.
9. The patient in room ten has a fever of one hundred and three degrees.
10. Please read pages one through forty by March third.

Using Abbreviations

Shortened forms of words are called abbreviations. Generally, in formal writing, abbreviations are not acceptable.

However, abbreviations are correct for most titles before and after names. Abbreviations may also be used for government agencies and for time.

Titles before proper names:	Dr., Rev., Mr., Mrs., Ms., Lt., Pvt., Cong., Gen.
Titles after proper names:	Jr., R.N., M.D., Ph.D., R.Ph.
Dates and times:	B.C., A.D., A.M., P.M.
Government agencies:	FCC, CIA, IRS, ICC

As you can see, periods are not used in the abbreviations of government agencies.

A title is abbreviated only when it is used with a person's name, as in *Cong. Don Jones*. For example, an abbreviation like this would not be acceptable: *The Cong. was not present*.

For certain titles, abbreviations are not correct. *Honorable* and *Reverend* are not abbreviated when preceded by *the*: *the Reverend C. D. Wolfe*. The titles of President and Vice-President of the United States are not abbreviated.

In general, abbreviations are not acceptable for the following: names of countries and states, months and days of the week, addresses, and company names.

Incorrect:	Nev. got its name from a Sp. word meaning "snow-covered."
Correct:	Nevada got its name from a Spanish word meaning "snow-covered."
Incorrect:	The Steely Dan concert is Sat., Feb. 17.
Correct:	The Steely Dan concert is Saturday, February 17.
Incorrect:	Katy works at the Gibson Co. on Wayland Ave.
Correct:	Katy works at the Gibson Company on Wayland Avenue.

In most writing, abbreviations are not acceptable for names of school courses and such words as *chapter*, *page*, *Christmas*. Abbreviations for measurements, like *in.*, *mi.*, *ft.*, and *min.*, are also unacceptable.

Exercise   Correct the errors in abbreviation in these sentences.

1. In the last qtr. of the game, we scored fourteen pts.
2. Give the baby one oz. of formula for each lb. of body weight.
3. The dr. said that some burns affect tissue under the skin.
4. The phys. ed. teacher told us to exercise for fifteen min.
5. Nature Foods Co. has an advertisement on p. 4.
6. The Rev. E. B. Rice spoke about conditions in SE Asia.
7. The Hon. Neil Griffin is a Fed. judge.
8. We invited some sr. citizens for Xmas dinner.
9. Does the Pres. appoint the dir. of the F.B.I.?
10. Porter discussed the issues with the two sen. from Ill.

A

Acknowledgments

William Collins Publishers, Inc.: For entries appearing on pages 12, 183, 185, 186, 188, 189, 306.

Photographs

James L. Ballard: ii, 199.

Illustrations

Ken Izzi: handwritten art, 208-224; special mechanical art. Amy Palmer: handwritten art, 147, 149; diagrams. Jeanne Seabright: handwritten art, 71-73. Montague Design: special mechanical art.